THE SCANDINAVIAN WAY
AND ITS LEGACY IN EUROPE

Edited by
Christine Ingebritsen

ISBN 978-0-9891528-5-3

1 2 3 4 5 6 7 ATP 18 17 16 15 14 13

SCANDINAVIAN STUDIES

Fall 2002 Volume 74 Number 3

Preface

THE COLLAPSE OF THE COMMUNIST STATES in eastern Europe along with the founding and expansion of the European Union will stand out in future historical reckonings as among the most remarkable social, economic, and political developments of the second half of the twentieth century. The demise of communism as a viable political and economic system and the easing of tensions between the eastern block and the western democracies had important ramifications for the Nordic region, which had long felt itself caught in various ways between the destructive potential of the two counterpoised superpowers. Although the wide-ranging consequences of these shifting ideological positions are, perhaps, more dramatic, the emergence of the European Union may well prove to have implications that more deeply permeate the fabric of both politics and commerce at the highest level as well as the texture of the daily lives of ordinary citizens of the region. Although the specific nature of this impact will be a function of a particular nation's relationship to the Union, everyone will in some way feel the consequences. The breadth and the depth of this influence on a host of cultural institutions, moreover, is such that it commands the attention of anyone with serious scholarly commitments to the area. What makes the region's varied modes of affiliation particularly engaging for specialists on politics and economics as well as readers with other areas of expertise is the broad range of attitudes to be found, expectations to be accommodated, reservations to be addressed, and national strategies to be integrated against the background of conflicting demands of Nordic unity and particularism.

The frequently shifting contours and nuances of the Nordic involvement with the EU have accordingly been taken up in the pages of *Scandinavian Studies* before. Scandinavia's relationship with the EEC, the immediate predecessor of the EU, was presented in a special issue (46.4) in the fall of 1974. Then, under the title, "Scandinavia and the New Europe," another special issue (64.4) appearing in 1992 provided analyses of several facets of the Nordic response to the European Community. Expertly edited by Peter Vinten-Johansen and Philip Vogt, it offered penetrating insight into the actual as well as the anticipated challenges of European integration in three longer and more comprehensive articles and eleven shorter essays on a wide range of specific topics. Much, however, has happened during the intervening years: some of it could, perhaps, have been expected but considerably more is surprising and suggests an emerging vision of the Union that goes well beyond what either supporters or skeptics could have reasonably imagined a decade ago.

Given the importance of the topic and the rapidity with which wide-ranging initiatives have been enacted—or in some cases rejected—the opportunity to revisit the question of the Nordic responses to the diverse demands of integrating the principles governing the flow of goods, labor, and capital is most welcome. Christine Ingebritsen has assembled an extremely engaging series of articles emerging from a conference she organized that critically examined the policies and practices of each of the Nordic nations and a number of derivative issues. Although scholarship is sometimes outpaced by rapid developments in political and economic policy, this special issue offers a timely, well conceived, and clearly focused examination of the diversity of Nordic thinking about European integration during the early years of the new millennium. Appreciation is expressed to Prof. Ingebritsen for gathering the work of distinguished specialists and making it available to *Scandinavian Studies*.

Because of their length and the complexity of their preparation, special issues are often costly and require modest funding in order to be financially feasible. Gratitude is, thus, expressed to the University of Washington, particularly the EU Center, the International Studies Center, and the Department of Scandinavian Studies, which have contributed to making this extended issue possible.

Steven P. Sondrup
Editor, *Scandinavian Studies*

The Scandinavian Way and Its Legacy in Europe

Christine Ingebritsen
University of Washington

If the test is the good life for the greatest number, and now, here in this immediate present and in the immediate future, not in some distant and debatable tomorrow, then one may well consider what has happened in these small countries.... For they have achieved a measure of peace and decent living that will serve, and for a long time to come perhaps, as a standard for larger nations.

Marquis W. Childs Sweden: The Middle Way, *xv–xvi*

IN HIS BEST-SELLING ANALYSIS of the Swedish model, Marquis Childs established the concept of the "Scandinavian" or "middle way" between American capitalism and Russian socialism. Childs describes capitalism in Sweden following the Great Depression as "hothouse laissez-faire," where "the state, the consumer, and the producer have intervened to make capitalism 'work' in a reasonable way for the greatest good of the whole nation" (161). Scandinavia's emergence as a group of "model" societies became a prominent theme of post-World War II scholarship—particularly among American and European academics who developed explanations for "the peculiar version of the mixed economy," which "combin[ed] concerns for social equity (both between classes and sexes) with private capitalism" (Mjøset 653). From the innovations of the cooperative movement in labor and production, to an organized farmer's movement, to the selective establishment of state monopolies—from

The author wishes to thank Peter J. Katzenstein, Johan Lilliehook, and the participants in the conference "The EU and Scandinavia Today," (Eric Einhorn, Lykke Friis, Ann-Cathrine Jungar, Annica Kronsell, Paulette Kurzer, Robert Rinehart, Lars Svåsand, and Baldur Thorhallsson) sponsored by the European Union Center and the Department of Scandinavian Studies, University of Washington, Seattle, Washington, 1–2 Feb. 2001, for helpful comments on an earlier version of this manuscript.

power generation to liquor control—Scandinavia has earned a reputation for its unique combination of dependence on the international system and innovation in its domestic institutions (see Katzenstein).

The pressures on Scandinavia to become more like other states are immense—from changes in global markets, to the revival of integration in Europe, to a growing individualism in international society, and a declining ideological commitment to taming market economies. Yet the legacy of the Scandinavian way persists—outside the territorial boundaries of Sweden, Denmark, Finland, Norway, and Iceland. As this article seeks to explain, the differences between Scandinavia and its European neighbors have become part of a new agenda in regional politics as Europe and Scandinavia become increasingly intertwined.

While formerly unattractive to Scandinavian social democrats who found Europe to be overly centralized and capitalistic, cooperation has become more appealing in recent decades. Scandinavian political and business leaders seek European cooperation as a means of reviving ailing domestic economies. Scandinavian defense planners view European-wide security collaboration as a pragmatic balance to countering both instabilities in neighboring Russia and to overcoming dependence on the North Atlantic Treaty Organization (NATO) during a period when American interest in securing Europe appears to be waning. Although not one of the five northern European states was present at the signing of the Rome Treaty, three of the five now participate in the major decision-making institutions of the European Union (Denmark, Sweden, and Finland), and the remaining two (Norway and Iceland) have pursued closer and closer cooperation with the EU—short of formal membership.[1]

Previous contributions to the study of Scandinavia's relationship to the European integration process have focused on the transformation of domestic institutions, policies, and values in northern Europe as a consequence of enhanced cooperation with the European Union. However, scholars in this volume pose a different question: to what extent has Scandinavia's accession to the European Union contributed to new agendas at the regional level? This article examines how the Scandinavian way provides an institutional legacy and reference point for deepening cooperation in four major issue-areas where European

---

[1] Denmark joined in 1973; Sweden and Finland joined in 1995. In all three states, a national referendum was held prior to entry.

policy making is being developed—from social policy and conflict prevention, to the environment and e-commerce.

After Sweden joined the European Union, Prime Minister Ingvar Carlsson announced in a ministerial meeting that "we don't do it this way in Sweden." In his statement, Carlsson was referring to the lack of gender diversity within European Union (EU) institutions. Sweden, and the rest of Scandinavia, outpace other societies in narrowing the gap between the number of men and women serving in national government. Carlsson's perception of social justice represents a prominent difference between standards of appropriate behavior (or "norms") in continental Europe, which contrast to egalitarian expectations of Sweden, and its Scandinavian neighbors (see Klotz; Ingebritsen *Scandinavia's Role* chapter 2).

As the crisis in the former Yugoslavia deepened, the Finnish president was asked to mediate between the opposing parties. A "neutral" northerner, respected for a tough yet even-handed negotiating style, became a preferred partner in European conflict resolution. Other more powerful states in Europe, such as Germany, were constrained by historical legacies and were unable to play a similar role.

When the United States negotiators met with European Union leaders in Kyoto at the summit that set parameters for greenhouse gas emissions, they encountered a tough-minded Dane at the head of the delegation. Denmark has adopted higher standards in its environmental regulations and has a distinguished record domestically and within the EU as a prominent proponent of "green norms."

As Finland's hi-tech firm NOKIA introduced the first internet-capable cellular phone, other producers sought to emulate Fenno-innovations. At the same time, Helsinki has converted itself into a "virtual city," with easy web access to travel information, educational opportunities, and other social amenities. Northern Europe is a prominent site for the European information industry, yet even these new technologies have been embraced with a social conscience.

These examples of the Scandinavian way illustrate how a group of states selectively and strategically play a role in European politics consistent with priorities long-held *within* these societies. The following discussion further develops an understanding of the four ways in which Scandinavian historical legacies have positioned this group of states to play a special role and then identifies how dimensions of the Scandinavian way are exported to Europe.

RETHINKING THE SCANDINAVIAN WAY AND ITS LEGACIES

In what ways has Scandinavia historically been viewed as distinct and to what extent does the sub-region serve as a "site" for understanding the possibilities of state engineering outside Scandinavia?

In an era of "globalization" when states encounter more powerful market forces and private or local solutions are often advocated over state ownership or intervention, Scandinavian innovations may seem to be out of step with changes in the international political economy.[2] However, in four distinct issue-areas, Scandinavian institutional choices have shaped the expectations of the current generation of policy makers who represent these countries in external negotiations. Their reference points and expectations are different as they engage European partners, and even though there have been profound changes within these systems, the legacy of past choices continues to guide Scandinavian foreign policy makers. And as Baldur Thorhallsson argues, small does not mean ineffective when it comes to EU participation. Administrative flexibility and the capacity to mobilize limited resources efficiently has given smaller states a comparative advantage within the EU decision-making structure (232–40).

The first, most prominent example of the Scandinavian way is the widely known "cradle to grave" system of welfare entitlements.

THE PERSISTENCE OF UNIVERSALISM

German international relations scholar, Michael Zurn, is skeptical about the prospects of retaining "national" social welfare systems in a globalized and increasingly individualized Europe. Yet even with cut-backs in the commitment of state agencies to social welfare programs, Scandinavia remains the *only* group of states that continues to provide assistance to all residents of the society—citizens and non-citizens. This model has not been exported to other parts of the world but is historically unique to the Scandinavian area (see Esping-Andersen *Three Worlds* and *Welfare States*). Although the size and visibility of immigrant populations

---

[2] "Globalization" refers to the intensification of interaction between market actors, political entities, and cultures. For Thomas Friedman, "globalization" represents a systemic change in international relations; for Saskia Sassen, it represents a decline in state sovereignty.

throughout Scandinavia has introduced the notion of "we" and "them," these societies are far from adopting British, American, or Continental systems of welfare provision.

The underlying assumption within Scandinavia is equality—everyone should be treated in the same manner, as a basic right in these societies. In addition, there is a strong sense of responsibility for the collective group, which exceeds the expectations of other societies. In order to understand this unique institution, Scandinavianists point to the historic experience of village life. As Swedish novelist Vilhelm Moberg argues, "[t]he most positive aspect of the village community was its unwritten laws for mutual aid and assistance. Here their fellowship was without flaw.... Anyone needing help must at once be given it. 'You help me, and tomorrow I'll help you,' was the rule" (11). Scholars in political science, on the other hand, tend to see the role of labor movements (Peter Swenson, Jonas Pontusson, and Bo Rothstein); or the influence of ideas (Ton Notermans) as formative in establishing the comprehensive Scandinavian system of benefits.

The new literature on the welfare state, however, is preoccupied with how to reform (read: cut-back) the welfare state as demands on these systems exceed available revenues. Although the days of welfare expansion appear to be over, the underlying principles necessary for retaining the system and the expectations internalized by those who have been socialized to expect state activism persist. Thus, even though there are institutional and policy reforms, the legacy of universalism makes it difficult for Scandinavians to accept lower standards of state commitment. What are the implications of differing perceptions of who *should* receive support as Scandinavia more closely engages its European partners?

Within the European Union, Sweden has actively pursued policies of equal treatment associated with an earlier period of social democracy. In addition, the Danes have advocated the adoption of a set of worker's rights, to be applied to all EU member-states. When Scandinavians criticize the "democratic deficit" within EU institutions, we are reminded of the distinction between deferring decisions to higher levels of authority vs. a preference for a more egalitarian structure of direct democracy. Sweden's request for greater transparency within European Union institutions as part of the agenda of the Swedish EU presidency (15 Jan.–15 June, 2001), is a deliberate attempt to export a national tradition.

A second legacy of Scandinavian exceptionalism is the preference for conflict avoidance—visible in virtually every dimension of daily life—but also a prominent "niche" for these states in a period when alternative means of conflict prevention are deemed more appropriate than traditional applications of military power.

CONFLICT RESOLUTION AND THE PROMOTION OF PEACE

Collectively, Scandinavia represents a group of states, which have only reluctantly agreed to participate in agreements viewed as compromising state sovereignty (from Norwegian, Danish, and Icelandic participation in NATO; to the 1995 accession of Sweden and Finland to the European Union). Decision-making in national security involves a relatively small circles of actors, and strategies of conflict resolution based on balancing against and cooperating with more powerful neighbors is a Scandinavian virtue.

In Scandinavia, conflict management is a way of life. In one sphere, the labor market, there have been distinctive innovations designed to "keep the peace" between capital and labor. These so-called "labor peace" agreements enabled workers to have greater say over their working conditions and wages, while agreeing to refrain from striking. Scandinavian style cooperation is unique in modern capitalist societies for bringing these two opposing parties into negotiated settlements. And even in a period of economic downturn, the extent of labor market policies continues to be much more inclusive than other societies (see Trehorning).

In another sphere, forging deals between political parties, Scandinavia has also had a distinct experience. The "Cow Deal," which was an alliance between the farmer's party (the Center Party) and the labor party (the Social Democrats) created in the 1930s, is a further example of the capacity to mediate between different interests. In exchange for providing political support for labor, the farmers were guaranteed subsidies for agricultural production. Thus, the capacity for negotiated solutions is part of the collective experience of these societies.

As evidence of this Scandinavian legacy, representatives from these states have been active players in conflict resolution abroad. Prominent members of these societies, such as Thorvald Stoltenberg and Knut Vollebaek (Norway), Martti Ahtisaari (Finland), and Carl Bildt (Sweden) have been regularly requested to intervene to mediate internal conflicts—not only within Europe, but also in the Middle East, Asia, and Latin America.

The efforts of Terje Rød-Larsen and his colleagues in getting both Israeli and PLO leaders to sign the "Oslo Accord," remains a breakthrough in international conflict management.

Conflict prevention has also taken new forms in Europe relying on initiatives from Scandinavia. For example, Sweden put forward the "EU Programme for Prevention of Violent Conflicts," which was endorsed by the Göteborg European Council in June 2001. This joint action plan commits the EU to new measures for mitigating conflict—from closer cooperation with collective institutions such as the United Nations (UN) and the Organization for Cooperative Security in Europe (OSCE) to developing new instruments for long-term and short-term prevention (Swedish Ministry 5–6). And as part of the negotiations to create a common European military (Common Foreign and Security Policy, or CFSP), Sweden and Finland contributed heavily to the text of the Amsterdam Treaty outlining new forms of conflict intervention referred to as the Petersberg Tasks. Even Norway, outside the EU, has committed a force of 3,500 personnel for new types of EU international operations—from rescue missions to internal policing (Norwegian Ministry 2). For Scandinavian governments, this type of participation is a logical extension of its domestic political experience.

A third aspect of the Scandinavian way has only become prominent in recent decades, reflecting changes in global and European priorities.

RESOURCE MANAGEMENT: SUSTAINABILITY IN PRACTICE

A lesser known dimension of Scandinavia's legacy as a group of states distinct from other capitalist, market economies, is the early and consistent management of natural resources. The term "sustainability" captures what has long been a Scandinavian practice of long-term restrictions on growth and development. This is evidenced by Finnish forestry management practices; Norway's decision to adopt restrictions on oil and gas production to save these resources for future generations; Sweden's role in cleaning up the Baltic Sea region; Iceland's restrictive fisheries management system; and Danish innovations in land reform and "green agriculture."

Two principles are central to Scandinavian environmental norms, which also frame the context of decision-making abroad. The rule known as "allemannsrett," which refers to the open access of all residents to natural areas; combined with a tradition of protecting the environment for recreation, or *"friluftsliv"* (Norwegian for outdoor recreation), are two fundamental codes of Scandinavian societies (see Vail 58; Ingebritsen *Europeanization*).

At the European level, Denmark has become the home of the European Environmental Institute. In addition, Danish court cases brought before the European Court of Justice have enabled the preservation of "sustainable practices," particularly in the area of recycled products. The labeling process adopted by the Nordic Council (the swan symbol) designates "environmentally friendly products." Such a system could be adopted by the European Union, as eco-concerns receive greater attention in EU politics.

As Annica Kronsell argues, the Swedes have cultivated a niche within European policy making as leaders in advancing more stringent collective measures to protect the environment. This is particularly evident in the adoption of rules governing the use of chemicals in Europe. The legitimacy of these states, as late and relatively clean industrializers, places Scandinavia in a unique position *vis-á-vis* its European partners.

A final area where the Scandinavian way differs from the priorities of other states is in the application of technology for the "good" of society.

HARNESSING TECHNOLOGY FOR SOCIAL PURPOSES

In a recent article, the *New York Times* described Scandinavia as a "digital Valhalla" referring to how these societies have become global leaders in cell-phone technology (Lewis). Ericsson (Sweden) and NOKIA (Finland) are market leaders in Europe. These companies challenge prominent American producers such as Motorola in providing global service and in developing new e-technologies. Not only have Scandinavian companies emerged as technological innovators, but they also lead the world in cell phone use per capita. Providing access to new forms of technology for a greater proportion of the society while monitoring the effects of technological change on society distinguish the cellular age in Scandinavia from the other parts of Europe or North America. For example, Scandinavians register concern over the consequences of wealth creation among an emergent group of young entrepreneurs; and national institutions have conducted more studies about the physical effects of mobile phones than in other societies. Scandinavian governments invest heavily in research and development and have fostered cooperative arrangements across national borders to facilitate greater competitiveness in world markets. As Seattle-based internet company vice-president Roger Gulranjani explains, "Nokia's success in transitioning from a forestry-based company to a mobile phone exporter depended on a sharing technological innovations with Swedish-based Ericsson." As demonstrated by the success of the Scandinavian Airlines System (a joint company created by Denmark, Sweden and Norway), cross-border economic partnerships have enabled Scandinavian companies to prosper internationally.

Consistent with other technological developments (Norway's development of a technological edge in offshore oil exploration and production; an Icelandic entrepreneur's creation of "DeCode," which enables DNA studies of genetic material; and Danish leadership in post-Fordist, hi-tech production), these innovations are perceived as *collective*.

Institutional relationships that preceded the age of the internet and the mass-produced cellular telephone permit Scandinavia to play a leading role in this sector of the world economy. Scandinavia has consistently invested a greater percentage of GNP in research and development, and universities in Scandinavia cooperate closely with the corporate sector. Thus, technological entrepreneurship is not limited to the west coast of the United States, but is also found in Europe's northernmost corner where a new generation of "e-vikings" are embracing new technologies and harnessing these to improve the economy and the quality of life in these societies.

CONCLUSION

As I have argued in *The Nordic States and European Unity,* the direction and substance of Scandinavian reforms constitute more than what prominent political scientist Peter Katzenstein referred to as "flexible adaptation" in his 1985 book, *Small States in World Markets.* European integration is imposing a logic of reform on the Scandinavian way of life, which moves it away from its past successes. Nonetheless, the fight to retain the norms of Scandinavia's "golden years" continues — outside the territorial boundaries of this group of states.

Thus, the legacy of institutions and policies adopted in an earlier era create expectations about how "Europe" should be governed as more and more Scandinavians engage the EU. Scandinavians have experienced systems with separate underlying principles, collective expectations, and a clear role for the state in society. As this article demonstrates, foreign policy making has become the format for expressing the legacy of the

Scandinavian model. In posing demands within the EU—from preferences for equality and social justice to mediating conflict—to working for more stringent environmental standards, to techno-sociological innovations the Scandinavian experience brings with it powerful legacies which Europe is now required to engage collectiely.

WORKS CITED

Childs, Marquis. *Sweden: The Middle Way.* New Haven: Yale UP, 1936.
Esping-Andersen, Gøsta. *The Three Worlds of Welfare Capitalism.* Cambridge: Polity P, 1990.
___, ed. *Welfare States in Transition: National Adaptations in Global Economies.* London: Sage, 1996.
"EU Programme for the Prevention of Violent Conflicts." Swedish Ministry of Foreign Affairs. The Swedish Presidency Home page. <www.eu2001.se/main/>.
Friedman, Thomas. *The Lexus and the Olive Tree.* New York: Farrar, Strauss, and Giroux, 1999.
Gulranjani, Roger. "Scandinavia in World Affairs." Presentation to SCAND/POLI SCI 326, U Washington, Seattle. Spring 2001.
Ingebritsen, Christine. "Europeanization and Cultural Identity: Two Worlds of Eco-Capitalism." *Scandinavian Studies* 73.1 (Spring 2001): 63–76.
___. Scandinavia's Role in World Politics. Unpublished manuscript.
Katzenstein, Peter J. *Small States in World Markets.* Ithaca: Cornell UP, 1985.
Klotz, Audie. *Norms in International Relations.* Ithaca: Cornell UP, 1995.
Kronsell, Annica. "Can Small States Influence EU Norms? Insights from Sweden's Participation in the Field of Environmental Politics." *Scandinavian Studies* 74.3 (Fall 2002).
Lewis, Peter. "Wireless Valhalla: Hints of the Cellular Future." *New York Times* 13 July 2000, late ed.: GI.
Mjøset, Lars. "The Nordic Model Never Existed, but Does it Have a Future?" *Scandinavian Studies* 64.4 (Fall 1992): 652–71.
Moberg, Vilhelm. "Life in the Villages." *Nordic Views and Values.* Eds. Patrick Engellau and Ulf Henning. Stockholm: The Nordic Council, 1984.
"On Norway and the European Security and Defence Policy (ESDP)." *Norwegian Ministry of Foreign Affairs, Thorbjrrn Jagland.* The Storting, 9 June 2000. <www.odin.dep.no>.
Rothstein, Bo. *Just Institutions Matter: The Moral and Political Logic of the Universal Welfare State.* Cambridge: Cambridge UP, 1998.
Sassen, Saskia. *Losing Control?: Sovereignty in an Age of Globalization.* New York: Columbia UP, 1996.
Thorhallsson, Baldur. *The Role of Small States in the European Union.* Aldershot: Ashgate, 2000.
Trehorning, Par. *Meaures to Combat Unemployment in Sweden: Labor Market Policy in the Mid-1990s.* Stockholm: The Swedish Institute, 1993.
Vail, Benjamin. "Toward A Green Tourism in Norway: Recognizing A Clash of Cultures." *Scandinavian Review* 88.1 (2000): 57–63.
Zurn, Michael. "The Challenge of Globalization and Individualization: A View from Europe." *Whose World Order? Uneven Globalization and the End of the Cold War.* Eds. Henrik Holm and Georg Sørensen. Boulder: Westview P, 1995. 137–163.

Just Enough ("Lagom") Europeanization
The Nordic States and Europe

Eric S. Einhorn
University of Massachusetts

I N AN AGE OF "EUROPEANIZATION" and "globalization," what remains of the "Nordic way"? This short survey looks at the far-reaching changes that have swept across northern Europe during the past decade following the sudden conclusion of the Cold War. As will be discussed below, the happy conclusion to the protracted conflict was not unproblematic. Not since 1918 have the geopolitics of northern Europe undergone a so sudden and unpredictable change. All of the Nordic countries have had to reappraise their political, security, and economic relations. A decade is too brief to draw conclusions about trends, but the coming decade is more likely to resemble the 1990s than the previous forty-year period. Of course history is full of surprises. As Monty Python put it, "no one predicted the Spanish Inquisition!" In early 1929, European politics (and much else) looked quite rosy. The 1980s started with a strong foreboding of doom, especially in Europe. Such precedents call for caution and humility, not paralysis.

Since 1990 the Nordic countries have reassessed their roles in European, Atlantic, and global politics. Four questions highlight the new perspectives of the regions.

1. How has the past decade changed regional, political, economic, and cultural identity in the Nordic countries?

2. What is Scandinavia's[1] place in evolving European economic and political cooperation, especially the European Union? What sort of "Europe" should they seek to build?

---

[1] Although strictly speaking "Scandinavia" refers to Denmark, Norway, and Sweden, I shall use it interchangeably with "Nordic" to include Finland, Iceland, as well as the autonomous territories of Greenland, Faeroe Islands, and Åland Islands.

3. How can Scandinavia encourage and support democratization and reforms in the European Union but also among her northern neighbors including Russia, the Baltic states, and Eastern Europe. This has been identified somewhat confusingly as the EU's "northern dimension."[2]

4. How can Scandinavia reconcile its European focus with its historical commitment to global cooperation and activism? Including Nordic support for the United Nations and other international organizations and development policies. The prominence of Scandinavian efforts in peacekeeping measures in the Balkans and in the Middle East suggests a tension between commitments and multilateral political cooperation.

The past decade has been tumultuous in Scandinavia as in all of Europe. First came severe economic crises in each of the Nordic countries well illustrated by the Swedish experience. By the late summer of 1992, the Swedish economy hit rock bottom and started to dig. The combination of domestic inflation, bank collapses, and a global recession ended the economic expansion of the 1980s. Domestic economic and political turmoil had reached a turning point when Swedish labor unions rejected the austerity measures of Social Democratic Finance Minister Kjell-Olof Feldt in February 1990. This paved the way for the non-socialist government of Carl Bildt after the September 1991 elections.

The Swedish economy spiraled downward until 1993 producing government deficits of over 13 percent of Gross Domestic Product (GDP). Unemployment soared to "double-digits" in the homeland of "active labor market" policies that had assured full employment even as most western countries accommodated high unemployment after the first oil "shock" of 1974. Although opportunistic currency devaluations had restored global competitiveness twice during the 1980s (as it had done in the early 1930s), the crown was under severe international pressure. Sweden's brief membership in the European Union's Exchange Rate Mechanism had lost credibility with the international financiers, some of whom ruthlessly speculated against those currencies they suspected of overvaluation. Unfortunately the Swedish crown was on their "hit list." The Swedish Riksbank (central bank) and the Ministry of Finance in their elegant Stockholm headquarters prepared to defend their currency, in part by hiking overnight interest rates to an amazing 500 percent,

---

[2] Confusingly because the focus is not really the "Nordic" states but rather northeastern Europe including the Baltic region and northwestern Russia from Pechenga/Kola south through the St. Petersburg region to the Polish-Lithuanian-Belorussian borders.

they could not resist the international tidal wave. The global economy had come to Sweden.

The Swedish currency (among several in Europe) was devalued, clever speculators made a quick killing, and the ideal of independent national monetary policy was knocked down several pegs. Even the less shaky currencies of Norway and Denmark swayed for a few days, reportedly in part because distant manipulators failed to distinguish between the several Scandinavian "crowns." Finland too was in severe economic crisis as a quarter of its export market in formerly communist eastern Europe imploded.[3]

Just as the European Economic and Monetary Union—the prize project of the recently concluded Maastricht Treaty on European Union—was to be launched, the brave new world temporarily faded. A few months earlier, Danish voters had shocked Europe (and perhaps themselves) by rejecting the Maastricht treaty by narrow 2 percent margin. Within weeks of this international economic turmoil, Sweden joined Norway and Finland and applied to join the expanding EU. In 1995, Finland and Sweden entered the EU while Norwegian voters again rejected membership by a decisive margin in a referendum. Danish voters accepted the Maastricht (European Union) Treaty with "four reservations" in 1993, approved the Amsterdam Treaty in 1998 but again narrowly defeated the "common currency" in 2000. The Nordic road to "Europe" remains rocky (see Ingebritsen 1998, especially chapters 1, 4, and 8).

In Scandinavia as elsewhere, foreign policy analysts and policy-makers compartmentalize issues and developments. Traditionally such "geopolitical" analysis focuses on historically significant geographic regions and states.[4] Such regional perspectives have included Nordic, Baltic, west European, east European, Atlantic, and numerous additional distinctions. Key countries also weighed heavily: Germany (1871–1945), Russia (continuously, but especially between 1945 and 1990), the United States

---

[3] Until the early 1990s Finland sent 20–25 percent of its exports to "ComEcon" (Council of Mutual Economic Assistance; the Soviet bloc trading organization). Trade was mainly with the Soviet Union and based on periodic trade agreements that basically exchanged Finnish industrial products for Soviet raw materials and energy. Other eastern European countries had also become significant after 1970. The sudden collapse of this market not only affected overall Finnish exports, but certain sectors (e.g. shipbuilding) that had specialized in products for the east European market.

[4] "Geopolitics" has had a deterministic and even ideological content during much of the twentieth century. Here the term is more simply descriptive.

(since 1945), etc. Typically national security issues have been the prime concern of geopolitics. Questions of "war and peace" remain important for Europe and Scandinavia especially given the proximity of several crisis regions (especially the Balkans, the Middle East, and to a lesser extent Russia, north Africa, and the Persian Gulf).

A more recent analytical framework has been called "geoeconomics," which reflects the prominence of economic issues in contemporary international relations.[5] These have mostly focused on "trade" issues, but now include finance, technology, strategic commodities, and international economic development. The currently popular "human capital" dimension adds human skills, education, innovation, and other factors that contribute to a country's economic strength and potential. Some would add another category: "geosocial" affairs to encompass some of the above human and social elements of international relations but also to recognize the importance of issues involving immigration, refugees, health and disease, criminal activities, and the transnational impact of social policies. Environmental and cultural factors also belong at least partially to this category.

To talk of Scandinavia and Europe is ambiguous: does one mean relation with the rest of the continent, and what is the extent of contemporary "Europe"? Should "Europe" focus on the issues and agenda of the emerging European Union, which is still overwhelmingly a west European community of advanced capitalist democracies? The complexity of overlapping international and regional organizations (NATO, the Organization for Security and Cooperation in Europe, Council of Europe, etc.) makes matters yet more complex. What about "special relationships" with the transatlantic connection to the USA and Canada the most prominent? Clearly the geopolitics of Scandinavia has changed but remains high on each country's political agenda.

The events of the past decade have reaffirmed that the Nordic countries remain distinct, independent actors on the European and global scene. They have not rejected the idea of sovereignty although they usually reject the mirage of isolated autonomy. Their economies remain ever more interdependent on their neighbors and the global economy. While such interdependence can exacerbate crises (as in 1992), it is the foundation for national prosperity. This essay will

---

[5] A provocative discussion of contemporary "geoeconomics" is found in Edward Luttwak's *Turbo-Capitalism: Winners and Losers in the Global Economy*. More traditional is Robert Gilpin's *The Challenge of Global Capitalism: The World Economy in the 21st Century*.

argue that the Nordic countries have developed a reasonably pragmatic—"lagom"—"just enough"—attitude toward regional integration and cooperation.[6] They rationally join international "communities" to maximize their political, economic, and strategic advantages or to minimize risks. They do not, however, see their nation-states as "obsolete" or dysfunctional.

BACKGROUND

The dramas of world politics seldom focus on the five Scandinavian countries: Denmark, Finland, Iceland, Norway, and Sweden.[7] These countries have had the good fortune of rarely being at the center of international crises or political turmoil. In recent years, world politics has "surfed" from one global trouble spot to another with few clear patterns or promising models of a more peaceful and just world order. The Scandinavian countries have a large stake in this "new world order," and perhaps some lessons on how to shape the course of events more positively. Their internal and regional efforts at conflict resolution, their dedication to international cooperation, and their small state perspective have much to offer a world anxious to balance international and domestic concerns, use scarce resources more wisely, and build institutions capable of avoiding new global conflicts.

The Scandinavian countries are among the world's most prosperous and democratic societies. International economic and social surveys consistently place them at the top in terms of their achievements. This attracts both foreign admiration but also criticism. Only a century ago, their poverty and social tensions stimulated a massive emigration to North America. Today Scandinavians venture abroad in massive numbers as tourists, students, artists, businessmen and women, and occasionally as "tax refugees." Their countries have attracted tens of thousands of immigrants and refugees. Some Scandinavians have been

---

[6] The Swedish expression "lagom" is not easily captured by English: "just enough" or dictionary alternatives: "just right, appropriate, in moderation, etc."

[7] The main "exception" during the past century was World War II, 1939–45. Particularly the "Winter War" when the Soviet Union attacked Finland in November 1939 and the German assaults on Norway and Denmark in April 1940 (the opening salvos of Hitler's western campaign) demonstrated Scandinavia's geopolitical vulnerability. Although the "Cold War" certainly affected the Nordic region, it was not the principal point of East-West confrontation.

quite visible on the world scene: the first two Secretaries-General of the United Nations were Trygve Lie (Norwegian) and Dag Hammarskjöld (Swede).[8] Contemporary politicians including former Swedish Prime Minister Carl Bildt, Norwegian Prime Minister Gro Harlem Brundtland, and Finnish President Matti Ahtisaari have continued that tradition. Today hundreds of Scandinavian military personnel serve as UN peacekeepers at dozens of global hot spots or as part of the NATO-led international force in the strife-torn states of former Yugoslavia. There are also police and civil servants serving as peacekeepers, truce observers, and emergency administrators. Like Dag Hammarskjöld and Folke Bernadotte dozens have given their lives over the past four decades in international service.

For nearly five decades, the view of Scandinavia as sharing a social democratic political economy but different foreign policies was generally accurate. Denmark, Norway, and Iceland joined NATO in 1949. Although they fulfilled their alliance commitments according to national preferences, they stood with the United States and the rest of western Europe. Sweden stuck to its non-alignment and traditions of neutrality. Cooperation with the West was discreet and focused on economic relations. Finland's position was unique and at times difficult. Finland escaped the terrible fate of the Baltic and eastern European countries by vigorously defending its independence and accommodating its politics to the concerns of Soviet Russia. Successful "reassurance" allowed Finland to maintain its internal democracy and close ties to the West (see Jakobson 1998, especially chapter 3).

Post-1945 Scandinavia sought security and prosperity through broad European cooperation. All wished to avoid new divisions despite the obvious differences between the western democracies and Stalin's Soviet Union. The term applied to this policy of reconciliation and optimistic diplomacy was "bridge-building." Bridges are built over chasms; the Scandinavian states recognized the fundamental conflicts that threatened the postwar order.

A useful way to view the past half-century of Scandinavian foreign policies is from *five* perspectives: Nordic, western European, Atlantic, eastern European, and Global. Such analytical shorthand is not precise,

---

[8] This was also true in the 1920s, where the Norwegian "explorer-statesman" Fridjof Nansen, Danish Foreign Minister Peter Munch, and Swedish Foreign Minister Östen Undén were prominent in the effort to make the League of Nations viable (see Lönnroth 1963, 86–99).

especially with the transition of many central and eastern European and Baltic states following the end of the Cold War. Such "geopolitical" shorthand must be an analytical tool rather than a doctrine of historical determinism.

NORDEN OR NORTHERN EUROPE?

In his provocative 1992 essay, Ole Wæver suggested that Nordic cooperation and even regional identity was threatened by the widening and deepening European Union. He analyzed "Nordic nostalgia" sympathetically but unsentimentally. He correctly noted that most Nordic political cooperation was developed as a "next-best" solution to broader European cooperation. The record of post-1945 Nordic projects that failed is impressive. The effort to create a Scandinavian Defense Union in 1948–49 failed when Norway and more reluctantly Denmark chose the Atlantic Pact (NATO). Efforts to create a Scandinavian Customs Union in the 1950s and a Nordic Economic Community (Nordek) in 1970 were overtaken by wider European economic communities. Only the Nordic passport union and common labor market—originating in the 1950s—were notable successes.[9]

After the Cold War, Nordic cooperation would have to find a "niche" within the European and global policy complex. Of course the Nordic Council survives and continues to foster pragmatic cooperation and policy coordination. With Norway and Iceland (as well as Greenland and the Faeroes) outside of the European Union (but within the European Economic Area), Nordic cooperation provides a useful form and symbol of regional identity. Even with Finland inside the full Economic and Monetary Union, public opinion is still broadly skeptical of the EU's ambitious plans on the economic, social, and foreign policy front. Denmark's September 2000 rejection of the common currency (while still maintaining EMU policy commitments) is more typical of an "à la carte" approach to globalization and Europeanization. It builds, however, on a longer tradition of foreign policy pragmatism.

---

[9] The passport and labor treaties allowed Nordic citizens to settle freely in any of the Nordic countries. It facilitated the immigration of tens of thousands of Finns primarily to Sweden between the late 1950s and early 1970s. Moreover it was later reinforced by agreements on equal access to social protection and benefits.

Nordic cooperation has traditionally been every Scandinavian country's "second" choice. Fortunately first choices have rarely excluded Nordic cooperation, but few "heavy issues" (e.g. security, economic, and trade cooperation, etc.) are anchored in this small region. While in the cultural and popular sphere there have been echoes of "Pan-Scandinavian" enthusiasm (primarily among the cultural and political elite), Nordic cooperation and integration has been a modest structure on a strong foundation. Nordic cooperation and global citizenship (e.g. the League of Nations and the United Nations) have been the two most broadly supported geopolitical dimensions in Nordic foreign relations. Although there were signs of such regional sympathies in the nineteenth century, it was not until the crisis of World War I that such efforts became real alternatives for the Scandinavian countries.[10]

The *Nordic* perspective reflects history, culture, but also deliberate choices. Scandinavia was never part of the ancient Roman Empire or its Germanic successors. As far back as the fifteenth century, Scandinavia was united in a loose dynastic entity known as the Kalmar Union. The next 400 years saw frequent and often bitter rivalry in the Nordic region until the current five independent states evolved in the twentieth century. Yet even as nationalism was shaping five distinct sovereign countries, there were calls for regional cooperation. They followed two lines: a "romantic" "pan-Scandinavianism" that argued for a federation of the increasingly democratic societies of the North, and pragmatic "functional" proposals covering a range of public policies common to the industrializing economies of the five states. After roughly 1720, none of the Scandinavian kingdoms could aspire to hegemony. They shared common interests in preventing other powers (Russia and later Germany) from dominating the Baltic-North Sea region.

While "Scandinavianism" ended historic rivalries, it did not prevent the further division of the region into the five modern nations. The practical policy approach proved most fruitful starting with a monetary union at the end of the nineteenth-century (which collapsed following World War I), an "inter-parliamentary union" in 1907, and frequent discussions between political leaders. After World War II, the more

---

[10] Reference here is to the tentative support for Denmark in its Schleswig-Holstein struggles—support was almost entirely "moral"—and the pragmatic economic cooperation of the Scandinavian Monetary Union launched in the 1870s. During World War I political, economic, and military cooperation helped support the three kingdoms' common goal of neutrality.

ambitious goals of Nordic advocates, illustrated by the "failures" noted above, repeatedly ran into two obstacles. First, the interests of the Scandinavian countries were often different and not infrequently competitive. This situation strengthened historical and nationalist desires in Norway, Finland, and Iceland to maintain full independence from the older Scandinavian states. Secondly, alternative political and economic ties outweighed Scandinavian possibilites. This situation was seen most dramatically in security policy after 1948 when Denmark, Norway, and Iceland chose the Atlantic alliance led by the United States, Finland accommodated its foreign relations to the narrow margins demanded by the Soviet Union, and Sweden reaffirmed its historical and successful non-alignment.

Later economic cooperation followed a similar path with broader European opportunities outweighing the potential of narrower Nordic proposals. Although intra-Scandinavian trade expanded significantly after 1950, access to European and global markets remained the higher priority. Despite these setbacks, in 1952 the Nordic countries established the Nordic Council—essentially an extension of the inter-parliamentary union, which would coordinate legislation and encourage Nordic initiatives whenever consensus could be reached. Since 1971 the Nordic Council of Ministers (linking the five/eight governments and civil servants) has become the principal instrument of Nordic cooperation.

Nordic cooperation thus functions at three levels: parliamentary, ministerial, and civil. The annual meetings of parliamentary delegations from the five countries (plus the three autonomous regions: Åland, Greenland, and the Faeroes) encourages pragmatic cooperation and deepens mutual understanding. Committee work fosters personal contacts across the region and a comparative perspective on policy issues. Ministerial contacts are more intense and continuous. Ministries develop expertise on Nordic affairs and also establish contacts among policy experts. Hence solutions to technical problems may be expedited by a direct phone call to a Nordic bureaucratic neighbor. In addition there are regular ministerial "summits," which bring together the top political and best administrative people for detailed discussions and planning. A common Nordic political culture that emphasizes consensus, fact-finding, pragmatism, and responsibility helps this process. Finally there are the various non-governmental (or autonomous) organizations in the educational, cultural, and scientific area that bring Scandinavians together on specific projects and interests. Again this invigorates Nordic cooperation at the "grass roots" but also mobilizes important interests in support of these activities. This is "soft" integration: rather than create a large "acquis communautaire" (code of laws, directives, and regulations), much Nordic cooperation is informal or loosely structured. A phone conversation between civil servants, quiet meetings of "experts," and more recently the continuous pulse of electronic communication ("Norden 2000").

Western Europe was a concept of the Cold War, but it increasingly gained real political and economic significance. The Nordic countries chose not to be part of the evolving European community that started with the Brussels Pact of 1948, the Schuman Plan of 1950 for a coal and steel community, and especially the Treaty of Rome in 1957, which sparked the development of a European common market. Yet all but Finland participated in the European Recovery Program (the Marshall Plan) and became part of looser institutional structures that were also favored by Great Britain. Likewise Denmark and Norway (and to a lesser extent Iceland) found that NATO membership brought them closer to the western European democracies and expedited reconciliation with the German Federal Republic. By the 1960s relationships with expanding western European institutions (notably the Common Market) became a permanent item on the Scandinavian political agenda.

The *Atlantic* dimension overlaps considerably with the western European but it suggests two important aspects. After 1940 the Scandinavian states developed sustained and intensive relations with the United States (and to a lesser extent Canada) with which they previously had important ethnic ties but no real "diplomatic history." Secondly it brought particularly the three Scandinavian NATO members into a much wider community in Europe (especially with the Mediterranean NATO members). Finally it evolved into a broader western community exemplified by the Organization of Economic Cooperation and Development (OECD) which emerged in 1960 out of the narrower Marshall Plan structure.

Relations with *eastern Europe* and the former Soviet Union reflects the legacy of the Cold War which also dominated Scandinavia for more than forty years. For the past two centuries Scandinavia has not had close relations with eastern Europe, and Russia was most often seen as a threat. After a period of "bridge-building" between 1944 and 1948, the Scandinavian countries chose different options to cope with the east-west struggle. Common to each was a desire to maintain relatively low tensions in the Nordic region and to develop autonomous Nordic relations. Since 1990 Scandinavia's "eastern question" has become far more complex. At present three aspects define the former eastern "bloc." First is the renewed independence of the Baltic states of Estonia, Latvia, and Lithuania. The Scandinavian countries have greeted this unexpected development with unusual activism. Coupled with this is the emergence of a democratic and increasingly dynamic Poland. Secondly, Russia's weakness and tentative steps toward democracy represents an unprecedented challenge for the Nordic states. The norm had been an authoritarian, powerful, but often conservative Russia. Finally, the emerging democracies of central and eastern Europe are moving toward a common European destiny but along varied paths. The Nordic countries support an inclusive and pluralistic future for eastern Europe but have focused on a handful of countries of particular concern. Clearly the disintegration of Yugoslavia and Balkan instability reflect Scandinavia's worst fears.

Finally there remains a *global* perspective that includes Scandinavia's historic commitment to the United Nations and other forms of international cooperation. The Nordic countries have global economic interests and collectively represent a substantial global economic power. They are among the most generous and steadfast contributors to international economic assistance and often champion the less developed countries in international organizations. Yet they are far from major actors whose decisions can affect global affairs. Here too a strategy of "bridge-building" can be constructive, as illustrated by the role of Norway and her late Foreign Minister Johan Jørgen Holst in facilitating the Israeli-Palestinian "Oslo" Accords.

NORDIC BALANCE

By the 1960s, Nordic foreign policies had established patterns that with occasional variations were maintained until the end of the Cold War in 1990. The geopolitical-political dimensions of Nordic, Atlantic, European, Baltic and eastern European, and global seemed reasonably defined. Each Nordic country had, of course, its own interests, priorities, and interpretation. At no time has there been a formal "common" Nordic foreign policy; each country has assessed the impact its foreign policy might have on an overall "Nordic balance." In addition, as the Norwegian analyst Arne O. Brundtland (1994) and others noted, each Nordic country has generally assumed that the success of one Nordic country's foreign policy would benefit the entire region and minimize tensions in the region, an assumption that was facilitated by Nordic cooperation.

Foreign policy was initially taboo for formal Nordic cooperation especially when Finland became a full partner in the system in the 1960s. Collaboration here developed nevertheless under more discrete conditions; indeed Finland's expansive President Urho Kekkonen pursued "active non-alignment" for twenty-five years in order to maximize his country's options and assure the Soviet Union of Finland's friendly intentions. His "pre-emptive" anticipation of Soviet requests elicited domestic and foreign criticism, including the notorious concept of "Finlandization." Coined by West German politicians but broadly used by western conservatives and critics of détente, it implied a passive regard for Soviet interests in lieu of western cooperation.

Swedish leader Olof Palme also rejected the discretion and restraint of his predecessors and tried to shape a Swedish "profile" of active non-alignment in international affairs.[11] Both countries put pressure on Denmark and Norway to minimize their engagement in NATO and to reconsider a more active Nordic security commitment. Many were tempted to follow such a line, but the choice of 1949 to rely primarily on broader western defense cooperation prevailed.

Nordic balance remained illusive and flexible during the Cold War. While NATO and particularly the American guarantee to western Europe formed the foundation of national security policy in Denmark, Iceland, and Norway, both Finland and Sweden counted on that ultimate source of assistance should things go wrong. All of the Nordic countries sought to reinforce the reality that northern Europe was *not* the main axis of east-west tensions. Norwegian restraint along their border with the USSR in the far north and the Danish regard for Soviet concerns in the eastern Baltic including the Danish island of Bornholm (which had been briefly occupied by the Russians after World War II) succeeded in keeping regional tensions under control. Recurring Soviet pressures and interference highlighted by the provocative submarine violations of Swedish territorial waters reminded most Scandinavians of the need for a credible security policy.

---

[11] Olof Palme became prominent and controversial as a Social Democratic cabinet minister in the 1960s. He served as Swedish Prime Minister from 1970 to 1976 and again from 1982 until his assassination in February 1986. Both as a junior minister in the 1960s and later as Prime Minister, Palme pursued "active non-alignment" vigorously and controversially.

While successfully restraining most Cold War tensions in their region, the Nordic countries never succeeded in creating a region truly distinct from the larger European context. In the security sphere there was insufficient power. In economic matters their ties to Europe remained supreme. Until the 1960s Britain was the most important market for the Scandinavian countries, and British reluctance to participate in the new European Economic Communities (EEC: the Common Market and Coal and Steel Community) restrained Scandinavia. The alternative was the European Free Trade Association (EFTA) that eventually also included Finland. By 1961, however, the dynamic Common Market was a serious issue in Scandinavia. West Germany had become again a vital market for the Scandinavian states. As security issues waned, economic questions demanded difficult choices: first between competing blocs and models (EEC vs. EFTA), and then over the extent of integration and its political consequences.

AN END AND A BEGINNING

By the mid-1970s, it was again clear that "Nordic Balance" would be mainly a passive policy. Nordic cooperation would be limited in the economic sphere to the common labor market (agreed in 1955) and to joint investment efforts (e.g. the Nordic Investment Bank). Only Denmark joined the European Community in 1973, while Norwegian voters rejected membership, and Sweden and Finland never applied. Denmark would preserve its Nordic links and would even promote regional interests in Brussels, but the limits of Nordic cooperation seemed clear.

Despite the different Nordic responses to the Cold War, each country sought to combine credible national security, conflict avoidance with the Soviet Union, and cautious steps toward relaxation of tensions between east and west. Since 1990, the Nordic states have become more "pro-active" in the new security design for their region. While the "Scandinavian" core remains well defined, there are complexities. First, Norway and Iceland are outside of the European Union but members of NATO. Sweden and Finland are in the EU but not NATO (although they are linked to both through the Partnership for Peace). While NATO has expanded eastward, it has not yet expanded northward. Arguably the continued reluctance of the four democratic "neutrals" (Sweden, Austria, Finland, and Ireland — along with perennial neutral Switzerland) to join the "new" NATO gives credibility to those who say that NATO is not the only credible source of security in post-Cold War Europe.

Secondly, the shape of the European Security and Defense Identity (i.e. the EU's common foreign and security policy) is still uncertain. It must compete not only with NATO—which still is the preferred instrument of the United States—but also the UN and the Organization for Security and Cooperation in Europe.

Thirdly, the Nordic area is highly engaged in Baltic regional cooperation as noted below. So just as the Nordic Council began to consider heavier political issues like security and common foreign policy initiatives, important "competitors" have emerged.

POST COLD WAR OPTIONS

After the collapse of the Soviet Union and its bloc, the strategic situation for the Scandinavian countries was radically changed. There were then similarities with the post-World War I period. The principle hostile power was down but Russia would remain a factor in European politics as it has been for at least three hundred years. Germany was reunified but under a liberal democratic constitution and with a political culture more like Scandinavia (the German Social Market welfare state had numerous similarities with the Scandinavian Social Democratic model) but with its 80 million people and economic mass would remain *the* factor in European politics. The other major western European powers—France, Britain, and to some extent Italy—enjoyed prestige and influence but were clearly limited in their unilateral options (a factor rarely admitted). The United States remained committed to European security and would become increasingly in the 1990s the core of the "new economy" (utilizing information technologies and other science based industries). US dependence on imported petroleum guaranteed a global role, especially when regional crises threatened global energy markets (e.g. the Persian Gulf, especially in 1990–91). But American responses to regional European crises (especially in the Balkans) were slow to gain coherence, and US engagement in Europe inevitably declined as the traditional military threats to the region receded.

A traditional Nordic role—first visible in 1946–47 as east-west cooperation broke down— would have relevance in post-Cold War Europe. The term "bridge-building" was applied to diplomatic efforts to reconcile the two blocs. In the 1990s the Nordic states, despite their economic problems, had the economic, political, and diplomatic resources to assert this role more forcefully than fifty years earlier. Economic assistance to the new European democracies was significant. Political and organizational aid to some post-Soviet states was important, especially to the Baltic states where democratic and economic institutions had been problematic even in their two decades of interwar independence. Humanitarian and pragmatic aid to Russia has been significant. The Nordic countries, especially Finland, have supported fully the "Northern Dimension" initiative of the European Union to improve relations and conditions in Russia and the Baltic states.

Clearly the Baltic Sea region has in policy terms become almost "co-equal" with the Nordic region. Estonia, Latvia, and Lithuania have become "quasi-Nordic" in political terms (though there is little modern historical reason for such a special relationship, except between Finland and Estonia). Military, economic, and administrative support—such as training the trilateral "Baltic Battalion" for peacekeeping duties—has been the Nordic effort to assist their eastern neighbors. The creation of the Council of Baltic Sea States in 1992 (including Poland, Russia, and Germany) has been another effort to "organize" northern Europe.[12]

EUROPEAN UNION

As noted, Scandinavia remained on the periphery of the European integration project for nearly twenty-five years after World War II. By 1961 regional trading blocs still seemed to be tightening. The Rome Treaty of 1957 had given birth to the European Economic Communities (then known as "the Common Market"), while Britain and the Nordic countries were instrumental in launching an alternative and much looser "European Free Trade Association." It soon was clear that the EEC would progress more dynamically than EFTA. The British ambiguous decision to apply for EEC membership forced the Scandinavian countries to reconsider their position. French President Charles de Gaulle delayed British entry for a decade, but when in 1969 the issue again became germaine, it was clear that the EEC was an economic and political success and that there would be no other significant European alternative. Just as the European option again appeared promising, the Nordic

---

[12] Baltic and Nordic developments in the 1990s are nicely summarized by Tom Schumacher (2000) in "The Emergence of the New Nordic Cooperation."

countries (now including Finland) had commenced negotiations on a wider Nordic economic community, which would possibly lead to a common Nordic entry into the EEC. This possibility threatened especially Finland's special regard for Soviet sensibilities, but Sweden too was concerned about its "non-aligned" status (a point already raised in 1963). In short, whenever a wider European option became promising, the Nordic countries found they each had different perspectives.

The result would be five Nordic roads to Europe, with Denmark's entry in 1973, Sweden and Finland in 1995, Norway's failed entry (the government agreed but the public rejected the option in national referendums in 1972 and 1994), and Iceland's continued peripheral status in the remains of EFTA. Just to complicate matters, the two Danish autonomous North Atlantic territories of Greenland and the Faeroe Islands remained outside of the EEC with Greenland actually withdrawing in 1982.

Since the 1970s the European Union has emerged as the focus of economic cooperation and integration in Europe. Nordic alternatives, initially attempted in the 1950s and not fully abandoned until after 1970, are no longer a factor. Even the "non-members" (Norway and Iceland) are anchored to the EU system as "outer planets" in the "European Economic Area." They have accepted most EU policies except in the agricultural and fishery areas. For this exceptional position, they sacrifice direct influence in the EU policy process.

All of the Nordic countries have contrived "special" relationships with the EU demonstrating both the reality of national politics and the flexibility of the confederal EU system. These national differences reflect two competing visions of European unity over the past half-century: confederal vs. federal. The first has been highly pragmatic and "functional." Cooperation aimed at removing barriers to free trade and investment as well as policy collaboration in areas of common concerns (e.g. environment, refugees, human rights, defense) has come to be regarded as "Europe *à la carte*."[13] States can pick and choose the collection of project in which they will participate. The alternative has been more grandiose: a United States of Europe with genuinely federal institutions would move significant portions of public policy into a European entity. National governments would still have residual powers, but like other federal systems, the whole would be more than

---

[13] The French metaphor has been "variable geometry" (referring obscurely to swing-wing aircraft). See Hubert Védrine and Dominique Moisi (2001) *France in an Age of Globalization,* especially 55–75.

the sum of its parts. Ancient cultures and states would be unlikely to disappear or become mere provinces, but the four hundred year tradition of state sovereignty would be largely ended in principle as well as practice. Without either historical ties to earlier European dynastic empires or an imperial past, this vision has little support in Scandinavia and much vigorous resistance.

ECONOMIC COOPERATION

As trading states, the Scandinavian countries have long been wary of economic isolationism. All suffered from the economic nationalism and mercantilism of the interwar period. In response domestic protectionism gained a foothold in the agricultural and other primary economic sectors. International and regional economic cooperation has had two important goals for the Nordic countries. First, to maintain access to main export markets. The extreme economic nationalism of the 1930s and the post-World War II restrictions on trade and capital flows challenged the Nordic economies. A priority has been to reduce barriers to trade particularly in industrial goods. For Denmark, exports of agricultural products have also been crucial. The past decade demonstrated to the Nordic countries that their welfare states were affected by European and global economic, political, and social changes. The economic "roller-coaster" of 1990–95 was one dramatic sign, as was the emergence of Nordic economic and technological leadership in telecommunications, offshore petroleum extraction, and alternative energy systems (other areas of global strength included pharmaceuticals, electrical engineering, and container transport).

Although Nordic economic prosperity has depended on global markets for more than a century, the share of *exports* to Gross Domestic Product (GDP) has increased by 50–60 percent in Denmark, Finland, and Sweden (from 25–28 percent to 35–40 percent of GDP). Norwegian exports grew only modestly but from a very high level: 37 percent of GDP in 1970 to 39 percent in 1999. (Statistics from OECD 2000:70). Membership in the European Union (European Economic Area for Norway) has also affected broad areas of policy beyond trade. Although only Finland has committed itself fully to the European Economic and Monetary Union, Danish monetary and currency policies are fully tied to the EMU, and Sweden has committed itself to closer cooperation with EMU (but still has modestly devalued its currency over the past two years). What this suggests is that the Nordic "difference" will be smaller in the future, but there is less "difference" in key welfare state areas to defend.

Few Nordic politicians talk openly about their country as "ordinary" European social market states, but that is increasingly the reality. Given the EU's growing emphasis on social policy "convergence" (thus far to the "highest common denominator"), there is little threat and perhaps significant support for the Nordic welfare model in western Europe. While the Nordic EU members have strongly supportive "social convergence" initiatives, it enjoys broad support across to the EU.

The second foreign economic policy goal has been to maintain stability of prices for commodities (especially primary raw materials such as wood, paper, metals, and more recently, petroleum). Although the relative share of such commodities has declined markedly, Norway, Sweden, and Finland are still significant exporters. Denmark and Iceland have been concerned about agricultural and fishery exports. Access to regional trading arrangements has offered protection for these interests.

RELUCTANT EUROPEANS

As the European integration project pursues "an ever closer union" in the wake of the Maastricht Treaty of 1991 (as amended in Edinburgh in 1992 and further in Amsterdam in 1997), the Nordic countries remain divided as much within as between. Iceland and Norway are tied through the agreement on a European Economic Area, which was negotiated in 1990, took effect in 1993, and essentially gives these countries access to the "Single European Market" in all areas excepting agriculture and natural resources and other issues of "vital national interest." Public opinion in the three member states is critical of various aspects of the EU, while only a small minority is opposed to the entire enterprise. The nature of the EU expansion to as many as twenty-seven members within the next decade assures that it will not soon become a functioning "supernational state." Yet, the current governance structure is complex and impenetrable to most citizens. Critics complain about "democratic deficits," but few want a genuine federal EU government and voting for the European Parliament (EP) remains surprisingly low.[14] Turnout for

---

[14] The EU parliament is not comparable to national parliaments, but neither is it a sham. In 1999 it dismissed the entire European Commission of President Santer over various scandals. But voting levels are about half those normally seen for parliamentary elections in the Nordic countries.

EP elections remains dramatically lower than for national elections. In 1999 turnout in Finland was 31.4 percent, in Sweden 38.8 percent, and in Denmark 50.4 percent.[15]

Increasingly the European Union resembles (metaphorically) the geometry of the solar system. The core states—especially the original "Six"—orbit the "sun" (Brussels?) tightly. Denmark along with Britain circles the EU at a distance, perhaps analogous to Mars and Jupiter. Both are signatories to Maastricht Treaty, but have significant (if different) reservations. Although the Danish economy is among the strongest in the EU and its currency has been closely tied to the German mark for more than fifteen years, Denmark has rejected monetary union. Neither does it fully accept harmonization of police and judicial affairs nor participation in key elements of the common foreign and security policy. Every significant change in European policy has occasioned a bitter fight in Denmark and resulting national referenda. Danish voters approved the 1997 Amsterdam revision of the Union treaty in 1998, but rejected (narrowly) full participation in the Economic and Monetary Union in September 2000. Likewise, a quarter of the delegate elected by the Danes to the European Parliament are anti-EU activists.

Sweden and Finland became EU members in 1995 after vigorous national debates and referenda. As new members, they were forced to swallow the whole EU system ("acquis communautaire") but not without protest and regret. Their EU parliamentary delegations have strong anti-unionists, and opinion at home is even more skeptical of the EU project than the doubting Danes. Although Finland has fully accepted the EMU, Sweden like Britain pursues an independent currency policy (including continuing modest devaluations). Neither is firmly committed a common European foreign and security policy. They are likely to prove as reluctant in further steps as the Danes, and together with other anti-federalists (especially in Britain, but throughout the EU) are likely to restrain overly ambitious projects.

The "outer ring" of the European "planets" includes Norway and Iceland (as well as Greenland and the Faeroe Islands). They reside in the European Economic Area and have essentially full access to the European market (including labor), but they have no direct influence on development of the European Union. The circumstances of both (Iceland's reliance on its national fisheries, and Norway's expensive

---

[15] An analysis of the 1999 European Parliamentary elections and statistics is found in Lodge (ed.) 2001.

regionalism resting on enormous petroleum reserves) have outweighed any drawbacks.

Nordic habits of non-alignment and independence along with their still vigorous sense of nationhood and self-confidence (reduced perhaps marginally in Sweden and Finland by the economic turmoil of the 1990s) color their view of Europe. Expansion of the EU eastward may ease federalist pressures, as the new democracies of eastern and central Europe will not be able to adjust to the EU system quickly. The Nordic EU bloc (of three) is likely to support pressures for a "social Europe," which are now supported by the Blair government in Britain. Principles of "subsidarity" and pragmatism will make all Scandinavians more comfortable in the European home. Public opinion surveys like those conducted biennially by the European Union's Statistical Office ("Eurobarometers") reflect this luke-warm attitude. The Nordic public feels much more "national" than "European" (but so do most EU citizens outside of France, Germany, Spain, and Italy). Yet these data are ambiguous: 74 percent of the Swedes and 66 percent of the Danes in late 2000 felt "very" or "fairly" attached to Europe, while many fewer currently support membership in the EU (*Eurobarometer* 54).

"JUST ENOUGH" (LAGOM) EUROPEANIZATION

The Nordic countries share five decades of Nordic, European, Atlantic, and global cooperation. This sketch has outlined the historical evolution of Nordic geopolitical orientations. Clearly the Nordic countries have no firm or determined goal in their European policies other than to avoid rigidity, determinism, or dogmatism. Every state seeks multiple options not only to protect its vital interests (especially in national security), but also in maximizing broader policy goals. What the Nordic countries share in response to "Europeanization" is a determination not to be "trapped" or excessively "entangled" in the expansive "acquis communautaire." There is an inevitable tension between the desire to maintain sovereignty while benefiting from the cooperation and even integration in specific policy areas. It is not a simple "free rider" strategy that may have characterized aspects of Nordic security policy during the Cold War. It is clearly "Europe *à la carte*" but one which reflects tentative and at times contradictory tendencies throughout evolving European cooperation.

In part because of their modest size, high socio-economic standard and general administrative competence, the Nordic countries remain remarkably "successful" states by almost any standard. While few contemporary Nordic statesmen will brag about these achievements in the manner of some of their predecessors (e.g. Olof Palme, Alva Myrdal, *et al*), the recovery of economic balance and growth in the 1990s has restored confidence in the region. Moreover, careful examination has revealed to a growing number of Scandinavians that their "middle way" does not diverge significantly in social and economic policy from the western European mainstream. They have built impressive social welfare states, and proven in the 1990s that with proper reform they can sustain these achievements. The same challenge confronts most western European states, and there is reason to be cautiously optimistic that they too have moved toward a sustainable course.

The Nordic countries understand the necessity to engage through the European Union (especially its Parliament, Commission, and other institutions) — even *à la carte* — as well as in NATO (Denmark, Norway, and Iceland), the Partnership for Peace, the Organization for Security and Cooperation in Europe, and the United Nations. None seeks to be submerged in the EU's inner circle. As illustrated by the ambiguous relationship with economic and security issues, pragmatism is a viable EU strategy.

In short, the Nordic countries generally accept the EU as "good idea" and a "work in progress," but not a "great idea." It is proving to be a stabilizing and creative force in economic and increasingly social policy. The EU is clearly a useful mechanism to manage "globalization" even if consensus within the EU is often difficult (e.g. the Nice Summit of December 2000). Scandinavian rationalism thrives in such situations. Each Nordic country has tailored its Europeanization to fit its apparent contemporary needs (though one can disagree how well). As reflected in public opinion surveys such as the *Eurobarometer,* support is conditional, contingent, and at best pragmatic. Scandinavians want "just enough" European integration to achieve political, economic, and social policy goals, but no more. As Stanley Hoffmann has reminded us, political enterprises, especially those as ambitious as the various European projects, do well to recall the caution attributed to Prince Talleyrand, *"pas trop de ziel!"*

286   SCANDINAVIAN STUDIES

WORKS CITED

Brundtland, Arne Olav. "Nordic Security at the End of the Cold: Old Legacies and New Challenges." *Nordic-Baltic Security: An International Perspective.* Eds. Arne Olav Brundtland and Don M. Snider. Washignton DC: Center for Strategic and International Studies and Oslo: Norwegian Institute of International Affairs, 1994. 1–30.

Eurobarometer 54. Autumn 2000.

Gilpin, Robert. *The Challenge of Global Capitalism: The World Economy in the 21st Century.* Princeton: Princeton UP, 2000.

Ingebritsen, Christine. *The Nordic States and European Unity.* Ithaca: Cornell UP, 1998.

Jakobson, Max. *Finland in the New Europe.* Westport, CT: Praeger, 1998.

Lodge, Juliet, ed. *The 1999 Elections to the European Parliament.* New York: Palgrave, 2001.

Lönnroth, Erik. "Sweden: The Diplomacy of Östen Undén." *The Diplomats 1919–1939.* Series: The Twenties I. Eds. Gordon A. Craig and Felix Gilbert. New York: Atheneum, 1963. 86–99.

Luttwak, Edward. *Turbo-Capitalism: Winners and Losers in the Global Economy.* New York: Harper Collins, 1999.

"Norden 2000—öppet för världens vindar." Nordic Council of Ministers. July 2001. <www.norden.org/vis/norden2000.htm>.

OECD (Organization for Economic Co-operation and Development). *Historical Statistics 1970–1999.* Paris: OECD, 2000.

Schumacher, Tom. "The Emergence of the New Nordic Cooperation." Copenhagen: DUPI, 2000. Working paper 2002/6.

Védrine, Hubert, and Dominique Moïsi. *France in an Age of Globalization.* Trans. Philip H. Gordon. Washington DC: Brookings, 2001.

Wæver, Ole. "Nordic Nostalgia: Northern Europe after the Cold War." *International Affairs* 68.1 (1992): 78–102.

Can Small States Influence EU Norms?
Insights From Sweden's Participation in the Field of Environmental Politics

Annica Kronsell
Lund University

IN A FORTHCOMING BOOK, Christine Ingebritsen challenges the view that small states lack power in international relations by pointing to the Scandinavian countries' influence on the setting of international norms. For example, since the early 1970s, Sweden has been particularly active in pushing for environmental norms in various international settings. The Swedish government announced it would continue to do so as well in terms of its EU membership. In 1995 the government promised a skeptical electorate that it would not compromise domestic environmental norms (Kronsell 1997A). Looking back at Sweden's six years of EU membership, we note some evidence that these ambitions have at least partly materialized. One important example is the EU acidification strategy (COM 2001); another, the efforts at common legislation on the control of the use of chemicals. The commitment to environmental issues was stressed further as the strategies for the Swedish presidency of the EU during the first part of 2001 were announced. The main goals of the Swedish presidency were enlargement, employment, and environment. The foundation for the arguments in this article is a set of interviews conducted with participants in EU environmental policy making,[1] as

I want to express my gratitude to the Swedish Research Foundation (HSFR) and to the Department of Political Science, University of Washington for making my year as a visiting scholar so successful. I am particularly thankful to Professor Christine Ingebritsen who encouraged me to pursue my research in the direction of this article and Dr. Baldur Thorhallsson for valuable comments. The most recent set of interviews, of November 2000, were done with the help of a financial contribution from a Project on the Presidency led by Bo Bjurulf and Ole Elgström at the department of Political Science, Lund University.
[1] During January and February of 1998, I conducted nineteen telephone interviews and in November of 2000 in Stockholm, seventeen interviews. All interviews were with key policy makers in the National Environmental Protection Agency, the Chemical's Inspectorate, the Ministry of Environment, with members of the Parliamentary EU committee, the Nature Conservation Society, and Greenpeace. I want to thank all of the participants for patiently answering my questions and inquiries. The interviews are documented and in the author's possession.

well as studies commissioned by the Swedish government.[2] The main goal in this article is to challenge the arguments that small states have little or no influence in global politics by analyzing Swedish relations to the EU in the area of environmental issues. The article will assess that relationship in terms of what kind of influence can be discerned.

SWEDEN IN INTERNATIONAL ENVIRONMENTAL RELATIONS

Ingebritsen (2001) suggests that small states like the Scandinavian countries can make important contributions to world politics as norm setters or as "entrepreneurs of good practice" even with limited power and resources. Norm setting can hence be a means of influencing world affairs. Like other international organizations, the EU too is a norm-generating arena, even more extensive than other international or regional organizations. If we take Ingebritsen's thesis as valid for the international context, it may be relevant to the EU as well. Before looking at exactly how Sweden has exerted influence in the EU, I want to briefly outline the background of Sweden's involvement in international environmental politics and highlight aspects that are relevant for the Swedish position on environmental issues in the EU today.

Over the years, the pollution problems perceived as particularly threatening and urgent by policy makers and the public have been problems of a transnational kind. Motivations for Sweden's active involvement in international environmental policy making have been largely associated with environmental vulnerability and a perceived threat to national interests. In other words, many of the environmental issues that Swedish policy makers have pursued internationally have also been issues related to environmental problems that could only be resolved by other nations also taking action.

---

[2] These governmentally-commissioned studies are based on extensive interviews and surveys with policy makers involved in EU work. The following government studies have been most valuable as empirical material for this study: Ds 1994:126, *Det svenska miljöarbetet i EU*; Ds 1997: 68 *Det svenska miljöarbetet i EU—uppföljning av 1995 års strategi*, Ministry of Environment; Statskontoret 2000:20, *Fem år i EU—en utvärdering av statsförvaltningens medverkan i EU-samarbetet*; Statskontoret 2000:20A, *Den svenska förvaltningsmodelen i EU arbetet*; Statskontoret 2000: 20B, *Fallstudier av tre EU-intensiva politikområden*, The Swedish Agency for Public Management; SOU 2001:4, *Kemikalieinspektionen—översyn av verksamhet, resurser och finansiering*, Ministry of Environment.

A TRANSNATIONAL AGENDA FOR THE ENVIRONMENT

In the 1960s, there was an increasing problem with urban air pollution in Sweden. Within a few years Swedish scientists had discovered that urban air pollution could be traced to high contents of sulfur in heating oil. When alerted to the problem, politicians simply outlawed the use of high-sulfur oil.[3] The urban air quickly improved but acidification remained a problem because the jet stream brought winds, particularly from Germany and Great Britain, with precipitation that polluted Swedish lakes and forests. Starting in the 1970s, policy makers and experts, who had exhausted what could be done within the borders, tried to come to terms with acidification by inaugurating international cooperation. The first UN conference on environmental issues was held in Stockholm in 1972, partly on the initiative of Swedish policy-makers, who also presented their position paper on acid rain to the conference.

Another more recent issue firmly based in the national interests of Sweden is the regulation of chemical products. Sweden is a country with comparatively strict chemical legislation. Many chemicals allowed in Europe and the rest of the world are forbidden or have their use highly restricted in Sweden. Such restrictions come into conflict with norms of free trade, particularly in terms of the integrated market of the EU. Swedish experts and policy makers have tried to play a prominent and active role in the work on international standardization of chemicals for a long period of time.[4] The interest of Swedish policy makers in the regulation in the field of chemicals and products has been particularly geared toward the desire to control the content of goods imported into the country. The urgency of convincing other member states to adopt regulations similar to Swedish policy is striking. If they are not successful in their efforts, previously banned chemicals might have to be reintroduced on the Swedish market as an effect of the standardization and harmonization of the trade in goods. An example is the use of the pesticide 2,4-D which was banned from the Swedish market in 1991, but because it is not banned in the EU countries, will now be

---

[3] That it went so quickly is in itself very interesting. In brief terms, it appears to have been due to an unusual relationship between experts and policy makers at this particular point in time.

[4] For a longer discussion on Sweden's ambition to set an example in international relations and the EU and how that relates to domestic developments in policy and polity see Annica Kronsell (1997a).

again allowed in Sweden, needless to say, a development much to the disappointment of policy makers.

The participation in international environmental cooperation is the rationale of the activities conducted in the EU arena, but it is carried out differently by the various actors involved. The Environmental Protection Agency (SEPA) and the Chemicals Inspectorate (ChemI) are the two main actors who provide expertise both in the Commission working group and to the political representation in the Ministry of Environment and to the Swedish representation in Brussels.[5]

In international politics, it is often argued that important power bases can be such things as the country's size, its population, natural resources, and military or economic status. The criteria certainly apply to the EU as well and give certain countries more esteem and legitimacy apart from what is granted by the institutional context exemplified by the number of votes in the Council. While it is always important and interesting whether one of the bigger member states is likely to be supporting or blocking an initiative—act as a laggard or a forerunner—it might be less important how one of the smaller states intends to act. However, voting strength is not the only way of making an impact. Most agreements are made in the many day to day negotiations carried out throughout the EU. Hence, most of the work is done in various meetings between people who are representing sometimes only vague notions of a national interest. This fact suggests that important power resources may be the ones employed successfully in that context. This claim, then, is the basis for the following argument that small states' influence may be enhanced by being active EU members.

SWEDISH GOALS FOR EU ENVIRONMENTAL POLICY

When it comes to environmental policies, the EU has developed into a far-reaching regime incomparable in scope and strength to any other international cooperative arrangement. This is mainly due to the

---

[5] The work of the two Agencies, the Chemical's Inspectorate and the Environmental Protection Agency, toward the EU differs substantially. This is because chemical policy is concerned with trade and hence is subject to standardization directives; environmental regulation, however, is normally based on minimum directives. This is important because standardization directives requires identical standards over the entire community while the latter allows for member states to go beyond minimum directives in their efforts at environmental protection.

process of integration, which seems continuously to increase the areas of jurisdiction and the mechanisms for enforcement at hand in the EU. Furthermore, it is an ongoing negotiating arena where the steady input of ideas, perspectives, and comments seem to be encouraged and, at least, always expected. Norms that have been used in national contexts have served as models for EU directives or proposals. The explicit intention of the Swedish government has been, even before membership negotiations, to try to push the EU in the direction of Swedish environmental policy. There seems to be a very strong conviction among policy makers today that this is also at least to some degree possible. However, as five years in the EU has shown, compromises are necessary, and Swedish environmental policy is not always perfect but has its own flaws and weaknesses.

Looking back, it is clear that Swedish policy makers have had some success in pursuing their goals in the area of environmental policy. Although causal links cannot easily be verified, the EU has nevertheless adopted an acidification strategy and has agreed to a revision of the existing chemical policy and recently launched a chemical strategy (KOM 2001:88). Policy makers also attest to a whole range of small-scale or partial successes within the negotiations of specific directives. Evidence of small successes are exemplified by such things as convincing the rest of the member states to adopt the Swedish version of the definition of BAT (Best Available Technology), or adopting central parts of the Swedish equivalent in the EU IPPC (Integrated Pollution Prevention Control) directive. What will be investigated in what follows is the type of influence that is important in this issue area and how that influence is asserted.

HOW CAN SMALL STATES INFLUENCE THE EU AGENDA?

The remainder of this article discusses the factors that have contributed to Sweden's modest success in making an impact on the formation of common EU environmental policies. Before going into these factors in more detail, it is necessary to say something about perceptions of "the nature of the EU." There are various theoretical examinations and equally as many views on what European integration is all about. Hence, there is no one way to study EU processes. One suggestion, however, is to approach EU as a case of new governance (Kohler-Koch 1996). From this perspective, the vision of the EU is as a new governance form resulting from a range of parallel processes such as states pooling their sovereignty, the influence of a discourse of integration over time, spillover effects, and path dependency in policy making. One key characteristic of new governance is that it takes place in networks, where relations between different actors are important (Kohler-Koch 1999). Policy making in the EU can, therefore, perhaps be best understood as an integrated system of multi-level negotiations and bargaining (Grande 1996). The difference from a national system and the uniqueness of EU is that there is not one central authority in a multi-level governance system. This may be particularly fruitful as we address how this multi-level governance system may empower new and different actors.

Here I want to suggest that small states have been partially empowered by this new governance system and have gained influence particularly as norm setters. I will consider four different aspects and discuss how they have contributed to Sweden's influence on EU environmental policy. They are: (1) reputation and expectation on behavior, (2) expertise and knowledge as an important resource in the environmental policy process, (3) the importance of national policies as examples of success, and (4) successful coordination of national interest. Each aspect will be discussed in turn.

REPUTATION: SWEDEN AS A FORERUNNER STATE IN ENVIRONMENTAL ISSUES

What reputation may mean for the relations between states has been extensively and theoretically analyzed, for example, in the field of conflict resolution. In the past, the concern in international relations has been largely overshadowed by super power relations and dealt mainly with those relations and much less with small states.[6] Nevertheless, such approaches tend to indicate that impressions and perceptions of the partners to the negotiation process are important for the outcome (Shelling 1960; Snyder and Diesing 1977; Axelrod 1984). The perception that the participants at any negotiation table have of one another seems to be a function of previous experiences and earlier interactions. Cognitive frames that are based on previous experience constitute the expectations that partners in any negotiations hold of

---

[6] There are obviously exceptions such as Peter Katzenstein (1985) and Baldur Thorhallsson (2000).

one another. Furthermore, reputation will have an impact on current relations because behavior is interpreted and judged against those frames. What is less understood is how those previous interactions are framed and exactly how they determine current activities (Mercer 1996). As Jonathan Mercer stresses, we need to be particularly cautious in drawing causal links between reputation and behavior because such processes are highly subjective and interpretive. While proceeding with some caution, we will here infer that Sweden's behavior is interpreted positively because of the general cooperative ambition between the EU member states.[7] Furthermore, we will presume that the expectations of Sweden's behavior in EU environmental relations during the past years have been informed by the reputation incurred in previous engagements in international environmental relations. Swedish policy makers concerned with issues related to the environmental field have been very active in international negotiations, cooperation, and organizations and hence enjoy a reputation of being "activists" or "forerunners" on such issues. This means that the behavior of Swedish negotiators in the field of environmental politics was likely subject to such pre-established interpretive frames at the time of membership. There were expectations that Swedish policy makers would pursue environmental goals and line up with the so called "forerunner states." Among the policy makers of the other EU member states—the partners in negotiations—there was already an established image-based on the domestic environmental record and, perhaps more importantly, previous engagement in international environmental relations. Based on this fact, we can conclude that reputation and previous relations can become important resources for small states in EU negotiations. Simply because, as in this case, it gave Swedish representatives and experts alike a certain legitimacy to act on such matters.

Many policy makers have confirmed in interviews that Sweden's history of international environmental cooperation has been to their advantage in the EU and is illustrated by the following quotations from a recent study of the Chemicals Inspectorate (ChemI). ChemI is one of the two administrative agencies responsible for the management and implementation of environmental policy, domestic as well as European. Many of those interviewed in connection with the study of

---

[7] Mercer discusses the different impact that the type of relationship has on cognitive frames of the actors and suggests that between enemies negative interpretation will prevail and between allies positive interpretations (1996:59–65).

ChemI "point to the fact that ChemI is perceived as having highly reliable expert knowledge and a high legitimacy internationally and within the EU." One policy maker is quoted as saying: "This means that we have won acceptance for more than what is motivated for a country the size of Sweden. Sweden and ChemI have a solid reputation internationally" (SOU 2001:58). Even though these quotations and the study in general focus on ChemI, similar views have been expressed with regard to the EU work of the Swedish Environmental Protection Agency (SEPA), which is the other agency responsible for environmental policy implementation.[8] While international reputation as an environmental forerunner might benefit Swedish representatives and outfit them with particular power resources wherever they find themselves in the multi-levels of EU governance, in time it may be limiting to a new member. As negotiation and network relationships develop within the EU, it is likely that intra-EU experiences will overshadow pre-EU relations. It is highly likely that Sweden's success or failure in handling the EU presidency is an important challenge which will also be an input to the way that Swedish policy maker's future behavior will be interpreted by other member states. Indeed, from the perspective of the policy makers involved, an important goal for the presidency was to demonstrate to the member states that Sweden is a very competent and dedicated EU member. A satisfactory performance of the presidency creates trust and legitimacy that is expected to benefit Sweden significantly in future EU relations. Again, it supports the proposition that reputation and previous relations can become important resources for small states in international relations.

THE IMPORTANCE OF EXPERTISE AND KNOWLEDGE

In the field of environmental policy, the need for expert knowledge is often addressed. Indeed, what we broadly call environmental concerns are often highly complicated issues demanding the input of technical and scientific experts. While the EU acidification strategy has a more general framework character and perhaps can adequately be handled by generalists, most of the EU directives require much more specific and detailed knowledge. For example, specific directives suggesting

---

[8] Both of the agencies play an important role in the transposition of EU environmental legislation partly due to the traditional division of labor between autonomous agencies and the ministries in Swedish policy making are partly due to the high demands on administrative capacity of smaller member states (see Baldur Thorhallsson [2000]).

ways of implementing the acidification strategy have to do with the limitation of exhaust in various vehicle types. Experts, who can provide facts about exhaust processes, are aware of current updated techniques and can provide cost-benefit calculations that become an extremely valuable resource in such a context. Triumphant about the success of including producer responsibility in the auto/oil directive, Anna Lindh, the former environmental minister, exclaimed, "we have been push-ing hard and stubbornly for standards according to a Swedish model. Although there was ample resistance, *facts* won in the long run." She goes on and repeats: "the small countries won with *facts*."[9] I have heard similar claims that scientific facts and expertise are crucial elements in environmental policy making ever since I started to work in the field of EU environmental politics in the early 1990s.

It may be expected that scientific knowledge is particularly influential in agenda setting or the initial stages of policy making mainly carried out in the Commission and its many expert committees. While this has certainly been shown to be true, it seems as if, at least for envi-ronmental policy making, expertise is crucial in all stages of the policy making process. For example, the proposed EU chemical's strategy is of a general nature and is accessible to the layman. However, the issues that will have to be resolved in order to realize the strategy will most likely demand qualified scientific input both with regard to scientific knowledge about a range of specific chemical products as well as exper-tise in methods and techniques of risk assessment and cost estimates. Such issues may also come up for debate at the decision-making level in the Council and the European Parliament.

What has been learned from this case so far supports Karen Litfin's claim in which she highlights the interdependence of knowledge and influence. In her work on international environmental negotiations, she points to "the central importance of knowledge ... as both a political resource and an arena for struggle" (1994:177). In my earlier research on the development of EU environmental policy, I argued along a similar vein pointing out that scientific knowledge has been particularly impor-tant for a growing environmental awareness in the EU polity (Kronsell 1997B). I suggested that scientific "facts" have had an important standing and at times have been absolutely crucial to the introduction of new environmental policy in the EU. There appear to be a number of ways in which experts can provide resources for successful environmental

---

[9] My translation.

negotiations. One is scientific knowledge, i.e. familiarity with natural processes such as how chemical compounds are broken down and why certain lakes have high pH levels, etc. Another type is technical expertise, the knowledge of cleaner technologies, how they work, and how they can be constructed. Still a third type of expert knowledge is generated from experience as, for example, with applying a particular kind of policy or knowledge about financial costs incurred when making a particular choice of policy, economic instrument, or technology.

Swedish policy makers may be fortunate in this respect because they have a foundation built on broad national expertise and more extensive experience with various environmental measures than many other member states. One specific example here is the assessment of biocides,[10] where only Sweden and seven other member states have any experience at all with biocide regulation. The other countries lack any legislation whatsoever on biocides. In such a context the potential for influence is high, simply because policy makers can draw on national experience (SOU 2001:201). In turn, the Swedish experiences have resulted from early involvement in environmental problem solving as well as a certain innovative aptitudes among Swedish policy makers. Not surprisingly, the acidification strategy, an initiative which originated in Sweden was the outcome of both the long experience internationally and the development of a strong competence and extensive expertise with regard to issues of acidification. Similarly, the chemical's revision and strategy would most probably not been possible had it not been for the Swedish representatives and particularly the resources of ChemI, which has been put to use in the Commission and in both multi- and bilateral negotiations with member states.

The importance of expertise might be particularly pertinent in the EU because the Commission, despite its role as an initiator of proposals, possesses only limited resources and, thus, often relies on expertise outside the EU institutions. The appointment of national experts who, for a limited time, work in the Commission is an important resource for the Commission. At the same time, the procedure gives member states an opportunity to appoint certain experts to work on topics with which they are concerned and for which they push. In the case of the

---

[10] A biocide is a biological or chemical product that is used to destroy damaging organisms, for example, pests or bacteria. In the EU, there is now a biocide directive 98/8/EC in effect since May 2000. Although biocide products can be similar in their composition to pesticides or insecticides used in agriculture, products used in agriculture are regulated in separate EU legislation.

EU acidification strategy, the Swedish government as early as 1995 had appointed a national expert who was to work on the acidification strategy of the EU. The national expert was Christer Ågren, also head of the Secretariat for Acidification, an organization based in Gothenburg with extensive involvement, high standing, and ample international experience with the problem of acid rain. The ministry recognized the importance of national experts and one comment highlighting the importance of national experts was voiced in 1998 by a civil servant in the Environment Ministry. "When it concerns chemicals policy, we have thought it important to have a national expert in DG III (Industry). The same expert is now permanently employed there, and that is good. Our ambition is also to get a Swedish head of unit (Chemicals) in the Commission." In 1997 it was an ambition, today a Swedish woman heads the unit on chemicals in DG XI (Environment). The placement of key individuals in the EU institutions is not only about making sure the expertise and knowledge on a topic become known to the Commission and the member states. It is also a response to the multi-governance structure where network relations are a key element. Therefore it becomes necessary to build inter-personal relations among a group of key individuals in an issue area.

We can hence conclude that facts from scientific sources or from experience gained with policies or particular technologies may be an important resource in trying to have an impact in setting the EU agenda. Such knowledge can serve as a legitimating force, as a resource for Commission work, or be put to use in the actual negotiation process. The importance of expert knowledge—particularly fitting for environmental politics—may derive from the way environmental issues are closely related to scientific discoveries about what chemicals and pollutants do to our bodies and to nature and technical innovations concerning what can reverse or compensate for environmental degradation. Only further comparative research can tell us whether this is relevant for other sectors of policy making as well.

NATIONAL POLICIES AS EXAMPLES
OF WHAT CAN BE DONE

Another way of influencing EU policy would be to try to "up-load" national policy to the EU level. Uploading can be explained as a way of successfully convincing the Commission that a particular national policy could and should be adopted as a standard or as a policy applicable in all the member states. The efforts to revise the chemicals' policy and the push for a community chemical strategy, possibly including an EU Chemical's Inspectorate facility, seem to be an attempt at this. This approach is really nothing new or out of the ordinary in that many policies in the EU actually have their origin in specific national policies. While it is probably rare that national policies are copied precisely as they were originally formulated, they are, in a moderated form, an important contribution to EU policy. The Commission often glances at national policies when preparing proposals, a procedure which was most definitively the case with the Fifth Environmental Action Program, which had as its major inspirational source the Dutch Environmental Action Plan (Kronsell 2000). Furthermore, two civil servants in SEPA recently argued that the Swedish national environmental policy partly inspired the IPPC directive even though at that time Sweden was not yet an EU member. More commonly, however, and also more difficult to trace and verify, parts of member state's legislation are adopted in a Commission proposal.

Various national studies on topics relating to environmental policy making may serve as important background information. This type of expertise can be used not only to influence actual negotiations and help persuade adversaries but may also form important input or contributions to EU strategies and policies.[11] One example is a national project carried out by SEPA on traffic and environment during 1995–96 (MATS), which served as an example for and initiated a similar European project that is to provide background information and suggestions to the Commission. We can note that the various Swedish governmental studies on environmental policies, for example the extensive work on chemical policy, have provided input into the work in DG XI (Environment).

A voice in the ministry expresses the usefulness of such studies in the following way during an interview in 2000: "Expert knowledge is important, it is crucial to have information and knowledge, and there we have a lot of experience in SEPA. It is great that there are substantial studies with English summaries that we can rely on." It is clear that these studies, their suggested strategies, and the expertise in the agencies

---

[11] An indication that the government takes such a strategical consideration is given in SOU 2001:4, where it spells out that proposals issued in a previous study were written as a direct input to the EU green paper on products (*Varor utan Faror* SOU 2000:53) .

generate important facts, experiences, and accounts that can successfully be drawn upon both while the agenda is being set in the Commission and while policies are debated, contested, and decided upon in the various EU institutions. However, since such studies are generally written in Swedish there are limitations on their applicability and usefulness outside the national context and that of the Swedish representatives in the Commission. It is notable that the Dutch Environmental Action Plan was published in English.

Member states, successful in uploading domestic policy to the EU, reap two-fold rewards. For one, they are able to influence EU norms, and secondly, they can avoid later complications in the transposition and implementation of EU directives. However, such up-loading may have unwanted consequences and even cause complications in the long run with the effect of delaying or stalling the integration process. "Policy misfits" can generate problems of compliance with EU measures (Börzel 2000). Such misfits arise because there are incompatibilities between different policy styles and instruments in the different member states. A policy, which looks too much like a national member state's, may generate a misfit rather than what was intended, more adequate common European environmental legislation.

NEGOTIATING FROM AN UNDISPUTED NATIONAL INTEREST

The decision-making body in the EU is the Council of Ministers. Although it can no longer be considered a classic intergovernmental body, since votes are weighed and qualified majority decisions taken on many issues, national interests are still important stakes in this venue of decision making. When negotiating in such a context, it is important to articulate and present arguments that closely reflect a clear and unified national position.[12] Failure to do so may lead to the exposure of domestic differences in points of view. When one member state's national interest is perceived as either non-existent, divided, or contested, it can be used strategically by adversaries in the negotiation process to undermine and weaken the arguments proposed.

---

[12] Here I draw on such classic work in international relations as that by Thomas Schelling (1960), which has also been confirmed in my own interviews.

As was argued earlier, scientific experts are extensively involved in the field of EU environmental politics. Much of the work that takes place in the various committees is often a preparatory step for policy making. Experts are gaining increasing influence since most of the groundwork on Commission proposals is carried out in such committees (Van Schendelen 1998). Theoretically, there should be a division of labor between the agencies and the ministry: the representatives from the agencies attend the working groups of the Commission and provide expertise while the representatives of the ministry attend the Council working groups. In practice, however, the divisions of responsibilities are much less clear. Experts also pay careful attention to national interests. No clear division of what is political and what is expert knowledge exists since what appears as a highly technical question is often laced with political considerations. Hence, it has become increasingly evident that this division can not really be strictly maintained.

This interpenetration of politics and science as evident in the EU may be termed the "scientization of politics" and "politicization of science." It has been observed and studied previously in international environmental cooperation (Haas, E. 1990; Haas, P. 1990; Litfin 1994; Bäckstrand 2001). The sheer complexity of such pre-negotiations taking place in the multi-levels of EU governance challenges the ability for member states to coordinate the various actors involved in representing the member states. Hence, there is obviously a potential that different and perhaps contradictory positions and views may be articulated by those who are to be representing experts or member states in those various bodies handling EU pre-negotiation, a situation that may lead to contradictory messages about what a specific member state's national position is.

Having noted that there is no clear dividing line between expertise and political considerations in environmental policy making, a governmental report addressing the issue comes to the conclusion that it is very rare that Swedish representatives, whether they are in expert committees or council groups, exhibit different views (Statskontoret 2000:20B:5–32). It seems as if experts and governmental representatives have a common understanding of what the Swedish interest are on a particular question no matter how technical.[13] The report argues that this is due to the way that the ministry and the agency personnel relate to one another. They have close, informal and frequent contacts, which makes coordination

---

[13] It was also confirmed in my interviews of November 2000.

not only possible but also easy. The Swedish government is small and the ministries need to work closely with the administrative agencies. In turn this creates a tightly knit network of actors familiar with each other. There is also a significant amount of interchange between the ministry and the agencies with regard to job positions. To illustrate, it is common that a civil servant from the Environmental Protection Agency takes on a position with the Ministry of Environment and, after a few years, moves on to permanent representation and a position as environmental attaché, only to return to the Agency again after a few years. It is also argued that the experience of international environmental relations prior to EU membership has contributed to this pattern of working (Statskontoret 2000:20B:6–7).

In the multi-level governance system of the EU, small states may be better equipped to coordinate a national position because of their smaller and more tightly knit polity. Even when questions arise that are highly technical but laced with political interests and complications, it seemed from my interviews that there was actually little difficulty in establishing a "Swedish interest." Either this was, as they told me at the Environmental Protection Agency, because everyone already knew what was in the Swedish interest or they would simply pick up the phone and talk to the one politically responsible for the issue. This suggests at least two considerations: there is some common understanding or are similar values within the close community of policy makers that deal with these issues, no matter whether they represent the agencies or the ministry; and, because small states also have a smaller adminis-tration and governmental apparatus, they may also be more efficient in coordinating the various representatives who are dealing with an issue in different venues of the EU. In the smaller setting, it is easier to establish a common understanding of what the national interest may be, something which also seems extremely important in order to achieve success in the negotiation process.[14] For Sweden the experi-ence of doing this many years prior to membership in the international setting of environmental policy was beneficial but may also suggest it does not necessarily apply to other policy sectors. The other side of the coin is that this transformation of bringing experts and governmental representatives into closer and more informal relationships, may have a detrimental effect on the transparency of the policy process associated

---

[14] These findings are also congruent with those of Baldur Thorhallsson's study.

with a lack of democratic control and possibilities to hold someone accountable for concessions made and decisions taken.

CONCLUDING REMARKS

Starting from the argument proposed by Ingebritsen that small states can wield power in international relations as norm-setters, this paper considered Sweden's experiences of trying to influence EU norms on environmental policy. The ambition was that in doing so something could be said about the possibilities of small states making an impact in an era of globalization and shifting sites of authority.

The evidence from Swedish policy makers' involvement with EU environmental policy making since 1995 point to four important factors: the first is the importance of actors' reputation based on the perception and expectation, which has emerged from previous activities performed by Swedish policy makers internationally. Swedish policy makers' active involvement in international environmental cooperation since the 1970s has been an important resource for the work of ensuing high environmental standards in the EU. Already at time of membership, the expectation of Swedish engagement seems to have been measured against the reputation and experience of this previous engagement internationally. Secondly, the important role of expertise and knowledge in the policy process, perhaps particularly striking in the field of environmental policy, was discussed. Long experience with environmental policy in the domestic setting has provided a resource base which negotiators in the EU context can use to their benefit. The acidification strategy is perhaps the most significant example that attests to this. Third, since national policies often serve as an inspiration for EU policy, Swedish policy makers may find themselves in an advantageous position. The well-developed domestic policy and the associated experiences provide considerable input to negotiations in the EU. The chemicals revisions and the proposal for a chemical's strategy were examples in this paper. The final argument was that small states might have a better negotiating position due to their smaller polity. A clear and well-defined national position, absolutely essential in the EU negotiation process, may be more easily obtained in a smaller polity like Sweden's because coordination is facilitated by close, informal relations between different actors affected and concerned with the policy in question. Some reservations need to be made regarding the possibility of speaking generally about small states' influence in the EU from one single case that draws exclusively from the environmental policy area, however, the conclusions generated here can be a fruitful starting point for future comparative research.

WORKS CITED

Axelrod, Robert. *The Evolution of Cooperation*. New York: Basic Books, 1984.
Bäckstrand, Karin. *What Can Nature Withstand? Science, Politics and Discourses in Transboundary Air Pollution Diplomacy*. Lund: Political Studies, 2001.
Börzel, Tanja. "Why There is No Southern Problem: On Environmental Leaders and Laggards in the EU." *Journal of European Public Policy* 7.1 (2000): 141–62.
COM (2001) 31 Communication. Brussels: The EU Commission.
Ds 1994:126. *Det svenska miljöarbetet i EU*. Ministry of Environment.
Ds 1997: 68. *Det svenska miljöarbetet i EU—uppföljning av 1995 års strategi*. Ministry of Environment.
Grande, Edgar. "The State and Interest Groups in a Framework of Multi-Level Decision-Making: The Case of the European Union." *Journal of European Public Policy* 3.3 (1996): 318–38.
Haas, Ernst. *When Knowledge is Power: Three Models of Change in International Organizations*. Berkeley: U California P, 1990.
Haas, Peter. *Saving the Mediterranean: The Politics of International Environmental Cooperation*. New York: Colombia UP, 1990.
Ingebritsen, Christine. "Scandinavia's Influence on International Norms: The Cases of Environment, Security and Welfare." Conference Paper. *EU and Scandinavia*. University of Washington, Seattle. February 2001.
___. *Scandinavia in World Politics*. Lanham, MD: Rowman and Littlefield, forthcoming.
Katzenstein, Peter. *Small States in World Markets: Industrial Policy in Europe*. Ithaca: Cornell UP, 1985.
Kohler-Koch, Beate. "Catching up With Change: The Transformation of Governance in the European Union." *Journal of European Public Policy* 3:3 (1996): 359–80.
___. "The Evolution and Transformation of European Governance." *The Transformation of Governance in the European Union*. Eds. Beate Kohler-Koch and Rainer Eising. New York: Routledge, 1999.
KOM (2001) 88. *Vitbok—Strategi för den framtida kemikaliepolitiken*. Brussels: The EU Commission.
Kronsell, Annica. "Environmental Policy in Sweden: Setting A Good Example." *European Environmental Policy: The Pioneers*. Eds. Mikael S. Andersen and Duncan Liefferink. Manchester: Manchester UP, 1997A.
___. *Greening the EU: Power Practices, Resistances and Agenda Setting*. Lund: Lund UP, 1997b: 50–7.
___. "A 'Sustainable' Impact on the EU?: An Analysis of the Making of the Fifth Environmental Action Programme." *The Emergence of Ecological Modernisation: Integrating the Environment and the Economy?* Ed. Stephen Young. London: Routledge, 2000.

Lindh, Anna. Press release. Ministry of Environment. Sweden. 23 June 1997.

Litfin, Karen. *Ozone Discourses: Science and Politics in Global Environmental Cooperation.* New York: Columbia UP, 1994.

Mercer, Jonathan. *Reputation and International Politics.* Ithaca: Cornell UP, 1996.

Schelling, Thomas. *The Strategy of Conflict.* Cambridge: Harvard UP, 1960.

Snyder, Glenn, and Paul Diesing. *Conflict Among Nations: Bargaining, Decision Making, and System Structure in International Crises.* Princeton: Princeton UP, 1977.

SOU 2001: 4. *Kemikalieinspektionen—översyn av verksamhet, resurser och finansiering.* Official Government Report. Ministry of Environment. Stockholm: Fritzes.

SOU 2001: 53. *Varor utan Faror.* Official Government Report. Ministry of Environment. Stockholm: Fritzes.

Statskontoret 2000:20. *Fem år i EU—en utvärdering av statsförvaltningens medverkan i EU-samarbetet.*

Statskontoret 2000:20A. *Den svenska förvaltningsmodelen i EU arbetet.* The Swedish Agency for Public Management.

Statskontoret 2000:20B. *Fallstudier av tre EU-intensiva politikområden.* The Swedish Agency for Public Management.

Thorhallsson, Baldur. *The Role of Small States in the European Union.* Aldershot: Ashgate, 2000.

Van Schendelen, M. P. C. M., ed. *EU Committees as Influential Policymakers.* Aldershot: Ashgate, 1998.

Can Scandinavian Member States Play a Leadership Role in the EU?

The Case of Alcohol Control Policy

Paulette Kurzer
University of Arizona

EW SCHOLARLY TOPICS provoke as much debate as the question of how or when member governments and domestic actors succeed in steering European Union policy outcomes, institutional design, treaty amendments, and initiatives into a particular direction. In this debate, it is often argued that small member states, like Finland and Sweden, are at a distinct disadvantage because they cannot throw their weight around the way in which the big players, for example France or Germany, can wheedle their European partners. But another viewpoint, counter to this seemingly commonsense observation, is that small states can marshal the resources to push forward narrow or specialized initiatives because they have cohesive administrative structures, staffed by a small elite, and are adept at cultivating ties with appropriate Commission officials. Owing to their tight-knit national administrative bureaucracies, smaller member states can attempt to accomplish a limited agenda of specific objectives at the EU (Thorhallson 2000).

This article examines these two contending views of how or whether Scandinavian member states have opportunities to be trend-setters and have the resources or opportunities to shape the basic substance of a specific issue by highlighting the controversy surrounding alcohol control policy. This particular constellation of measures occupies a very significant role in the history of the Scandinavian welfare state and differs from how other countries regulate the commodification of alcoholic beverages. Indeed, anti-drinking measures set off several rows between the new Scandinavian members and the EU with the final outcome that Finland and Sweden acquiesced to deregulate and liberalize their restrictive anti-drinking measures. Although Finland and Sweden (and Norway to a lesser extent) had no choice but to yield to EU expectations, they were given an adjustment period of just about a decade to implement the new rules.

Examining this issue at greater length allows us to raise two questions. First why did anti-drinking measures become a source of tension between the new Scandinavian member states and the EU? What constituted the original point of disagreements between these countries and the rest of Europe? Second, and a related question, is how to interpret the failure of Scandinavian officials to shield alcohol control policy from Community law and single market directives. Can we generalize from this case study to draw broader conclusions with regard to the ability of governments of smaller member states to protect essential national arrangement from external influence? Or do we need to view this particular issue through a different prism, resist any broad generalizations, and treat it as an exception to the general rule?

Anticipating my own argument, I will argue that for Finland and Sweden the room for agenda-setting and policy influence in this particular instance was limited because of a certain configuration of domestic conditions. By the time that the discussion about alcohol control policy had begun, public opinion had already turned against the merits of preserving the entire set of institutions to regulate alcohol consumption. This explains why the failure to arrest the erosion of alcohol control measures did not provoke voter disenchantment or an electoral backlash. Elite and mass opinion diverged and the majority of citizens in fact welcomed intervention by the EU on behalf of greater availability and lower prices of alcoholic beverages. Alcohol control policy is possibly a unique situation in that the public desires a European formulation of a domestic policy regime and happily trades a Scandinavian system of doing things for a European course of action. My argument is therefore that the Scandinavian public invited EU activism and urged reluctant national governments to adjust to EU standards and rules. As other authors in this volume demonstrate, under the right circumstances, Scandinavian officials can be trend-setters and influential actors. Yet, to accomplish anything at the EU level, policy officials need at the minimum the enthusiastic support of the voter. Otherwise, they are in no position to bargain with the Commission or Council and cannot effectively employ pressure tactics to persuade reluctant officials or partners to pay heed to their demands.

To illustrate this point further, this article begins with a short survey of the origins of alcohol control policy. It then examines the encounter between a European and Scandinavian mode of regulation of intoxicants. The third part of the paper looks at the decline of public support for tight restrictions on drinking. The fourth section speculates whether there is any possibility for Finland and Sweden to influence the formulation of a European-level anti-drinking campaign.

SCANDINAVIAN ALCOHOL CONTROL SYSTEM

Detailed government intervention in the market of alcoholic beverages in order to promote public health separates the Scandinavian countries from the rest of the EU. Finland, Norway, and Sweden created and sustained a regime of anti-drinking measures to curb and modify alcohol consumption. A brief glance at per capita alcohol consumption taken from the mid-1990s confirms the claims of Scandinavian policy officials that restrictive drinking measures lead to low alcohol consumption and low incidence of alcohol-related morbidity and morality (see Tables 1 and 2). Denmark, which does not share the temperance culture and state ideology of its Scandinavian partners, has indeed a higher per capita consumption of alcohol and higher rates of cirrhosis of the liver.[1]

	Finland	Norway	Sweden	Denmark
Total	8.5	5.3	5.9	12.1
Wine	1.5	1.3	2	4.25
Spirits	2.2	1	1.3	1.35
Beer	4.45	2.95	2.6	6.5

Table 1. Liters of 100% alcohol per inhabitant 15 years or older. 1997. *Nordic Studies of Alcohol and Drugs* 16 (1999):147.

	15–44	45–64	65+
Finland	3.3	21.5	24.6
Norway	1.4	12.8	20.5
Sweden	2.7	22.5	30.7
Denmark	3.7	27.9	38.6
France	7.5	95.2	149.4
Italy	6.7	79.5	173.7

Table 2. Male cirrhosis mortality rates of different age groups per 100,000. 1950–95.[2] Ramsted 200:21.

---

[1] Denmark has relied extensively on high excise taxes to discourage excessive drinking and has used this as an alternative to restrictions on the physical availability of alcohol.

[2] These figures cannot be taken at full face value because mortality rates depend on national diagnostic and coding practices. In addition, liver cirrhosis can be caused by other factors aside from excessive drinking.

At present, this whole system of regulation is at risk in the name of European integration. Commercial trade policy is forcing the two member governments to ease restrictions on alcohol imports, which could drastically cut domestic revenue from state-monopoly wine, beer, and spirits sales. If the government agrees to lower taxes to make domestic purchases competitive with neighboring countries, then it would also lose tax revenues. In each scenario, moreover, consumption of alcohol would rise. By 2004, furthermore, Swedish and Finnish consumers are at liberty to take home in the form of personal imports the equivalent of one hundred and ten liters of beer, ninety liters of wine, and ten liters of distilled spirits. With that, Finnish and Swedish consumers can basically avoid the domestic high tax/restricted availability regime by purchasing all their liquor needs abroad, where liquor prices are lower because many governments impose a very modest tax on beer and do not subject wine to any excise taxes (for example, Austria, France, Germany, Italy, Luxembourg, Spain, and Portugal). Other potential difficulties arise from the broader consequences flowing from the decision made by the European Court of Justice in March 2001 with respect to *Konsumentombudsmannen* (KO) *and Gourmet International Products* AB (GIP) [C-405/98]. The significance of the ruling centered on whether the Swedish prohibition on alcohol advertising in certain publications was consistent with the EC law. The Court ruled that it was for the national court to determine whether the prohibition on advertising meets the condition of proportionality, which is required in order to justify the ban on advertisement. With that decision, the European Court basically permits Sweden to ban alcoholic beverage advertisements so long as the Swedish authorities can demonstrate that protecting public health against the harmful effects of alcohol cannot be achieved by other means with less impact on intra-Community trade. It may be difficult for the Swedish government to prove that only a ban on alcohol advertisements in popular publications is the most effective way to moderate alcohol consumption.

Finland is under the same constraints as Sweden, with the exception however, that state agencies and the public have embraced a continental-like or liberal viewpoint.

Owing to its participation in the European Economic Area (EEA), Norway is less exposed to anti-discrimination suits emerging from trade liberalization. But whenever liquor prices fall in Sweden, Norwegian consumers travel to their next-door neighbor to purchase alcoholic beverages in Swedish retail outlets (Nordlund and Österberg 2000).

Traveler's imports, however, are not covered by the EEA agreement and Norway is under no obligation to relax its ceilings on personal imports. Nonetheless, Norway and obviously Finland and Sweden face various challenges that have already transformed a century-old regime of drinking regulations.

BACKGROUND

Insofar as there exists a specific Scandinavian model, its main outline consists of a strong state, highly organized and centralized social actors, strong commitment to egalitarianism and solidarity, and the political dominance of social democratic parties. Denmark does not fit this definition and deviates from the strong state-strong interest group model in several ways. The Danish state is more wedded to liberalism and to solutions reliant on private market actors. Denmark's social democratic party did not gain the same kind of political influence or hegemony as in Sweden (and to a lesser extent in Norway and Finland) while interest group organizations were weaker and the political landscape more fragmented. Above all, temperance or teetotaler movements did not succeed in passing legislation that would result in the creation of a vast system of intervention to curb alcohol consumption. Because of its different approach to state intervention and greater reliance on private solutions to address social problems, Denmark does not share the same alcohol control history as its Scandinavian partners. The latter group of countries (which includes Iceland) constructed comprehensive and coherent alcohol control systems that consisted of state alcohol monopolies, high excise taxes and prices, inspection systems, tight marketing regulations, various restrictions on alcohol use in public spaces, elaborate educational campaigns, and regulated serving and retail hours. Earlier, Norway and Finland enacted prohibition and Sweden, where a referendum on prohibition was narrowly defeated, legislated a rationing system. After the repeal of prohibition, in all three countries, public agencies, voluntary associations, and professional communities oversaw the administrative reforms and implementation of alcohol control system and molded its ideological framework.

Alcohol control systems survived until the present in each of the three countries thanks to their centrality in the formative stages of the modern democratic state. Temperance mobilization coincided with the political emancipation of the labor movement and intersected with the construction of the Scandinavian welfare state. Both the welfare state and alcohol control policies signaled progress and civilization as alcohol use symbolized poverty, degradation, and social disorder and was antithetical to the ideals associated with responsible citizenship and a just community. The state was an instrument for lifting the common people to a higher plane in which their material needs were met, thereby providing everybody the opportunity for acquiring education and civilization. Labor movements in Finland, Norway, and Sweden acquired a strong temperance orientation because drinking was considered one of the main barriers to material and spiritual improvements. Subsequently, reliant on the mass mobilization of the working class, social democratic parties actively lobbied for the suppression of the profit principle in the liquor trade once they had gained parliamentary representation. The elimination of private market actors in the liquor trade assumed the status of moral conviction by 1918 and justified the creation of state monopoly in the retail, distribution, and production of alcoholic beverages several decades later. Especially in Finland, which struggled to liberate itself from a decaying Russian empire, prohibition gained the same prominence as statehood.

Scores of Western countries became obsessed with the "liquor question" in the late nineteenth-century. The United States along with the Scandinavian countries, Australia, the UK, and Canada began to devote considerable efforts to ban public drinking and distilled spirits. Popular mass movements agitated for prohibition while temperance became a popular cause in selected Western societies. Generally, we can say that the countries, which sought to restrain drinking and to proscribe hard liquor, shared two common traits. Teetotaler movements and temperance cultures were found in the English-speaking world and Scandinavian countries, and they share a Protestant ethic and a taste for distilled spirits.

By definition, spirits are associated with different drinking rituals from wine, which is usually consumed during mealtimes and accompanies food. Distilled spirits are drunk outside mealtimes and are consumed to celebrate some kind of event. Taken out of context, the popularity of hard liquor in the Scandinavian and Anglo-Saxon drinking repertoire fails to illuminate why people joined temperance movements to effect a total alcohol ban. Poland and Russia, for example, were also part of the vodka belt yet temperance activism in these countries was modest. Therefore, historians of the anti-alcohol movement speculate that temperance cultures found a markedly warm reception in societies where Protestant ethics dominated (Eriksen 1993; Levine 1992). The entire idea of temperance appealed to cultures that already put much emphasis on restraining one's appetites and on exercising individual self-control. More so than Catholicism or Eastern Orthodoxy, Protestant-Christian ethos stressed individual accountability and warned against the risks of an unrestrained pursuit of simple desires. This vision was especially fashionable among evangelical Protestant sects (Methodists, Baptists, Swedish and Norwegian Free Church members). Whereas traditional Protestantism (Lutheran and Calvinist churches) was more inward-oriented and less likely to challenge state prerogatives, revivalist movements in opposition to established churches urged a more activist stance and desired to effect social change. For them, discipline became a cure for many modern ills while sobriety benefited the general community. Industrialization and urbanization underscored the dangers of unrestrained drinking and the hazards of spirits. The modern rhythm of life required discipline and willpower so that abstinence came to be considered a first step in dealing with new social problems caused by the breakdown of rural life and the emergence of an industrial, urban economy.

What set the Scandinavian countries apart, however, is more than a shared tradition of evangelical Protestantism and a liking for hard liquor. In many Anglo-Saxon societies, temperance activism disappeared after World War II and governments more or less withdrew from direct meddling in individual consumer choice.[3] In Scandinavia, by contrast, the repeal of prohibition in Finland and Norway paved the way for another system of restrictions and temperance as a mode of living and as a guidance post for state policy survived more or less intact (Johansson 2000). What differentiated Scandinavia from Anglo-Saxon cultures was the institutionalization of a temperance value system long after drinking had ceased to be a social issue.

The consolidation of a temperance worldview came about as the teetotaller movement fostered strong ties with social democracy. The fledgling labor movement in all three countries loudly supported prohibition and fiercely opposed the private market in alcoholic beverages. Workers were exhorted to abstain from alcohol in order to seek betterment and self-improvement, and private actors in the liquor markets

---

[3] After the failure of the "noble experiment," the American federal government delegated the task of regulating the alcoholic beverage markets to state and local authorities with the result that the US still has a patchwork of widely different liquor laws.

were depicted as wicked capitalists bent on destroying working class aspirations. In Finland, the mobilization against liquor intersected with the growing aspirations for independence from Russian rule. The Russian administration thwarted the ratification of prohibition legislation by the Finnish parliament so that national sovereignty became a prerequisite for stamping out boozing and became a vehicle for expressing the growing yearnings for independence (Sulkunen 1985).

The values and ideals of the teetotaler movement found wide resonance thanks to its ties with the labor movement and, in the case of Finland, to its links with national independence. It was widely believed that restraining the circulation of alcohol in society could solve social despair, criminality, or the destruction of traditional communities. General prohibition on production and sale of alcoholic beverages became part of the manifesto of the Finnish, Swedish, and Norwegian social democratic party in the period prior to 1914. The parties of the left partly appropriated temperance demands for prohibition and restriction to appeal to impoverished rural workers and the urban working class, groups that had been deprived from cheap drink and had turned radically anti-alcohol. In turn, the overt support of the left for prohibition and restriction strengthened popular sentiment against drinking.

After 1945, when prohibition was no longer a viable option, each country had established a system of control similar in structure. The objective was to eliminate the private profit principle and the state controlled imports, exports, sales, and production of alcoholic beverages via national monopolies. In Sweden, *Systembolaget* and *Vin & Sprit* dominated the liquor market. *Alko* served the same monopolizing role in Finland and *Vinmonopolet* operated in Norway. Compared to other European countries, the three Scandinavian nations had the strictest formal alcohol control policy from 1950 to 1990. Presently, in spite of the adoption of more liberal drinking legislation, the three countries still pursue a more extensive and comprehensive alcohol control policy than any other EU member state (Karlsson and Österberg 2001).

NATIONAL IDENTITY AND BINGE DRINKING

Compared to other European countries, per capita alcohol consumption in the Scandinavian countries was in fact modest at the turn of the century. France, for example, drank twenty-two liters of pure alcohol per capita compared to five liters in Sweden and a negligible one and a half liters per capita of pure alcohol in Finland in the period 1906–10 (Johansson 2000:30). Thus, it would be erroneous to attribute the success of the temperance movement to the outsized thirst for intoxicating beverages among the male population of each of the three countries. Then how do we account for the appeal of temperance in the three countries?

Apparently, the relationship between temperance values, anti-alcohol measures, and alcohol consumption is reversed from what we would expect. Because alcohol consumption in the three countries was already low, many people lent support to temperance and its anti-alcohol programs. This raises another question. Why would people rally behind voluntary associations whose main objective consisted of banning all alcohol when alcohol-related problems were not the main motivation?

Most observers claim that it was the style of drinking popular in the Scandinavian countries, that aroused indignation. What mattered was not *how much* was drunk but rather *how* it was drunk. The main grievance of temperance activists related to the misuse of spirits and the widespread ritual of boozing or drinking until intoxicated (Kurzer 2001:54–8).

The Scandinavian drinking culture was perceived to be highly destructive because it involved binge drinking. At the turn of the nineteenth century, destructive drinking styles were mostly attributed to the urban masses. The first measures proposed by the temperance movement was therefore to close working class pubs in the belief that this would put an end to spirit drinking. By 1900, in all three countries, most restaurants or pubs ceased to serve alcoholic beverages. The disappearance of public venues where people could drink led in fact to an increase in private drinking binges since most people drank at home alone or in small groups and from the bottle instead by the glass. The closing of public venues did not address the perceived problem of intoxicating drinking habits. The temperance movement, therefore, shifted its focus to banning all alcoholic beverages. One more issue needs to be examined, however. Why have Scandinavian people such an unhealthy relationship with alcohol? Why can they not drink in moderation and be like the French or Germans? Why do they gravitate towards binge drinking?

Here, the answer for most experts rests with the peculiarities of the Scandinavian mentality. The latter is not capable of showing emotions and of displaying easy sociability. Scandinavian people cope with communication anxiety and find it painful to relax with others. To ease sociability, therefore, they drink excessive amounts of alcohol, which helps shed inhibitions. In turn, social occasions become the perfect inducement for binge drinking. Since many people perceived themselves to lack internal self-control, they accepted external state restraints (Daun 1996).

This patronizing view was especially prominent in Finland. Finnish intellectuals spoke of taming the "primitive troll" inside the working person and bemoaned the lack of manners, civility, and respect. Methods to reach out and civilize the working man included individual controls, the promotion of wine, and the opening of more public premises serving alcohol (Sulkunen 2000:73). Much of the early discourse on alcohol control policy was clothed in terms of forcing men to be free and of civilizing ignorant folks so they can make the right choices for themselves. The state was regarded as the agent most likely to be able to carry out this task of protecting people from themselves and of forcing them to be independent, civil, and productive.

In short, alcohol control policies meshed with the social engineering ambitions of Scandinavian social democratic parties, which subscribed to the view that the state could be an instrument of emancipation if it adopted scientific principles. After World War II, alcohol control systems shed their moralizing tone and became a rational method of intervention to modify drinking styles and reduce alcohol consumption. The institutions and policy measures complemented the aim of creating a just, egalitarian society in which the individual made small sacrifices for the benefit of the collective.

By the late 1960s, the condescending intervention of the state was no longer acceptable to the majority of Finnish, Norwegian, and Swedish citizens. One major reason for the change in attitude was the growth of a professional urban middle class. As more people joined city life, their outlook and priorities shifted with the acquisition of new skills. Another element was the rise of the tourist and catering industry, which lobbied hard for deregulation in order to serve alcohol beverages on the premises. The actual operation of the monopoly system also fuelled resentment. It openly discriminated against women and lower class people and each state had instituted involuntary treatment programs for supposed alcoholics (Sulkunen 2000:74–5; Tigerstedt 2000:96–8). In response to growing resentment, many rules were relaxed and much of the stigmatizing rhetoric disappeared in the late 1960s. Governments in each of the three countries abolished the mandatory treatment system, phased out personal inspection of buyers, and Finland permitted the sale of beer in private stores. The focus of the policy establishment shifted from protecting individuals against themselves to the new target of moderating total consumption generally. Greater faith was placed on informing and educating people against excessive drinking and on promoting wine and beer at the expense of spirits, which are closely associated with boozing. Alcohol control measures fell under the label of protecting public health because it prevented alcohol-related diseases, accidents, deaths, injuries, family discord, abuse, vandalism, occupational mishaps, etc.

THE EUROPEAN UNION AND ALCOHOL CONTROL SYSTEMS

Non-Scandinavian countries take a radically different approach to the circulation of alcohol in society. The Commission or Brussels views alcohol either as an agricultural or an industrial item. The common agricultural policy (CAP) governs wine production. The aim of the EU is to keep production in check in order to maintain the standard of living of wine growers while aggressively seeking to expand the market for European wines both in and outside the EU. Distilled spirits are an industrial item manufactured by giant beverage companies. Beer is a national taxation issue. The first and most basic clash is thus that Brussels assigns no special importance to alcoholic beverages. It falls under the single market regime or is part of the heavily-subsidized agricultural domain.

Second, the EU and member governments do not share the public health perspective of the Scandinavian countries. They consider problem drinking a private affair and urge people to seek private solutions. For centuries, alcohol has been part of Europeans' daily life and governments in other countries pay scant attention to alcohol-related problems. Neither do experts in the rest of Europe support the view that alcohol is the cause of untold accidents, injuries, psychological disorders, antisocial behavior, etc. Professionals in other countries treat problematic drinking more like an intermediate variable that is often found in cases where other social, psychological, physical factors already impede a normal, productive, responsible life style. They do not assign independent causality to alcohol. Experts, policy officials, and politicians outside the Scandinavian region do not understand the arguments advanced by Scandinavian authorities. Awareness of link between alcohol and harm is weak except when a reference is made to adolescent drinking and driving under the influence of alcohol.

In addition, revenue from high excise taxes and state monopoly were employed to address alcohol-related health issues. Sweden and Finland supported a dense network of treatment centers to cure alcoholics and also used money to finance aggressive anti-drinking information campaigns. Other countries have less of a tradition of identifying addiction as a disease and spend fewer public resources.

But above all, the principal mission of the EU has been the creation of a single internal market with the free movement of goods, services, people, and capital. State monopolies contradict that basic mission and have been forced to de-monopolize. Since alcoholic beverages are treated as normal commodities, they fall under the rules of the single market.[4]

With hindsight, the temperance organizations and policy officials in all three countries gave little consideration to the consequences of EU accession (Finland and Sweden) and EEA membership (Norway) for the regime of alcohol control measures ("Conversation" 2001). In 1990, the Swedish temperance movement announced that its membership would reject EU membership if the state monopoly was dismantled, but it ultimately refrained from endorsing an official position in the EU referendum of 1994 (Warpenius and Sutton 2000:61). In Finland, there was hardly any reflection of how the EU would constrain alcohol control policies. The temperance organization had fallen apart and been absorbed into youth and lifestyle groups. Its funding was halted and the joint magazine of the umbrella temperance movement ceased publication in 1992. Alcohol policy was not on the Finnish agenda.

In Norway, the temperance movement pursued a multi-pronged strategy that focused on national politics and EU-level lobbying tactics. Norwegian delegates of the temperance alliance underplayed the absolutist abstinence message and mostly aimed to persuade key EU policy officials on recognizing the health hazards of alcohol. Although Norway would ultimately vote not to join the EU, only the Norwegian organization cultivated ties with like-minded interest group agencies in Brussels. In addition, the authorities themselves kept quiet about

---

[4] All free trade agreements are harmful to alcohol control policies (see Grieshaber-Otto, Sinclair, and Schacter 2000).

the possible incompatibility between alcohol control system and Community law. Yet there were good grounds for suspecting that the EU would not look kindly on the scores of measures in place to curb alcohol consumption (Lund, Alavaikko, and Österberg 2000:211–2). The Commission had an established record of rejecting import/export monopolies. The European Court of Justice, since 1975, issued several rulings that found foreign trade monopolies incompatible with the Treaty of Rome. The Single Market, moreover, guaranteed the free movement of people and goods, and the alcohol systems could also be construed as hostile to the four freedoms (Ugland 2000).

The parliaments of the Scandinavian countries evaluated the future effects of the EEA agreement in late 1992. At that time, the authorities had not yet made the decision to apply for full membership. In Sweden and Finland, parliamentary commissions did not raise a red flag with respect to the future of the alcohol control system, and the ensuing debates failed to mention state monopoly system. The situation in Norway was strikingly different. Opponents of the EEA could possibly have blocked the ratification of the treaty because they needed to marshal only forty-two out of one hundred sixty-five votes to torpedo the whole affair. The Christian Democratic party was a strong supporter of restrictive alcohol policy and enjoyed a pivotal role in the Norwegian parliament. The party leader called upon the members to support the EEA and most elected officials did so. But they insisted on inserting extra insurances in the agreement to protect alcohol control policies from Community law.

In 1993, by which time all three countries had applied for EU membership, the Commission invited them to exchange ideas on the state alcohol monopoly. Sweden responded to the invitation and entered into direct dialogue. Norway ignored the letter of the Commission and Finland pursued another strategy by going ahead with an ambitious plan to amend existing alcohol legislation to bring it into conformity with Community law.

Finland first and then Sweden agreed to demonopolize the import, export, wholesale, and production divisions of *Alko* and *Vin & Sprit* (the Swedish monopoly producer of spirits and international distributor). *Alko* was a powerful actor in the alcohol field because it controlled production, distribution, prices, foreign trade, and licensed private actors. The latter needed to cooperate with the monopoly since it set prices for alcoholic beverages produced by private manufacturers and set compensation for the catering industry. In addition, because *Alko* regulated foreign trade, it also protected domestic sector from international competition. The 1994 Alcohol Act drastically reduced the influence of the state monopoly in the alcohol policy field because all exclusive rights except the off-premise retail monopoly were abolished (Alavaikko and Österberg 2000). Sweden, too, demonopolized *Systembolaget* so that it would meet its most important social and health principles but would no longer dominate wholesale distribution and foreign trade. The Commission was sympathetic to the notion of preserving the retail monopoly and permitted both countries to retain a slimmer version of the previous state monopoly. Presently, *Systembolaget* is a more powerful actor than *Alko* because Swedish law stipulates that all beverages with alcohol content above 3.5 percent by volume can only be sold in its state stores. In Finland, the policy regime was already more liberal in that alcoholic beverages with maximum alcohol content of 4.7 percent by volume were sold in private grocery stores (Holder 1998).

The Commission also sent a letter to Norway outlining the compromises reached with Finland and Sweden in the hope of spurring Norway into action. The Norwegian authorities in 1994 continued to maintain that *Vinmonopolet* was compatible with EEA Treaty obligations and that it existed to protect public health. The Norwegian state alcohol system was also, compared to its Swedish and Finnish counterparts, less commercial and more faithful to its public health mission. Because of the less commercial character of the state monopoly, Norwegian officials insisted that its alcohol policy differed from that of Finland and Sweden and that public support for anti-drinking restrictions was higher. The issue was brought to court (Restamark) and the EFTA Court in December 1994 ruled on behalf of the Commission and told the Norwegian government to abolish the state monopoly on the import, export, and wholesale trade of alcoholic beverages. Norway decided to keep the production monopoly on spirits, but it was detached from the retail monopoly (Ugland 2001).

As a result, the situation after January 1, 1995 had changed dramatically because new market actors emerged to compete in a much more liberal environment. After dragging its feet, Norway was forced to introduce the same changes in 1996 in conformity with the stipulations of the European Economic Area (EEA). In 1998, Sweden and Finland introduced new excise duties in conformity with the principles prevalent in the rest of the EU that dictate higher excise taxes on beverages with higher alcohol content by volume. Nevertheless, the biggest challenge lies in the immediate future. Starting in 2004, Sweden and Finland will no longer be able to enjoy an exemption from Community external trade policy and will have to adopt EU-wide rules on tourist imports. In preparation, the authorities have already increased maximum allowable limits on travelers' imports. Beyond that, officials need to design an entirely new anti-alcohol strategy that is not reliant on the physical restrictions on the availability of liquor. Rather, public health officials and social welfare agencies will need to employ more indirect tools to educate the public and discourage bad drinking habits.

While state policy is taking a new orientation, earlier steps have already fostered a new climate and institutional structures. There are more venues licensed to sell alcohol and their business hours have become less regulated. Tax levels have come down, and the state retail monopolies make enormous efforts to please their customers. Finland has removed the ban on advertisement for alcoholic beverages with an alcohol content of 22 percent or less per volume. All in all, the legal adjustments and smaller cosmetic changes have removed the special aura associated with alcoholic beverages. In terms of image and availability, alcohol has lost much of its exceptionalism and is becoming more like other consumer items.

The dramatic departure from a century-old commitment to eliminating the private profit motive from the alcoholic beverage trade and to curb or modify drinking seems to be a direct outgrowth of participation in a supranational organization basically hostile to the principles and motivations of alcohol control systems. Community law and the intransigence of the Commission anxious to consolidate the gains of the Single Market spurred amendments to the alcohol legislation in all three countries and brought into play new private actors. The restructuring of the state alcohol monopoly in combination with the emergence of new players in the alcohol field has built inexorable momentum for further liberalization. The European Court of Justice or Community law is an important force in this development because it repeatedly questions the existence of particular instruments that are used by Scandinavian officials to steer alcohol consumption.

Although persuasive, this kind of analysis misses an important piece of the puzzle. It would be erroneous to attribute all the changes of the last five years to external pressures emanating from the EU. Rather, legal obligations flowing from active participation in a supranational institution on top of domestic shifts accounted for the transformation of the alcohol control system. The EU extended its influence over Scandinavian alcohol control systems precisely because the conditions were ripe for increased liberalization of alcohol control policies and market-driven solutions. The reason is simple. By the early 1990s, consumers in all three countries expressed growing dissatisfaction with the situation at home; public opinion became less accepting of state intervention in the matter of personal consumer choices.

For example, 11 percent of Finnish consumers favored incremental liberalization of alcohol control policies in 1981. In 1989, this number has risen to 40 percent although Finnish alcohol policy had become more liberal during the intervening years. Likewise, in a time series analyses done between 1962 and 1992 of a hypothetical referendum on the introduction of different alcoholic beverage arrangements, Norwegian respondents displayed a distinct shift toward liberalization. In a Swedish survey, 66 percent of the respondents characterized alcohol problems as very serious in 1981. In 1994, this figure had dropped to 13 percent (Tomasson 1998:496).

The Scandinavian authorities were not immune to the growing discontent with alcohol control policies. In the 1990s, Sweden permitted restaurants or pubs to serve alcohol without food. In Finland, monopoly stores adopted self-service in order to avoid queues and appease customers. In all three countries, the number of public drinking places grew. Newspapers started wine columns, television programs included tasting programs of new vintages, and each country had beer associations of people who promoted the further liberalization of the beer market (Sulkunen 2000:84–5).

People's attitudes forced the monopoly system to respond by becoming more service-oriented and customer-friendly. In turn, by de-emphasizing the public health dimension of alcohol control systems, drinking opinions became more liberal or relaxed. This trend predated any encounters with Community law and Commission rules. But until the final round of negotiations for accession and the subsequent legal wrangles, the legitimacy of the entire structure of rules, programs, and institutions of the alcohol policy regime went unquestioned. After all, there was no genuine alternative to the packet of drinking restrictions in operation for the last fifty years. It was virtually impossible to imagine the dismantlement of the retail monopoly. But the frictions with the EU uncovered new realities and set in motion new trends of discourse and scrutiny that influenced public opinion to demand more and more deregulation and liberalization.

DECLINING LEGITIMACY, GROWING CONSUMERISM

The mid-1990s were a real watershed. Public opinion in Sweden, for example, decisively swung in favor of wine in grocery stores, and newspaper articles increasingly wrote on behalf of the consumer. In Norway, in the late 1990s, newspapers minimized the effectiveness of alcohol control policy, complained about the high taxes, and called for greater availability of spirits and wine. In Finland, newspaper articles called for the abolishment of *Alko*, something that would have seemed totally outrageous just a few years earlier. More surprising, perhaps, is the willingness of politicians and thus opinion makers to challenge the institutions of the alcohol policy regime. The Finnish climate is definitely more liberal or Continental than that of either Norway or Sweden, as seen from the following examples. In 1996, the minister of Social Affairs and Health received a letter signed by fifty-nine members of parliament and seventy-nine candidates for the European parliament that was published in the largest newspaper. This appeal called for a rise in excise duties in many low-tax countries and a reduction in high alcohol taxes in Finland. The petition also mentioned the abolition of the off-premise retail monopoly, except for spirits. In 1997, 101 out of 200 members of parliament signed a written question, asking the government about its plans for closing down *Alko* (Nordlund and Österberg 2000:575; Olsson, Nordlund, and Järvinen 2000:238). The "dismantle the retail monopoly" movement suffered a partial defeat in late 1997, however, after the European Court of Justice found the Swedish retail state monopoly not inconsistent with EU legislation. The Norwegian retail monopoly was also brought before the EFTA court (Case E-6/96 *Tore Wilhelmsen AS vs. Oslo Kommune* and Case E-1/97 *Fridtjof Frank Gundersen vs. Oslo Kommune*) in a case that concerned the legality of the exclusive right of the Norwegian retail monopoly to sell strong beer (alcohol content of 4.75 percent or more by volume) and wine. The Court considered the restrictions to be in line with EFTA article thirteen—which is identical to EC article thiry-six—which makes allowances for discriminatory practices for the sake of the protection of health and life of humans.

Nevertheless, endless speculation about the possible interpretation of the European Court of Justice gave rise to new expectations. When no alternative seems possible, people resign themselves to the prevailing situation. But in the 1990s, public debate mentioned the likely dismantlement of the alcohol control system, thereby legitimizing the possibility of further liberalization. In Sweden, 40 percent of the people surveyed supported the sale of wine in regular grocery stores from 1967 to 1992. Suddenly, in 1993, 75 percent of the Swedish population favored wine in grocery stores. The enormous rise in support for this position is related to the changed perception of the utility of *Systembolaget* and new debates on European integration. Politicians from the political right also felt free to criticize the retail monopoly in public, something that was rarely done before 1992 (Olsson, Nordlund, and Järvinen 2000: 229–30).

Prosperity, exposures to global ideas and foreign travel, education, and professionalization have all conspired to transform the previous temperance-oriented moral viewpoint to a consumerist outlook. The state's role in regulating private life is simply no longer fully accepted. Citizens are not just subjects of the state but also sovereign consumers. In essence, the liberalization of alcohol policy reflects the triumph of liberal discourse about individual responsibility. A collectivist welfare state perspective assigns the state the task of protecting society against alcohol-related problems and of implementing restrictive drinking measures. According to the liberal viewpoint, the sale of alcohol should be unimpeded for the sake of the freedom of consumers to choose. The public has not yet fully embraced this perspective, but it has certainly moved closer to the liberal definition of a just state (Törrönen 2000). Not all groups reject the temperance-based policy instruments. Rural residents and Christians, especially in Norway, continue to treasure the success of alcohol control measures.

Aside from these specific groups, the universalism of the earlier drinking metaphors no longer works because alcohol habits and life experiences have changed. Whereas spirits were still the dominant beverage in the early 1970s, wine in Norway and Sweden and beer in Finland became the favorite alcoholic beverages twenty years later. Since much of the risk of drinking is traced to boozing with hard liquor, many urban professionals no longer consider themselves binge drinkers. If they drink like other Europeans, why do they need state intervention in the liquor market?

Acting upon these beliefs, the volume of personal or traveler's imports rose significantly after 1995. Traveler's import accounted for around 10 percent of total alcohol consumption in Norway and Finland and for 15 percent of total consumption in Sweden (Nordlund and Österberg 2000:558). If home brewing or distilling is included in addition to large-scale smuggling, then unrecorded consumption probably is closer to 30 percent of total alcohol consumption. Unrecorded alcohol consumption has important consequences for alcohol control policy. It reduces tax revenue, undermines the effectiveness of restrictions on physical availability, and raises hard questions as to the utility and rationale of anti-drinking restrictions.

SCANDINAVIAN INFLUENCE ON THE EU?

Can the governments of Sweden and Finland convince EU member governments to take a favorable look at their restrictive drinking policies? Will they be able to export some of their ideas and policies to the rest of Europe? The answer to these questions is firmly negative. The Scandinavian countries are not in a strong position to lobby the EU to adopt more restrictive policies toward the retail sales of alcohol, ceilings on personal traveler's import, and taxation. The European partners are not amenable to such arguments while the Scandinavian public does not support such a course of action. Public opinion registers great ambivalence, to say the least, about many aspects of the national alcohol control system. On the one hand, many people recognize the hidden costs of health care for abusers as well as lost labor efficiency and drinking's contribution to violent crime. They continue to think that alcohol problems are not just a problem for the individual but for the whole society. On the other, they desire to see a Continental style of alcohol market where wine and beer are available in grocery stores at substantially lower prices. Since so many consumers are unwilling to wait for domestic changes, they shop for cheaper liquor across the border. For example, retail sales in southern Sweden slumped after a new bridge to Denmark was opened in July 2000 (Lund, Alavaikko, Österberg 2000:219).

If the public is not pushing for a "Nordization" of European alcohol policy, while European agencies themselves are highly resistant to such an agenda, the governments of Finland and Sweden face insurmountable obstacles. Even if the two member governments will decide to attempt to persuade the EU to consider the benefits of restrictive drinking policies, a further impediment is the underdevelopment of the public health field at the European level. Member governments have been reluctant to transfer this responsibility to the EU. The new section on public health added to the Amsterdam treaty is mostly aimed at consumer protection and at dealing with crises like mad-cow (BSE) disease.

If these arguments are not sufficient grounds for concluding that Scandinavian alcohol control systems are not transferable to the European level, then there is one final consideration. Scandinavian alcohol control systems grew out of a particular constellation of circumstances that fused the ascendant social democratic model with a highly popular temperance movement. Both movements matured more or less at the same time, and social democratic activists embraced temperance ideology in order to appeal to rural voters, to uplift the standard of living of the urban working class, and to seek a healthier or better society. Other European countries do not share this particular historical and cultural legacy. The whole discourse on alcohol, therefore, raises eyebrows outside the Scandinavian region because officials there simply do not understand why Scandinavian authorities fret about drinking when actual consumption levels are low. Even Denmark, which shares many values with her Scandinavian neighbors, scoffs at the apprehensions expressed by Swedes or Norwegians. This skepticism is now shared by Finland, which has taken distance from its earlier anti-alcohol roots. Finnish public opinion is more liberal than Norwegian or Swedish opinion, and officials are more willing to contemplate radical transformations. Sweden would not be able to count on Finnish political support if it tries to cajole the EU to take up the alcohol problem as a European-wide public health challenge. Finally, Norway has been the most cautious and is the most likely to back up Sweden in the matter of drinking restrictions, but its influence in the EU is limited due to the fact that it opted to sign EEA instead of becoming full member.

At present, there are European organizations involved in the dissemination of information on alcohol-related problems in Brussels. Eurocare, an offshoot of the International Order of Good Templars, has an office in Brussels and publishes action papers with the (faint) hope of persuading the EU to take a firmer stance against alcohol misuse. But Eurocare carries virtually no policy weight, especially not against French or Austrian wine growers, gigantic multinational beverage companies, and the free market philosophy of the Commission.

In January 2001, Sweden took over the presidency of the Council of Ministers and announced its intention to promote tougher drink-driving rules in the EU (*Financial Times* 1 Nov. 2001:3). The Swedish cabinet did not indicate any desire of convincing Brussels to adopt a typical Scandinavian view of alcohol. Instead, the strategy was to frame drinking and general substance abuse in terms of youth problems. During its term as president, Sweden convened numerous meetings of the Council of Ministers of Health to generate both recommendations and actual regulations.

Earlier in June 2000, the Commission had submitted to the Council a new six-year program on improving health information and knowledge, enhancing the capability to respond rapidly to health threats, and addressing the determinants of health. The Swedish presidency pushed for an inclusion of a section on smoking, drinking, and drug abuse and the Commission submitted to the Council a reworked action plan that made references to the problems of underage drinking. It is especially youth drinking that has received most of the attention. The Commission suggested that member states ought to promote research into all aspects of this problem, raise awareness of the effects of drinking alcohol, increase young people's involvement in youth health-related policies and actions, and encourage co-operation with the producers and the retailers of alcoholic beverages and relevant non-governmental organizations to discourage the targeting of alcoholic beverages at children and adolescents.

In June 2001, the fifteen health ministers of the European Union approved a plan that would tighten enforcement of laws on alcohol sales and educate young people about the dangers of drinking. In addition, the EU agreed to work with the alcohol industry on codes of conduct to ensure that alcoholic beverages are not designed or promoted to appeal to children.

CONCLUSION

Alcohol control systems are the victims of cultural change growing out of the transformation of Scandinavian societies from agrarian to post-industrial economies. The ascendance of neo-liberal concepts, which limit the role of the state in setting priorities and simultaneously assigns much greater individual responsibility to personal choices, also shaped Scandinavian views on scores of areas of state activism. The changes imposed by EU membership coincided with an emerging sentiment among the responsible-drinking majority in all three countries that it is their own business—not the government's—how much they consume in the safety and privacy of their own homes. Until the arrival of the

EU with its own aggressive free market agenda, the public in the Scandinavian countries could not openly articulate a genuine alternative to the status quo. Nor could they easily avail themselves of an exit option until the arrival of the borderless Europe. Frictions with the Commission and incompatibilities with Community law opened new vistas that, among other things, pointed to a future of liberal Continental-like alcohol policy regimes.

Thus, to return to the original question why has the erosion of alcohol control policy occurred and why did it fail to mobilize a political backlash, the answer is that the Scandinavian public, with notable exceptions such as in remote areas of Norway, embraced Europeanization and welcomed outside interference by the EU. In contrast to other policy areas, Scandinavian citizens accepted a EU-type regime of liberalization. Finnish and Swedish state agencies, however, express greater ambivalence about alcohol control adjustments in part because they collect sizable revenues from the monopoly system. Can state officials pursue an activist agenda in the EU to arrest adaptational pressures? In the case of alcohol, the odds of success are small because the EU is not amenable to strict anti-drinking intervention and the public is eager to see domestic reforms of the current framework of intervention. Above all, Scandinavian consumers would like to have wine and beer sold in ordinary stores at lower prices. Their view of spirits is more nuanced; they associate hard liquor with binge drinking and most consumers prefer to have alcoholic beverages with high alcohol content sold through public monopoly companies. The package of policy instruments that form the backbone of anti-drinking intervention cannot withstand the pressures of market forces firmly supported by the EU for fostering harmonization.

Market integration has already spurred the formation of a more fragmented and liberalized alcohol control policy. But this development was not simply foisted upon Scandinavia against the popular will of its citizens. The public in all three countries no longer supports the earlier definition of a good life in which the state dictates what individuals should do. Parliaments no longer fully support drinking restrictions. Temperance movements have virtually disappeared in Finland, while their influence in Norway and Sweden has been greatly diminished. Political support for drinking restrictions has declined (Lund 2000: 248). None of the trends described in this article are reversible; a celebrated experiment in the public health field is poised to undergo changes, which to some extent is troubling because there seems little doubt that alcohol is a powerful intoxicant that causes untold misery.

WORKS CITED

Alavaikko, Mika, and Esa Österberg. "The Influence of Economic Interests on Alcohol Control Policy: A Case Study from Finland." *Addiction* 95 (2000, Supplement 4): 565–79.

"Conversation with Gabriel Romanus." *Addiction* 96 (2001): 383–93.

Eriksen, Sidsel. "Drunken Danes and Sober Swedes? Religious Revivalism and Temperance Movements as Keys to Danish and Swedish Folk Cultures?" *Language and the Construction of Class Identity.* Ed. Bo Stråth. Gothenburg: U Gothenburg, 1990.

Financial Times 1 Nov. 2001: 3.

Grieshaber-Otto, Jim, Scott Sinclair, and Noel Schacter. "Impacts of International Trade, Services, and Investment Treaties on Alcohol Regulation." *Addiction* 95 (2000, Supplement 4): 491–504.

Johansson, Lennart. "Sources of the Nordic Solutions." *Broken Spirits: Power and Ideas in Nordic Alcohol Control.* Eds. Pekka Sulkunen, Caroline Sutton, Christoffer Tigerstedt, and Katariina Warpenius. Helsinki: NAD, 2000.

Karlsson, Thomas, and Esa Österberg. "A Scale of Formal Alcohol Control Policy in 15 European Countries." *Nordic Studies on Alcohol and Drugs* 18 (2001): 117–29.

Kurzer, Paulette. *Markets versus Moral Regulation: Cultural Change in Europe.* Cambridge: Cambridge UP, 2001.

Levine, Harry. "Temperance Cultures: Concern about Alcohol Problems in Nordic and English-Speaking Cultures." *The Nature of Alcohol and Drug Related Problems.* Eds. Malcolm Lader, *et al.* New York: Oxford UP, 1992.

Lund, Ingeborg, Mika Alavaikko, and Esa Österberg. "Deregulating or Reregulating the Alcohol Market?" *Broken Spirits: Power and Ideas in Nordic Alcohol Control.* Helsinki: NAD, 2000.

Nordic Studies of Alcohol and Drugs 16 (1999).

Nordlund, Sturla, and Esa Österberg. "Unrecorded Alcohol Consumption: Its Economic and Its Effects on Alcohol Control in the Nordic Countries." *Addiction* 95 (2000, Supplement 4): 551–64.

Olsson, Börje, Sturla Nordlund, and Saija Järvinen. "Media Representations and Public Opinion." *Broken Spirits: Power and Ideas in Nordic Alcohol Control.* Helsinki: NAD, 2000.

Ramstedt, Matts. "Per Capita Alcohol Conusmption and Liber Cirrhosis Mortality in 14 European Countries." *Addiction* 96 (2001).

Sulkunen, Pekka. "The Liberal Arguments." *Broken Spirits: Power and Ideas in Nordic Alcohol Control.* Helsinki: NAD, 2000.

Thorhallsson, Baldur. *The Role of Small States in the European Union.* Burlington, VT: Ashgate, 2000.

Tigerstedt, Christoffer. "Discipline and Public Health." *Broken Spirits: Power and Ideas in Nordic Alcohol Control.* Helsinki: NAD, 2000.

Tomasson, Richard F. "Alcohol and Alcohol Control in Sweden." *Scandinavian Studies* 70.4 (1998): 477–508.

Törrönen, Jukka. "Mundane Social Policies in the Context of the Fragmentation of Welfare-State-Oriented Alcohol Policy in Finland." *Contemporary Drug Problems* 27 (2000): 137–62.

Ugland, Trygve. "European Integration and the Corrupting Gaps of the Systems." *Broken Spirits: Power and Ideas in Nordic Alcohol Control.* Helsinki: NAD, 2000.

___. *Policy Integration and Re-Categorization: Europeanization of Nordic Alcohol Control Policies.* Oslo: ARENA, 2001.

Warpenius, Katariina, and Caroline Sutton. "The Ideal of the Alcohol-free Society." *Broken Spirits: Power and Ideas in Nordic Alcohol Control.* Helsinki: NAD, 2000.

The Re-Emergence of the EU Issue in Norwegian Politics

Lars Svåsand

University of Bergen

Background

N orway's relationship to the process of European integration has
been characterized as one of "skepticism bordering on hostility"
(Pharo 1999:23). Pharo describes how Norwegian governments
were gradually drawn toward closer European cooperation, but driven
by a feeling of necessity and fear of isolation, rather than a belief in the
value of European integration itself. In the early 1960s Norway followed
Britain's and Denmark's application for membership, but the initiatives were blocked by French opposition. Membership again became
a possibility in the late 1960s, but when put a vote in a referendum[1] in
1972, it was defeated by 53.5 percent of the electorate. After that, the
issue disappeared from the political agenda.[2] The issue reappeared in
the late 1980s but was again defeated in the 1994 referendum by 52.2
percent of the electorate, almost identical to the 1972 result (see Map 1
in the Appendix.) The rejection of EU membership on two occasions
makes Norway something of an anomaly in Europe. As we shall see,

I thank Axel Rød for excellent research support for this paper and the Norwegian Social
Science Services (NSD) for production of maps and for supplying data. Some of the data
used in this paper is drawn from the EU-referendum survey 1994. Anonymized data
have been made available through NSD. Initial data collection and preparation were
carried out by the Central Statistical Office of Norway (SSB). Neither the SSB nor NSD
is responsible for the analysis of the data or for the interpretations of the data made in
this paper. I thank Christine Ingebritsen and Lykke Friis for constructive comments on
an earlier draft of this manuscript.

[1] There are no provisions for referenda in the Norwegian constitution. Thus, this mechanism is used rarely and is (in theory) only "advisory" to parliament.

[2] Perhaps it is indicative of how peripheral the issue had become that it took fifteen years
(1987) before a government again presented a report to parliament on Norway's relationship to Europe (Pharo 1999:23).

Norway is closely tied to Europe, and even to the EU and EU-affiliated institutions themselves and participates in European organizations, yet has rejected full membership. Toward the end of 1999, the issue of Norwegian membership in the EU was again being debated and the issue was debated in most political parties prior to the parliamentary election in 2001. The re-emergence of the issue must be understood against the backdrop of the EEA-agreement, which took effect in January 1994, the developments in the EU itself, and the fall-out from the end of the Cold War, in particular the prospect of the enlargement of the EU.[3]

This article centers the discussion of the EU issue in Norwegian politics around the political parties. These are the prime movers with respect to re-opening a debate on Norwegian membership in the European Union, although they may not be able to control the outcome of a debate.

The article takes as its point of departure the referendum in 1994 and discusses to what extent the positions of Norwegian political parties on the issue have been affected by developments in the years after the referendum. This discussion focuses on, first, the experience of the EEA-treaty which came into effect in 1994 as well as by some other linkages between the EU and Norway and, second, the changing nature of the EU itself as a result of the deepening of the integration process in the EU and the plans to enlarge the union.

NORWAY'S EU-RELATED LINKAGES

Although Norwegian membership was rejected in the 1994 referendum, Norway is not completely cut off from the EU as such or from other forms of European cooperation in which the EU member states also participates. Its position has been characterized as "a non-member inside the EU" (Andersen 2000). Some of these linkages originated in the period between the two referenda while others were agreed upon in the years following the last referendum.

Of all the linkages to the EU area three have been, and still are, controversial:

- the EEA treaty
- the Schengen treaty
- the associate membership in WEU

---

[3] These changes will not be discussed as such in this paper, only the role they play in arguments in the Norwegian debate.

YEAR	EVENT
1972	*EU-membership rejected in referendum by 53.5 percent of electorate*
1985	Norwegian membership in the EUREKA program
1987	Norwegian membership in ESA (European Space Agency)
1990	Norwegian participation in the COMMITT program
1992	Norwegian participation in EU's educational and research programs
1992	Norwegian associate membership in WEU (West European Union)
1993	Norwegian parliament ratifies EEA-treaty (European Economic Area)
1994	*EU-membership rejected in referendum by 52.3 percent of electorate*
1996	Norway signs Schengen treaty
1999	Revision of Schengen agreement following treaty's integration in EU[4]
2001	Norwegian contribution to the EU military force

THE EEA-TREATY

I will deal mostly with the EEA treaty because this treaty is different from the others:

- it is the most comprehensive of all Norwegian-EU linkages
- it is dynamic
- it created new institutions

The EEA treaty was developed in the years after the EU had decided upon the Single European Act (SEA), which created the internal market in the EU. The EFTA countries, Iceland, Lichtenstein, Norway, and Switzerland[5] agreed with the EU to a treaty that regulates the EFTA countries' access to this market, and vice versa. The treaty implies that EU-directives regulating the four freedoms of movement (goods, services, people, capital) are incorporated into the EFTA countries' legislation. In addition to the four freedoms of movements, Norway participates in thirty-one EU programs in eight different areas as part of the EEA agreement (*Nytt fra EU* 2000):

1. Research and tecnological development (Innovation)
2. Information services and security arrangements for such services (e-Content: two programs)

---

[4] Took effect as of 25 Mar. 2001.
[5] The Swiss participation in the EEA never materialized as the treaty was defeated in a referendum.

3. Education (Socrates [five programs] and four other programs)
4. Social and consumer issues (four programs)
5. Small and medium sized business (three programs)
6. Culture (two programs)
7. Environment and energy (three programs)
8. Public health (seven programs)

The EEA-treaty does not apply to:

- Trade policies with third parties
- Agriculture and fisheries
- Taxation and duty policies
- Monetary policy
- Justice
- Foreign and security policies

The main motivation for signing the EEA treaty was to ensure access for industrial products and various services to the EU market while at the same time shielding agriculture and fisheries, two sectors which are important to Norway both politically and economically. The EEA treaty provides Norway an alternative between full membership and associative membership.

The dynamic nature of the treaty makes it different from other treaties. As new directives are passed by the EU in fields covered by the treaty, they must be incorporated into Norwegian laws and regulations. As of 2001 only 8.8 percent of the EU directives have not been implemented by the EEA countries (Norway, Iceland, Lichtenstein) compared to 12.8 percent for the EU member states (*Nytt fra EU* 2001). Some directives have been more difficult for Norway to accept than others, such as the so-called gas-directive and the directive on artificial food additives.[6]

The EEA treaty also created special institutions. That was necessary for several reasons. The dynamic nature of the treaty required mechanisms for the "transfer" of new EU directives into Norwegian laws as Norway is not directly subject to EU institutions, such as the EU court of justice. Therefore, an EEA-committee was created to function as the body linking the EU and the Norwegian government. Second, the implementation

---

[6] The Norwegian government has been dragging its feet over these directives and applied for an extension of their implementation, much to the irritation of the EU (see *Nytt fra EU* 2000 and the interview with Chris Patten in *Aftenposten* 9 Jan. 2001). The *Storting* voted on 19 January. To incorporate the food additive directives into Norwegian law. The Socialist Party and the three center parties opposed while Labor, Conservative, and Progress supported the measure. The gas directive will lead to amendments of the petroleum act later in 2001.

of the directives is not supervised by the EU but by a special agency ESA, European Supervisory Agency, and an EFTA court.

While the EEA treaty has taken care of an important economic concern it nevertheless has raised a number of objections. The opponents of the EEA treaty argue that the treaty subjects Norway completely to EU regulations, just as membership would do. This makes the treaty supra-national and therefore erodes Norwegian sovereignty.[7] The sovereignty issue was an important argument for the parties that opposed EU membership in 1994, such as the Center and Socialist Left parties. These parties therefore see the EEA agreement as violating the intent of the majority of the voters in the referendum.

However, the most significant problem with the EEA treaty is the way it functions in practice. Norway participates in expert committees at the preparatory stages in the development of new directives but can not of course take part in the final decision making. At the same time, the treaty obliges Norway to incorporate directives into Norwegian laws. In the Norwegian *Storting*, the government consults with the parliamentary EEA committee in advance of the meetings in the EU/EFTA committee.[8] The EEA committee does not have the option as other parliamentary committees do to propose changes in the regulations, only to reject them. In theory, each EFTA country has the power to veto a new directive. However, this option has never been exercised, and it is unclear what would happen to the EEA-treaty if a directive were vetoed. In practice, therefore, all directives are implemented. This, according to the critics, is "worse than membership" since it suspends the constitutional law making process in Norway. One legal scholar has called the EEA treaty "a constitutional catastrophe," while others characterize it as "mixing oil and vinegar" and as trying to reach for the "nearly impossible" (Graver 2000). In a recent report, two constitutional lawyers concluded that

---

[7] This view is also shared by Graver (2000:4) who says: "despite the fact that the agreement has been characterized as a treaty under public international law, it contains clear elements that go beyond most such treaties towards elements of supranationality."

[8] The parliamentary committee is composed of the members of the standing *Storting* committee on foreign policy and constitutional matters and members of the Norwegian parliamentary delegation to the EEA parliamentary assembly. Dag Arne Christensen (1997) argues that compared to the Swedish and Danish parliament, the Norwegian *Storting* is particularly ill organized in order to play a significant role in Norway's relationship to the EU. Since Norway is outside the EU, the parliament can not instruct the government which negotiating position to take in the EEA committee; it can only to recommend "yes" or "no" to new directives. Documents in the parliamentary EEA committee are secret for one year.

Norwegian authorities' freedoms of manuevarability under the EEA treaty are not significantly greater than they would have been as a regular EU member. In some cases, it may be even more unclear what Norway's options are than if Norway was subject to the EU laws. "The concequence of this is that there is less room for exercising influence than in case of EU-membership. This impression is reinforced by the EFTA countries limited influence on decisions made by the EU, decisions that are later included in the EEA treaty (Arnesen and Graver 2000). Graver also argues that over time the EEA treaty is less and less suitable for the purpose it was originally established. The reason, he says, is that the agreement does not contain any mechanisms for taking into account the consequences of changes that are made in "the revisions and amendments of the treaties establishing the Community and the European Union." Thus, "the EEA is eroded a little bit every time treaty amendments of the EU take effect influencing corresponding rules in the Community" (Graver 2000:8).

SCHENGEN

Norway's accession to the Schengen treaty was motivated by the need to preserve the Nordic passport free zone in existence since 1956.[9] In May 1995 the Nordic prime ministers agreed that all the Nordic countries should be connected to the Schengen cooperation. The Schengen treaty became a hotly debated issue in Norwegian politics. The Labor government was supported by the Conservative and the Progress parties, but all the no-to-EU membership parties opposed. As of 1 May 1996, all five Nordic states obtained observer status in the Schengen cooperation. Until 1999, the Schengen agreement functioned as a separate cooperation program between participating countries, but as Schengen subsequently became integrated in the EU treaty, adjustments of Norway's participation was needed. Norway continues to take part in the preparatory work to Schengen related issues but can not participate in the actual decisions themselves. However, it is assumed that decisions are implemented as if Norway were a member.[10]

---

[9] However, motivations changed during the process to include greater police cooperation to fight international crime. See Hans E. Andersson (2000).

[10] The contact meetings between Norway and EU/Schengen used to take place in advance of the EU/Schengen committee made its decisions. However, during the Finnish EU-presidency these meetings were changed to *after* the EU/Schengen committee had met.

West European Union and the EU Defense Cooperation

In 1992, Norway became an associate member of the WEU. In the *Storting*, only the Socialist Left Party opposed membership. As the WEU was partly integrated into the EU structure in Nice and merged with a new defense dimension (ESDP), Norway faced a similar problems as with the Schengen agreement. Although the WEU itself has not been terribly important, its incorporation into the EU impacts the defense and security also of non-EU NATO members. Norway will contribute to the EU defence force with air, naval, and ground forces, but in order to do so has argued for access to the new decision-making structures. This has now been secured, although once an operation has been decided further decision making is left with the EU institutions where Norway cannot participate.

The linkage between Norway and the EU in this area has been supported by the "yes" to EU parties, but—predictably—opposed by the anti-EU parties. Thus, the Center Party, generally highly supportive of Norwegian participation in NATO and in peace making operations, is opposed to the possibility of Norwegian forces being under EU command and will only allow Norway to participate in EU lead operations when there is a UN mandate. The Socialists are similarly opposed to Norwegian participation in EU operations. In the party's proposal for a new election program, it is argued that an "independent" EU military capability might make Europe less dependent on the US, which the party would support. However, the party argues that at the present stage such an EU force would still have to rely on US support and could also lead to increased conflicts among European states.

As indicated above, Norway is closely linked institutionally to the European Union. Such linkages are underpinned by numerous other memberships in IGO's in which Norway interacts with the EU member states and the EU itself. Two other forms of EU-relationships further strengthen the linkages. Just as the state itself is connected to the EU, so are virtually all major interest organizations and civil society groups. The political parties themselves are members of European Party organizations (with the exception of the Center Party), and the Labor Party is even a full voting member of the PES, Party of European Socialists (Heidar and Svåsand 1998). Both the main trade union federation and the employer's federation are members of their respective European-wide organizations and also maintain offices in Brussels, as do several Norwegian regional authorities.

The EEA-agreement provides Norway with membership in the committees preparing new directives but excludes Norway from the political decision making. Thus, Norway participates in more than 200 committees dealing with the development of directives for the single European market.[11] Norway has also been included in committees that are "relevant" for the EEA-treaty, although not specifically related to it. Here EU has become more restrictive toward the EFTA countries. This restrictiveness is linked to the planned enlargement of the EU. Prospective member states do not enjoy "membership" on EU committees, as the EFTA countries (*Aftenposten* 24 Feb. 2001). Thus, EFTA countries—with no intention of becoming EU members—have had more access to the EU than prospective member states. Norwegian politicians are increasingly aware of how the enlargement process, although in general supported by several Norwegian parties, in this way also has a less advantageous effect on Norway's own EU-relationship. There is also a fear that enlargement will make the EEA-treaty less relevant. Already, the EEA treaty is imbalanced, with the three small EFTA members, Norway, Iceland, and Lichtenstein vs. the EU. But this imbalance will be worse with every new additional EU member.

Thus, the prospect of an uncertain future for the EEA-treaty as well as a deepening of the EU-competencies in defense and foreign policy are for some parties the main motivations for again advocating a membership debate. Underlying these concerns is the strong economic ties between Norway and the EU.

Figure 1 displays the EU-area's share of all Norwegian export and import from 1970 onwards. As the EU has grown through enlargements, so Norwegian export and import to the EU area have increased as a share of total export and import: first, in 1973 when Britain and Denmark joined the EU and then again in 1995 when Sweden and Finland joined. Particularly import levels are related to these enlargements while export has grown independent of the extension of the EU, probably due to the importance of the oil and gas sector. As of 2000, only 10 percent of Norwegian imports and exports are now with non-EU countries, and this figure will be further reduced as the EU expands with new members over the next years.

---

[11] Similar mechanisms are in place for the Schengen agreement and the security cooperation.

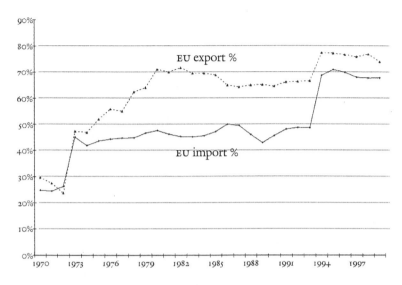

Fig. 1. Percent of Norway's Export/Import with the EU.

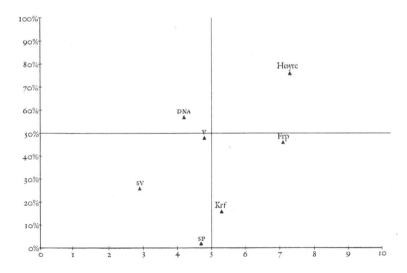

Figure 2. Left-right and pro-vs. anti-EU, by party.

POLITICAL PARTIES AND THE EU POLICY

What prospects are there that Norwegian voters again will be asked to vote "yes" or "no" to membership and which outcome is likely?

The political parties are the crucial actors in both deciding when the issue again will be presented to the voters and the prospects of a clear "yes" or "no" to membership. But the timing as well as the outcome depend on several considerations. It is an axiom in the study of political parties that their most important goal is to survive (Panebianco 1988: 7–13). Therefore unity in the party may be more important than the desirability of EU membership itself, a consideration that will clearly affect the timing of the issue as well as the strategies chosen by the parties in the campaign itself.[12]

It is quite common in comparative analysis of party policies to locate the policy position of parties along a left-right continuum. But in the EU issue correlates only partially with the left-right alignment.

In the diagram the parties are positioned along two axes. The left-right axis is operationalized by using the average self-placement of each party's electorate. This scale runs from 0 (far left) to 10 (far right). The other dimension is the pro- vs. anti-EU membership. Although this is a dicothomy as far as the official party policy is concerned, a party's location on the axis is determined by the proportion of each party's voters who voted in favor of EU membership in 1994. Since the membership issue is ultimately to be settled in a referendum, what matters is not only which positions parties adopt, but also how well this position is supported by its voters. Internal party cohesion has traditionally been a problem for the parties in formulating an EU policy, and as the vertical dimension in the Figure I indicates, there is only one party, the Center Party, that is completely united on this issue with regard to the voters as well as to the parliamentarians.[13]

With the passing of the EEA-treaty in 1993 and the debate on EU-membership extending until the referendum in 1994, the following combination of party positions can be identified (see Table 1).

What has happened with these positions since 1994? As we have seen, the EEA-agreement has been controversial. On the one hand, it

---

[12] For an excellent analysis of party strategies in the 1994 referendum campaign, see Saglie (1999).

[13] For how well parliamentary members reflect the policy positions of voters, see Don Matthews and Henry Valen (1999).

EEA-treaty

		FOR	AGAINST
EU-membership	FOR	*Labor* *Conservatives* *Progress*	
	AGAINST	*Liberals* *Christian Peoples Party*	*Socialist Left* *Center*

Table 1. Party positions relative to the EEA-treaty and EU-membership.

Future EU-membership?

		FOR	AGAINST
EU-membership 1994	FOR	Labor (*Post-2005*) Conservatives (*Now*)	Progress (*The issue is not relevant during the next four years*)
	AGAINST	Liberals (*Maybe a need for debate*) Christian Peoples Party (*No reason to change the status quo*)	Socialist Left (*No*) Center (*No*)

Table 2. Past and future EU-membership positions.

has ensured Norwegian access to the EU market. On the other hand, it has been accompanied with a almost total acceptance of all EU directives without active Norwegian participation in the decision-making process except in the developmental phase. Prospective EU expansion to countries in central and east Europe means the organization will be more pan-European than before, and the increasing role of the EU in security policy, such as dealing with regional crisis, like Yugoslavia, have altered the role of the organization. The combination of these changes has motivated a reopening of the membership issue.

In Table 2 the parties' position on future EU membership is compared to their previous position, an inevitably a difficult comparison in that we can not deduce from what the parties current positions (2001) are what they will be once the issue is firmly placed on the political agenda. The current debate is more a debate about a debate, than a debate on whether to re-open the membership issue as a priority issue. The location of the parties on the "future EU membership" variable is based mainly on the parties' electoral platform for the 2001 parliamentary election. As the EU issue is part of a broader electoral platform in a regular parliamentary election, the issue must "compete" with other issues for political attention. Thus, the parties' overall strategy in the election will determine how eagerly they will push the membership issue. These problems are discussed in the following paragraphs.

We will start with the Center Party because this is the most united party on the issue and has been consistently opposed to Norwegian EU membership since the very start of the debate during the 1960s. In the current debate, the party repeats it opposition to EU membership and substantiates it by two concerns (see Haga). The party sees the EU as a regional bloc that distorts the need to address global issues. The most crucial issues in the world are not issues that can be solved at the European level, but only through a global institution like the UN. A second concern for the party is the nature of EU developments. Since 1994 the EU has, in the party's view, developed toward more union and less democratic governance. The EMU and the German Foreign Minister's speech about a "European federation" imply for the Center Party that the distance between ordinary citizens and the governing elites will increase in a federal Europe. To the Center Party the EU is therefore not consistent with the need to strengthen national or international solidarity. In the 1994 referendum campaign, the main issue for the party was "the democratic deficit" in the EU. Thus, for the Center Party the geographic extension of the EU to include countries in central and east Europe does not alter its perception of the EU as mainly a regional institution. On the contrary, the party's election program for 1997–2001 argued that membership in the EU for the newly democratized countries in central and east Europe will create more social inequality and lead to worsened environmental conditions because of the market-based economic thinking, as expressed in the Maastrich treaty. Deepening EU integration means membership is even less attractive than it was as more issues will be determined by majority voting and more policy sectors will come under the EU umbrella, developments contrary to the decentralization of political power advocated by the party. The Center Party's evaluation of the EEA-agreement as well as the changes in the EU itself has lead the party to conclude that there is no reason for the party to take a different view of membership: all developments in the EU itself has, according the party program for 2001–05, strengthened the worst aspects of the EU: centralization and supra-nationality.

The same arguments are shared by the Socialist Left Party. Although this party accepts the principle of supra-nationality as such, the way the EU works is not in accordance with the Socialist Party's priorities; environmental protection and employment.[14] Also the EEA treaty should be replaced by a new treaty, but to the Socialist Left Party, the EEA treaty is still to be preferred to a full EU membership.

The Center Party's partners in the 1997–March 2000 government— Christian People's Party (Kr.F.) and the Liberals—deviate only slightly from the Center Party. Kr.F. argues that there is no reason to change the non-membership status for Norway. The EU as an institution has not become more attractive, at the same time as the EEA treaty has functioned satisfactorily, while the Liberals' proposed election program for 2001–05 argue that no application for EU membership should be sent unless there is support for it in the population. While supporting the status quo, the party also argues that there should be a public debate on the issue and that the "processes within the EU ... make it necessary to evaluate and discuss Norwegian EU-membership" (*Center Party*). Compared to the previous program, this position is a slight modification of its opposition to membership. In the previous program, the need to develop the EEA treaty and to make this attractive as an alternative to prospective EU members from east and central Europe as well was the main issue. Of the three coalition partners, the Center Party is the only one that has reinforced its opposition to EU membership, while both the KrF and Liberals are open to discussion of the matter.

The Conservatives have always been the most pro-EU party in Norway. The experiences with the EEA treaty and the changes in the EU itself have reinforced this preference. The party argues that the EEA treaty is inadequate due to the changes in the EU and that the prospects of WEU being integrated into the EU will have a negative effect on Norwegian security policy. The party's position, therefore, is to argue for Norwegian EU membership "as soon as possible" (Election).

The Progress Party was deeply divided on the issue of EU membership in 1994, although officially adopting a pro-membership position. The party's position today is "neutral." It argues that the issue is not on the agenda and should not be on the agenda until a shift in public opinion calls for the issue to be debated again. A motion debated at the party's

---

[14] There are, though, different opinions within the party. Five of twelve members of the party program committee favored a discussion in the party about EU membership (*Dagsavisen* 3 Nov. 2000).

executive committee and national committee concludes that there are good reasons for as well as against EU membership. According to the party, the issue is not to be decided by the parties or the parliament, but by the people in a referendum.

The pivotal party in any EU debate in Norway is Labor. The issue has twice divided the party from top to the bottom. The elite in the party have generally been more favorable to membership than the rank and file, but the split has run from top to bottom. When EU-membership was rejected in the 1994 referendum, the Labor government did not resign, as it did in 1972, but continued in office until the election of 1997. The EU issue was sidelined in the political debate but was again placed on the agenda during 2000. The party leader and the current foreign minister, Torbjørn Jagland, has argued for a change in the party's position allowing the party leadership some more freedom of maneuvaribility. The party's 2000 convention adopted (unanimously) a motion that allows for a new EU application process:

> during the next parliamentary period, implying an application earli-
> est 2005–2006. A new evaluation of whether or not to apply for EU
> membership is only relevant if EU extension is actually going ahead
> and a new membership application presuppose a significant change
> in the Norwegian people's attitude to this issue. ("Landsmøtets edtak
> om Europa og EU")

The Labor Party's EU compromise links a shift in Norwegian EU policy to a "significant change in public opinion." Is there such a change? Figure 3 displays the public opinion on the issue since 1994.

In the period immediately following the defeat of the EU membership proposal, public opinion reinforced the "no" side, which then stabilized. From 1997, the "yes" side again made some progress, perhaps as a result of the plans for the enlargement and the ambitions for the Euro. Progress for the "yes" side seems to take place when the membership issue is not on the agenda, but as the EU debate again is picking up, the opposition to EU also is mobilized. As of 2001, therefore, it is not possible to detact any "significant change in the public opinion," which is hardly surprizing as most party leaders — also the EU-enthusiasts — tread carefully on the issue. There are several reasons for them to be wary of the issue. First, as table 3 displays, the voters of two parties, Labor and Liberals, are split in almost equally, while others suffers from minorities one way or the other, except for the Center Party.

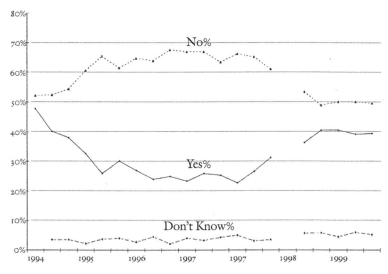

Figure 3. Percent "yes," "no" and "don't know" to EU membership. 1994–2000.

	Socialist	Labor	Center	Chris-tian	Liberal	Con.	Progr.
Yes	26	50	5	13	46	69	33
No	65	45	92	83	49	26	61
Dk	9	5	3	4	5	6	6

Table 3. Opinion on EU membership, by party. 11 Apr. 2001. Source: "Målingene siste år—når 'Vet ikke' holdes utenfor."[15]

Because of the size of the Labor Party, its linkage to the trade union movement, and its role as the dominant governing party, the issue of EU-membership is "dead" unless Labor decides otherwise and the change in the formulations in party's election program for 2001 was met with strong opposition inside the party. It is therefore likely that

---

[15] This survey also shows that the center-periphery contrast is as strong as ever.

it will take some time before the party leadership again will push the membership issue higher on the party's agenda.

During the spring of 2001, the Progress Party suffered serious splits and divisions over party strategy as well as personal rivalries. An additional divisive issue, like the EU, is the last thing the party would like see happen. But even the Conservatives, who are advocating EU membership "as soon as possible" have reasons to be careful. Parties have multiple goals in addition to surviving. One of them is to become a governing party. Only the Labor Party is able to assume this role on its own. On the non-socialist side, coalitions of one form or the other are needed. The Conservatives would like to build a coalition government with Liberals and the Christian Peoples Party. Government participation is important for the party in order to avoid being marginalized in parliament. After the 1997 election, a so-called center government was formed by the Center Party, Christian People's Party and Liberals. Even after resigning from government, these three parties have stuck together as an alternative. Several conditions must be fulfilled for the Conservative Party to break that alliance and to replace the Center Party with themselves as the coalition partner of the two others, but to do so membership in the EU cannot be part of such a government's policies, at least for now. Thus, the combination of the need for party unity (Labor, Liberals and Progress) and the coalition-seeking strategy of the Conservatives may push a change on Norway EU-membership still some years into the future.

This brief overview of Norwegian parties' position on possibly future EU membership demonstrates that the parties' interpretations of what the EU is and what the experiences of the EEA treaty are vary and lead them to completely different conclusions. The two parties that in the past were the most homogeneous, either as a "yes" party (Conservatives) or as a "no" party (Center) have reinforced their original position. Parties that experienced a greater or lesser split among its voters try to accoommodate the differences. The extreme version of this is the Progress Party's "no-opinion" stand. Norwegian parties confirm Marks and Wilson's (2000) arguments about the linkage between party family and preference for or against European integration to a great extent. But there are also some differences. Both the Liberal and Christian People's Party are on a sliding path towards accepting EU membership and even in the Socialist Party the anti-EU position is not as solid as before.

TOWARDS THE THIRD (AND FOURTH?) REFERENDA?

The issue of EU-membership has previously been settled in referenda arranged after the government has negotiated an accession treaty. If the membership issue is placed on the political agenda again, the referendum instrument will be used once more. However, it is also possible that the procedure will not be exactly like it has been on the two previous occasions.

It is unthinkable that EU membership would be decided solely by parliament, although it is within its prerogatives to do so, but the non-constitutional nature of referenda does not mean that it can be avoided. On the contrary, because referenda have already been arranged to settle the issue in the past, it is "mandatory" to use this mechanism again. But, potentially there could be two changes depending on how soon the issue re-emerges.

First, Norwegian political leaders have twice had their policy preference on this issue overturned by the electorate. It is therefore possible that there will be two referenda; one on whether to apply for EU membership at all, and one, on the accession treaty. This two-stage process may serve several purposes. The most important is that there will be a spill-over effect from the first to the second referendum.[16] This option was proposed by the Progress Party in the 1992–94 debate. Now, also the Conservative and Christian People's Parties advocate this alternative, and although the Liberals do not expressly propose the same, its program is clearly open for this possibility.

The second potential change is the status of referenda in general. Under the current rules, a referendum can be arranged by parliament, formally by passing a law in each case. The constitution requires that the final decision is made by parliament. The status of the referendum is only advisory. Accession to the EU involves a transfer of sovereignty to a supra-national body. Currently, there must be a three-fourth majority of MP's voting in favor for such a transfer to take place. Therefore, even if a majority of the electorate endorsed a EU-membership, a quater of the

---

[16] It was imagined that there would also be a spill-over effect in 1994, with the Norwegian referendum coming after that of Finland and Sweden where it always looked more likely that the "yes" side would win.

MPs would be sufficient to block it.[17] Depending on future changes in the constitution, the status of referenda may change. There has always been a minority arguing in favor of a constitutional status for referenda. However it is not likely that such a constitutional change would have an impact on the next EU referendum because the procedure for changing the constitution is cumbersome and the no-fraction in parliament will have little incentive for voting in favor of such a change.

When the membership issue was on the agenda in 1994, it was partly as a consequence of changes beyond the control of Norwegian political leaders. The decision by Finland and Sweden to apply for membership obviously affected the Norwegian position as well. This time there is less urgency and there are no political or economic problems that call for EU-membership as the solution, such as the severe economic problems experienced by Finland and Sweden early in the 1990s. The Norwegian state is flush with revenues from the oil sector and unemployment is low. The linkages between Norway and the rest of Europe are well developed, and to the electorate, this may very well remove any feelings of isolation. The Danish electorate's rejection of the Euro and the negative EU opinion in Sweden after it joined the EU have obviously not helped those in Norway arguing in favor of membership. At the same time, the EEA treaty is being defended by most political leaders as taking care of the most important needs for Norwegian industry and commerce. All of this has made it difficult for Norwegian political leaders to convince the electorate of the need for full EU membership.

The experiences of defeat in the 1972 and 1994 referenda and the fear of the issue leading to internal party divisions have cautioned politicians against rushing to make the membership question a top political issue. Particularly within the Labor Party the leadership is hoping that time is on their side and that by approaching the issue step-by-step, the party (and the electorate?) may be convinced that EU membership is right. But, they have been wrong before and may certainly be so again.

---

[17] A Conservative MP has proposed a constitutional change that will allow EU membership with a two-third majority, as currently applies to all constitutional amendments, on the assumption that there will also be a referendum on the issue, but the Labor Party has indicated that they do not support this idea.

APPENDIX

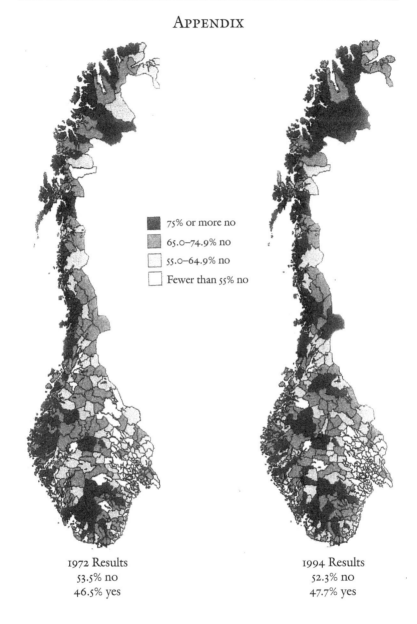

75% or more no

65.0–74.9% no

55.0–64.9% no

Fewer than 55% no

1972 Results
53.5% no
46.5% yes

1994 Results
52.3% no
47.7% yes

Map 1. Referendum on EU membership, 1972 and 1994.
Source: Norwegian Social Science Data Services/Statistics Norway.

WORKS CITED

Aftensposten. "Interview with Chris Patten." 9 Jan. 2001.

___. 24 Feb. 2001

Andersen, Svein S. 2000. "Utenforlandet i EU." *Nytt Norsk Tidsskrift* 3: 263–75.

Andersson, Hans E. 2000. "Den nordiska passunionen eller Schengensamarbetet?" *Norden i sicksack. Tre spårbyten inom nordiskt samarbete.* Eds. Bengt Sundelius and Claes Wiklund. Stockholm: Santerus Forlag, 235–51.

Arnesen, Finn, and Hans Petter Graver. 2000. "Rettslige sider ved Norges EU-rettede avtaler, Oslo." *Makt-og demokratiutredningen 1998–2003.* Rapportserien, 19.

Center Party. <www.venstre.no/programmet/utkast1/kap5.html>.

Christensen, Dag Arne. 1997. "Europautvala i Danmark, Sverige og Noreg: Sand-påstrøingsorgan eller politiske muldvarpar?" *Nordisk Administrativt Tidsskrift* 2 (1997): 143–62.

Dagsavisen. 3 Nov. 2000.

Election Program. Conservative Party. Norway: 2001–04.

Graver, Hans Petter. 2000. "Supranationality and National Legal Autonomy in the EEA-agreement." *ARENA working papers.* WP 00/23. 8 Jan 2001. <www.arena.uio.no/publications/wp00_23.htm>.

Haga, Åslaug. "EU-et fredsprosjekt?" *Dagsavisen* 28 Sept. 2000.

Heidar, Knut, and Lars Svåsand. 1998. "Nordiske partiers samarbeidsmønstre—med hverandre og med Europa." *Europa i Norden. Europeisering av nordisk samarbeid.* Eds. Johan P. Olsen and Bjørn Otto Sverdrup. Oslo: TANO. 290–317.

"Landsmøtets vedtak om Europa og EU." *Norwegian Labor Party.* 15 Nov. 2000. <www.dna.no/internett/politikk/vedtak/3641/ce9485.html>.

"Målingene siste år—når 'Vet ikke' holdes utenfor." *Nationen.* 4 May 2001. <www.nationen.no/40/60/96/1.html>.

Marks, Gary, and Carole J. Wilson. "The Past in the Present: A Cleavage Theory of Party Response to European Integration." *British Journal of Political Science* 30, Party 3 (July 2000): 433–60.

Matthews, Donald R., and Henry Valen. 1999. *Parliamentary Representation: The Case of the Norwegian Storting.* Columbus: Ohio State UP.

Nytt fra EU. Nyhetsbrev fra Europakommisjonens delegasjon for Norge og Island. No. 6/7, 2000.

___. No. 1, 2001.

Panebianco, Angelo. 1988. *Political Parties: Organization and Power.* Cambridge: Cambridge UP.

Pharo, Helge. 1999. "Ingen vei utenom? Norge i integrasjonsprosessene i Europa 1946–1994." *Utenfor, annerledes og suveren? Norge under EØS-avtalen.* Eds. Dag Harald Claes and Bent Sofus Tranøy. Bergen: Fagbokforlaget. 15–38.

Saglie, Jo. 1999. *Standpunkter og strategi. EU saken i norsk partipolitikk 1989–1994.* Oslo: U Oslo, Dept. of Political Science.

The Skeptical Political Elite Versus the Pro-European Public
The Case of Iceland

Baldur Thorhallsson
University of Iceland

OR MORE THAN A DECADE, surveys in Iceland have indicated considerable support among the population for membership application to the European Union. However, not a single political party at present advocates membership, and very few politicians publicly support membership. This has to be explained, particularly as European integration has had an elitist character in the other Nordic states, where leading politicians have advocated involvement in the European project but have had difficulties in convincing the public (Katzenstein 1997:258).[1] Also, interest groups in Iceland have been more reluctant to campaign for membership application contrary to many of their counterparts in the other Nordic states. The aim of this paper is to explain the *elite-electorate gap:* why political parties are reluctant to advocate membership in the EU while around half of the electorate want to start discussion with the EU about membership.

An intense debate on whether Iceland should join the EU has not taken place. There was a considerable debate concerning Iceland's membership in the European Economic Area in 1992 and 1993, but the question of membership in the EU has never seriously been on the agenda. However, Iceland is deeply involved in European integration as an associated member of the EU by the EEA-agreement. Iceland adopts around 80 percent of EU law and regulations through the EEA[2] but has very limited chances of influencing EU decision-making.

---

[1] Ninety percent of the elite in EU member states support European integration (see European Comission).

[2] Information from the Ministry for Foreign Affairs in Iceland. However, it is difficult to state precisely how much of EU law and regulations the EFTA/EEA states have to implement.

The paper will argue that the skepticism of the political elite in Iceland toward membership in the EU can be explained by three factors: first, the influence of the primary economic sectors combined with the electoral system and the role of interest groups in decision making of the government; second, the Icelandic political discourse concerning independence and sovereignty; and finally, the geographical location of Iceland and the defense treaty with the United States. The willingness of around half of the electorate to apply for EU membership is explained by the looser connection of the populace with the primary sectors compared with the political elite, the electorate's greater concern with their economic prosperity than the political discourse of the elite, and the electorate's anxiety about isolation from Europe, particularly the other Nordic states.

The paper is divided into four sections. It will start by examining the polices of the political parties toward EU membership and compare their polices with those of their sister parties in the other Nordic states. Secondly, the paper will analyze why the political elite are reluctant to adopt a pro-European policy. Thirdly, it will examine the public attitude toward EU membership. Finally, the paper will examine reasons behind the growing discussion in Iceland about EU membership. It will analyze why two of the political parties, the Alliance and the Progressive Party, as well as the main labor market organizations have been revising their policies toward European integration.

POLICIES OF POLITICAL PARTIES TOWARD EU MEMBERSHIP

Political parties in Iceland have adopted one of two approaches toward the question of EU membership: a firm approach against membership and a "wait and see" approach. The strategy of the Independence Party and the Left Green Movement is to reject EU membership altogether. They also reject any challenge to put EU application on the agenda. On the other hand, the Alliance and the Liberal Party have adopted a "wait and see" approach. This is also the case of the Progressive Party as it has moved from its firm opposition to EU membership toward a "wait and see" approach. The main argument by politicians against EU membership has been that Iceland would lose control over its waters by joining the Common Fisheries Policy (CFP).

	Support percentage	Total MPS	Regional MPS	Reykjavík MPS
Independence Party	40.7	26	11	15
The Alliance[3]	26.8	17	8	9
Progressive Party	18.4	12	8	4
Left Green Movement	9.1	6	4	2
Liberal Party	4.2	2	1	1
Others and outside parties	0.8	0	0	0
Total	100	63	32	31

Table 1. Results of the 1999 General Election to the National Parliament, Althingi. Statistics Iceland. Election Statistics. <www.hagstofa.is>

The policy of the Independence Party[4] toward membership in the EU has moved from a "wait and see" (Kristinsson 1996:150)[5] approach to firm opposition to EU membership. The Independence Party opposes EU membership on the grounds that by joining the EU Iceland would have to give up the control of its fishing grounds. The party has also stated that the EU's increased taxes and regulations on companies are against the party's economic policy. Furthermore, its party chairman and prime minister, David Oddsson, has repeatedly rejected any transfer of sovereignty to the EU. Oddsson, with his firm opposition to any debate about EU membership, has been successful in preventing the issue's being put on the agenda within the party.[6]

Until the mid 1990s, the "wait and see" approach of the party was a reactive approach to the uncertainty of the EEA-agreement and the question as to whether the political elite in Norway, Sweden, and

---

[3] In the 1999 general election, several left-of-center parties formed an electional coalition as the Alliance: the Social Democratic Party 11.4%, the People's Alliance 14.3%, the Women's Alliance 4.9%, and the People's Movement 7.2%. All together they received 37.8% and 23 MPS.

[4] The Independence Party is a center-right party and the largest political party in Iceland with around 40 percent support during the last decades.

[5] Kristinsson argues that the cautious approach to European integration is epitomized in a "wait and see" attitude.

[6] Oddsson took over as a party chairman in 1991 and as a prime minister two months later. He is the longest serving prime minister in the history of Iceland. He is also at present the longest serving prime minister in Europe and one of few center-right prime ministers.

Finland would be able to convince their electorate to join the EU. Also, the "wait and see" approach was a convenient policy for the leadership of the party as factions of the party wanted EU membership on the agenda while others, such as farmers and vessel owners, spoke against any discussion of membership. The move toward firm opposition to membership came at a time when the EEA-agreement was thought to guarantee Icelandic economic interests. Also, David Oddsson, who had faced some hostility as a party chairman in the beginning, had taken firm control of the party.

The policy of the Independence Party is not in line with its voters as over 40 percent of them support membership application according to an opinion poll in 1999 (see Chart 1). Also, nearly one-third of them are undecided toward the question of membership while just over a quarter follow the party line.

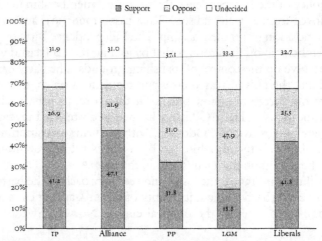

Chart 1. Do you support or oppose an Icelandic application for the EU. Icelandic Election Study (1999). Courtesy of Ólafur Th. Harðarson. IP: The Independence Party, PP: The Progressive Party, LGM: The Left Green Movement.

The founding members of the Left Green Movement[7] are the most outspoken critics of membership in the EEA and NATO. In general, the

---

[7] The Left Green Movement was mainly formed by former members of the People's Alliance and the Women's Alliance. They disapproved of the electoral coalition these two parties established with the Social Democratic Party in 1999.

Left Green Movement is the most skeptical of the political parties favoring Icelandic involvement in any free-trade area or other economic or international federations.[8] The Left Green Movement is more in tune with its electorate than the Independence Party as nearly 50 percent of them oppose EU membership application. However, nearly 20 percent of them support it, and one-third are undecided (see Chart 1).

The Alliance[9] has not yet taken a decisive stand on the EU question despite findings that nearly half of its voters support EU application. Furthermore, nearly one-third of the Alliance's voters are undecided concerning EU application, and just over 20 percent oppose application. In 1999, the Alliance stated in the election campaign that it would not apply for membership in the EU during the new parliamentary term that will end not later than 2003. However, the party demands an informed debate on the pros and cons of Icelandic EU membership. This policy was a compromise among the founding parties that had very different views on Iceland's involvement in European integration.[10]

The Alliance is, at present, revising its policy toward Europe. Factions of the party are already proposing a policy that demands that the government call for a referendum on EU application. In this regard, the party is likely to come up with objectives for Iceland in membership negotiation with the EU. Also, leading members of the Alliance have stated that the Common Fisheries Policy of the EU might not be unfavorable to Icelandic interests.

In its 2001 conference declaration, the Progressive Party[11] for the first time did not rule out EU membership. An internal European affairs committee of the party concluded in 2000 that the government should try to strengthen the EEA-agreement, but if that is not possible, Iceland then has to look for other means to secure its interests and a

---

[8] The party's skepticism toward political and economic integration in Europe is well demonstrated in a draft resolution that the party put forth in the Althingi in November 2000. The resolution states that Iceland should not be a member of any free-trade area but should make special trade agreements without membership.

[9] In the 1999 general election, several left-of-center parties formed an electoral coalition as the Alliance: the People's Alliance, the Social Democratic Party, and the Women's Alliance. In May 2000, these parties formally formed a political party: the Alliance.

[10] The Social Democratic Party supported EU membership while the People's Alliance and the Women's Alliance rejected membership altogether. They also opposed Iceland's membership in the EEA.

[11] The Progressive Party has traditionally been labeled a farmers' party and has defended the interests of farmers and the more sparsely populated regions in Althingi. It has been the coalition partner of the Independence Party since 1995.

membership negotiation is one of the options that has to be considered ("Telur samningsmarkmiðin raunhæf," *Morgunblaðið* 24 June 2001:10). The report also states that if a decision is reached to apply for membership, a national referendum should be held in which voters have an opportunity to choose between realistic options that Iceland has regarding European integration (Evrópunefnd Framsóknarmanna 2001).[12]

This policy change is a result of the efforts of the party leader and foreign minister since 1995, Halldór Ásgrímsson. He has systematically been working to get EU membership on the political agenda since early 2000. Ásgrímsson appears to be leaning more and more toward a pro-European position. However, he has had difficulties in convincing the party's MPs. None of the twelve MPs of the party, six of whom are ministers, in fact advocates membership, and most of them rule out membership in the EU at least for the time being. However, Ásgrímsson seems to have considerable support among the party's voters to revise its policy toward Europe. Nearly one-third of them support membership application, and 37 percent of them are undecided. On the other hand, nearly one-third of them oppose membership application (see Chart 1).

The newly founded Liberal Party[13] is willing to consider the membership alternative if Iceland can guarantee sole rights over its waters.[14] The party leader has also stated that he is in favor of a national referendum on EU application ("Yfirlit en ekki stefnumörkun," *Morgunblaðið* 24 Jan. 2001:12). A considerable number of voters in the Liberal Party support EU application—over 40 percent—while one-fourth of them oppose it, and the rest are undecided.

THE DISTINCTIVE APPROACH OF ICELANDIC POLITICAL PARTIES TOWARD EUROPEAN INTEGRATION

The policy of the Independence Party toward membership in the EU is in sharp contrast to other conservative parties in the Nordic states. They were among the earliest advocates of EU membership. Moreover, the

---

[12] The report also states that if a formal agreement is reached between Iceland and the EU on membership another referendum should be held where the voters have the chance to accept or reject membership.

[13] In 1998, a former MP and cabinet minister in the Independence Party founded the Liberal Party after he had been sacked as a governor from one of the two publicly-owned banks in Iceland for corruption.

[14] The Liberal Party homepage is available at < www.xf.is/evropumal.htm >.

other Nordic conservative parties have been among the most integrationist parties; furthermore, the elite of the parties have also reflected the opinion of their electorate. For instance, in Sweden, Norway, and Finland, only 13 to 18 percent of the conservative electorate voted against membership (Svåsand and Lindström 1996:215). These figures are comparable with the opposition among voters in the Independence Party since, as stated earlier, just over a quarter of them reject membership application. This is the case despite the skeptical view of the party elite toward membership.

The Alliance does not follow its sister parties in the Nordic states.[15] The social democratic parties in Finland and Norway campaigned enthusiastically for EU membership (Svåsand and Lindström 1996: 205–19). The leadership of Danish Social Democrats has also proved their pro-European policy in government since 1993. The leadership of the Swedish Social Democratic Party is somewhat more divided toward participation in European integration. However, a good majority is in favor of membership. Nowhere in these four Nordic states have factions of Social Democratic parties opposing involvement in the European project prevailed since the early 1990s (Svåsand and Lindström 1996: 208). Furthermore, voters of the Alliance seem to be as enthusiastic about European integration as other Social Democratic voters.

The Progressive Party has also been more skeptical toward EU membership than other agrarian parties in the Nordic states except for the Norwegian Center Party. The Danish agrarian party has been one of the most federally inclined parties. The Finnish and Swedish parties have both suffered from internal division, but they came out in support of EU membership before the referenda on the issue. Furthermore, the electorate of the agrarian parties in Sweden and Finland was less supportive of EU membership than the party elite (Svåsand and Lindström 1996:212). This is in direct contrast to the voters of the Progressive Party and its elite. Nearly one-third of the party voters support membership application, and 37 percent of them are undecided despite the skeptical view of the party's MPs.

The electorate of the Left Green Movement is more willing to consider the membership alternative than supporters of left parties in the other Nordic states. Between 80 and 90 percent of the left parties' supporters voted against EU membership in Finland, Sweden, and Norway and the

---

15 However, the Social Democratic Party came out in favor of EU application in 1994. This was not the case of the People's Alliance and the Women's Alliance.

Treaty of the European Union in Denmark (Svåsand and Lindström 1996:213). In Iceland, 50 percent of the electorate of the Left Green Movement oppose membership application, one-third are undecided, and nearly 20 percent support it.

WHY ARE THE POLITICAL ELITE RELUCTANT TO ADOPT A PRO-EUROPEAN POLICY?

Three main factors explain the reluctance of the political elite in Iceland to join the European Union: first, the influence of the primary economic sectors in Iceland reflected in the electoral system and the role of interest groups in Iceland; second, the Icelandic political discourse concerning the independence and sovereignty of Iceland; third, the geographical location of Iceland and its special relationship with the United States.

The Pivotal Role of the Primary Industries: The Electoral System and Role of Interest Groups

The reliance of Iceland on fish exports is extreme, as it constitutes around 63 percent of its exported goods as Chart 2 demonstrates.[16] Ingebritsen,

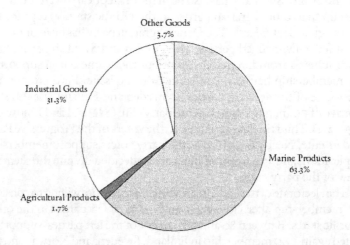

Chart 2. Export of goods. Statistics Iceland. Iceland External Trade.

---

[16] See <www.hagstofa.is>.

in her sectoral approach in explaining the Nordic states' response to the EU, argues that the balance of economic interest-group preferences in Iceland and Norway weighs against membership (1998:127). Fisheries and farmers' interest groups tend to be more influential in policy-making of governments in Iceland than in the other Nordic states. Thus, the primary economic sectors play an important role in the response of political parties to European integration.

The Icelandic Vessel Owners Oppose EU Membership

Because Iceland would lose control over its territorial waters and the Common Fisheries Policy (CFP) of the EU is unfavorable to Icelandic interests, fisheries do not support membership (Hjartarson 6 October 2000; *Fiskifréttir*). The Farmers' Organization also opposes EU membership because of the CFP and the danger of livestock diseases. Furthermore, it argues that Iceland would face difficulties concerning the Economic and Monetary Union (EMU) and the proposed changes to the Common Agricultural Policy with regard to the forthcoming enlargement of the EU (*Freyr* 97:3 [2000]:30). Agriculture is not one of the leading economic sectors in Iceland, but the electoral system and characteristics of the national administration enhance the influence of farmers in government policy-making.

A vast majority of the Icelandic population lived in the rural areas when the electoral system was designed. Iceland was largely a farming community during the first quarter of the twentieth century though fishing slowly took over as the main industry and greater numbers of people gathered in small villages around the coast. This is still reflected in the electoral system. A minority of the electorate—32 percent—from rural regions hold a majority in parliament, as Table 1 indicates. Parliamentarians from these regions have close links to the farmer and fishery interest groups where opposition to EU membership is stronger than in the urban areas. Nearly 60 percent of the respondents in Reykjavík and its surroundings support membership application while only 45 percent of the respondents in the countryside support it (see Chart 5 and more detailed discussion below).

The dominant interests of the regions are those of agriculture and fisheries, and they are better represented within all the political parties except the Alliance. For instance, 55 percent of the Progressive Party MPs had connections to agrarian interests and 20 percent of its MPs to fishing and fish processing between 1991 to 1999. Also, around 20 percent of members of the Progressive Party's central committee currently have connections to agriculture. Two of its six ministers are farmers, in addition, one has close ties to agrarian interests, and two are closely allied with fisheries' interests. Five out of its six ministers come from these regions. Twenty-nine percent of the Independence Party MPs had connections with fisheries' interests, and 14 percent had connections to agrarian interests between 1991 to 1999. Moreover, two out of six MPs of the Left Green Movement have ties with agriculture, and over 15 percent of members in its executive committee have connections with agrarian interests. Furthermore, a majority of parliamentarians in the fisheries and agricultural committees in Althingi had connections with these interests from 1991 to 1999 (Vignisson 2001). As a result, the parliamentarians from the rural regions are more likely to support the status quo and reject EU membership application.

The Althingi has made changes to redress the imbalance of seats that will take effect in the next general election. After the changes, the regions and areas around the Keflavík airport, 38 percent of the electorate, will hold thirty seats in Althingi. Thus, Reykjavík and its immediate surroundings will for the first time hold a majority in parliament. The changes do not fully redress the imbalance in the distribution of seats, but they may change the composition of the parliament in that fewer parliamentarians will have close ties with the primary sectors. In the 1999 general election, farmers far outnumbered candidates in other occupations in the Independence Party, the Progressive Party, and the Left Green Movement (Vignisson 2001). The changes in the distribution of seats in parliament and a new generation of parliamentarians, as some MPs are expected to retire because of the redrawing of the constituencies, might change the landscape of politics in Iceland.

The national administration has not been the forum for decisive policy-making in Iceland. This has contributed to the influence of the primary sectors. The administration was created late and developed slowly, which partly explains its weakness. Also, the small number of officials and the limited working conditions made ministers very dependent on external assistance (Kristinsson 1993:321–54). This led to the strong influence of pressure groups in the policy-making of the government, particularly those of fishing and agriculture. Their relationship with the government was so close that it was not always possible to see where the role of the state ended and that of pressure groups began (Kristjánsson 1979:349).

The main labor market organizations, the Confederation of Icelandic Employers and the Icelandic Federation of Labor, have not been as integrated in the policy-making of governments in Iceland as in the Scandinavian states. This is because policy-making in Iceland is characterized by sectoral consultation instead of corporatism (Kristinsson, Jónsson, and Sveinsdóttir 1992:43). This has enforced the influence of existing pressure groups in the primary sectors on policy-making as they have kept their ties with the political parties, as indicated earlier.

The Political Discourse Concerning Independence and Sovereignty
The second factor that explains the reluctance of the political elite to join the EU is the importance of preserving the traditional independence of Iceland. The leaders of the Independence Party and the Left Green Movement, which firmly oppose EU membership, most frequently refer to the independence of Iceland and the sovereignty of the nation.

The struggle for independence in Iceland took place in the late nineteenth through the early twentieth century. Iceland, however, did not become fully independent until 1944 and has since fought three Cod Wars with Britain—the last in 1976—which are fresh in Icelanders' memories. Hálfdánarson argues that the nationalistic rhetoric of the independence struggle, "its myths and ideas," has defined "all political debates" in Iceland (2002:335). He argues that in order to understand "absence of a critical and rigorous debate on the European integration in Iceland, we have to examine the logic of the Icelandic political discourse, its history, frames of reference, and ultimate goals" (2002:335). Hálfdánarson's arguments coincide with those of Neumann and his analysis of the Norwegian "no" in 1972 and 1994. Neumann states: "There is something about the way Norwegian discourse is set up, when it comes to institutional lay-out and also the shape of political debates, that has a preserving influence on policy outcomes" (2001:92).

Hálfdánarson argues that two particular features characterized the creation of Iceland as an independent state. First, the freedom and sovereignty of the nation was seen by politicians "as the indisputable and fundamental objective of all Icelandic political efforts in the past and, hence, its preservation as its ultimate goal in the future" (2003:337). Second, politicians argued with firm conviction that the Icelandic state was founded on the basis of the Icelandic Commonwealth of the tenth to the late thirteenth century. The new republic was seen as "an *Icelandic* idea rather than a European import" (2002:337). Iceland is one of the most homogenous countries in Europe on all levels, and politicians commonly refer to the unified nation. Hálfdánarson argues:

> One important effect of this imagined political unity in Iceland is the strong conviction that democratic sovereignty is vested in the nation as a collective unit rather than in its individual members, and therefore, Icelandic sovereignty cannot be divided between regions, shared with other countries or partially transferred to international organizations. (2002:344)

This said, it is quite a contradiction that politicians in Iceland have accepted the EEA-agreement. Hálfdánarson argues that Icelandic politicians are unable to discuss the implications of the EEA-agreement. They cannot admit that international treaties limit the legislative power of Althingi.

> In their [politicians'] parlance, sovereignty and independence were the foundations of Icelandic prosperity, and they are resources that have to be guarded in the same manner as the fishing groups. Thus, they see the preservation of these resources as their sacred duty and the final goal of Icelandic politics, and to compromise them would be a betrayal to Icelandic past and future generations. (2002:345)[17]

The debate about the EEA-agreement clearly demonstrates this belief. The government argued that no transfer of power was to take place from Althingi to the EU and EEA institutions. This was because the government could influence proposals at their initial stages in the European Commission and the Althingi could reject EU law and regulations, which were to be implemented in the EEA. The opposition in parliament disagreed, and the most intense debate took place in the Althingi since the discussion about EFTA membership in the late 1960s. Moreover, over 34,000 voters signed a declaration against the agreement, which constitutes around 19 percent of total number of voters. The feeling was such that the president even considered refusing to sign the agreement. She ultimately made an announcement explaining that she did so because of the traditional non-political role of the presidential office. Most politicians have made it clear that once again they are not

---

[17] Hálfdánarson also argues the security policy and environmental policy in Iceland tend to polarize voters around nationalistic themes. See also Hálfdánarson (1999) and Ingimundarson (1996).

prepared to subject themselves to a debate that might split the nation in order to join the EU.

The intense debate in Norway about EU membership makes Icelandic politicians even more wary of putting the issue of membership on the agenda (Thorhallsson 2001). As Neumann argues,

> one of the key reasons why the Norwegian nation returned a 'no' vote in 1972, and again in 1994, was that the peasant and the farmer were able to present themselves as the embodiment of the nation.... We are talking here about the power of identity. (2001:92)

The Icelandic government presented itself as the savior of the nation when it signed the Schengen agreement and guaranteed the right of Icelanders to travel freely to the other Nordic states. The government argues that a formal transfer of power from Reykjavík to Brussels has not taken place because Iceland participates in decision making in the Schengen Council.[18] The criteria for the traditional political discourse of the political elite are met. The government joined Schengen without publicly admitting that others directly make decisions that affect Iceland. Once again, Iceland's strategy is to become half engaged in European integration in order to secure its immediate interests without an official commitment to the supranational character of the EU.

The Influence of the Special Relationship with the US

The third reason why the political elite have hesitated to adopt a pro-European policy is the fact that Iceland was in an important geographical position during the Cold War in the middle of the GIUK-gap (Greenland-Iceland-United Kingdom). This geographic situation has had important consequences for the security policy of Iceland and its response to European integration. In 1951 the government signed a defense treaty with the United States that made Iceland's relations with the US different from that of all other members of NATO. The bilateral treaty and the NATO membership have ever since been the basis of Icelandic security policy (Ásgrímsson 1996:12).

Political parties in Iceland have never shown any interest in participating in the Common Foreign and Security Policy of the EU. Ministers

---

[18] Iceland participates in the working groups of Schengen, and the Icelandic minister of justice takes part in meetings of justice ministers within the EU when Schengen issues are on the agenda. However, Icelandic representatives have to leave the meetings when formal decisions are made and thus fall short of full participation in the decision-making process.

of the Independence Party have stated that Iceland does not need to look to the EU to bolster its security because the defense of Iceland is guaranteed by the US. This position is contrary to that of the Labor and the Conservative Parties in Norway. The Norwegian response to the uncertainty after 1989 was to call for a collective approach to security threats and to reconsider the EU as a source of security (Archer and Sogner 1998:127). The CFSP was seen as a reason for joining the EU, which was not the case with the Icelandic political elite. They did not seek an active role in the decision shaping of the new security structure of Europe as politicians in Norway. The defence treaty with the US has made security a non-issue with regard to the question of EU membership.

THE PUBLIC ATTITUDE TOWARD EU MEMBERSHIP

The purpose of this section is to analyze the public attitude toward membership in the EU. There is considerable support for EU application in Iceland according to opinion polls: for example, in an opinion poll conducted in May 2001, almost 54 percent of Icelanders wanted to initiate discussion with the EU on the question of membership while 30 percent did not; 16 percent were undecided or refused to answer the question.[19]

In the late 1980s and '90s, opinion polls indicated that Icelanders could be divided into three relatively equal groups concerning the question of EU application, each accounting for around one-third of respondents. However, whether supporters of EU application outnumber the opponents differs from year to year as surveys indicate a considerable fluctuation in the public attitude (Kristinsson 1996:155–7).

Opinion polls conducted in December 1998 and 1999 on whether Iceland should apply for EU membership indicate the strength of the three groups (see Chart 3). The wording of the question was slightly different from that conducted in 2001 as voters were asked directly whether they want to apply for membership. The groups were relatively stable and equal in size. Around one-third of the population supported an application, one-third was against, and the rest were undecided or

---

[19] In May 2001, the question was posed, "Do you think Iceland should start discussions with the European Union concerning membership?" 53.8 percent responded "yes," 30 percent said "no," and 16.1 percent were undedecided or refused to answer (PricewaterhouseCoopers).

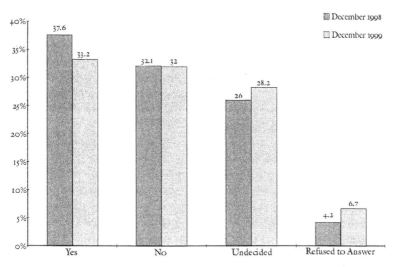

Chart 3. Should Iceland apply for membership? Verslunarráð Íslands 1999 and 2000.

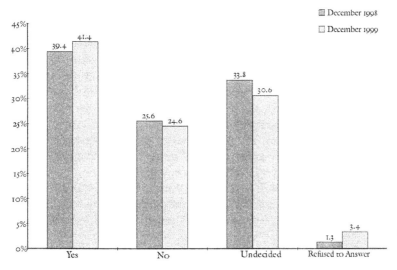

Chart 4. For those who said no, should Iceland apply for membership if fisheries are excluded? Verslunarráð Íslands 1999 and 2000.

refused to answer the question. Support for membership application declined a little between 1998 and 1999, but opposition remained the same; more people are undecided or refuse to answer the question.

On the other hand, when voters who said no to the question as to whether Iceland should apply for EU membership were asked whether Iceland should apply if fisheries were excluded, around 40 percent of them stated that Iceland should do so, and only a quarter of them were against EU application (see Chart 4).

The survey in May 2001 provides detailed information about the attitude of respondents to the question whether Iceland should start discussions with the EU according to regions, age, gender, and income. Chart 5 shows that support for membership is strongest in Reykjavík and its surroundings. However, this fact is not reflected in the Althingi since the distribution of seats is skewed toward the less populated regions. Around 30 percent of respondents in the regions are against discussion with the EU while only around 25 to 29 percent of the respondents in Reykjavík and its surroundings are against discussion. Also, voters in the regions are more undecided than those in Reykjavík and its surroundings. However, respondents in the regions are more likely to support discussion than oppose them—around 45 percent as opposed to 35 percent (see Chart 5). As a result, there is a majority in favor of discussion with the EU concerning membership in all regions if those who are undecided or refuse to answer are excluded.

Chart 6 indicates that the younger generation is more supportive of discussion with the EU concerning membership than the older generation. Support is greatest in the age group between 30–49 years old—nearly 60 percent—while around 25 percent of the age group oppose discussion with the EU. Around 52 percent of the age group between 18–29 years support discussion, and just over quarter of the age group oppose them. The older generation is most skeptical toward discussion with the EU as only around 46 percent support discussion, and nearly 40 percent oppose discussion with the EU.

The survey does not demonstrate that the same gender gap concerning attitudes to EU membership exists in Iceland as in the other Nordic states.[20] Chart 7 indicates that though more men than women favor

---

[20] A majority of women in Finland, Sweden, and Norway opposed membership in the 1994 referenda while a majority of men supported it. Also, men in Denmark favor European integration to a greater extent than women (see Svåsand and Lindström 1996:212).

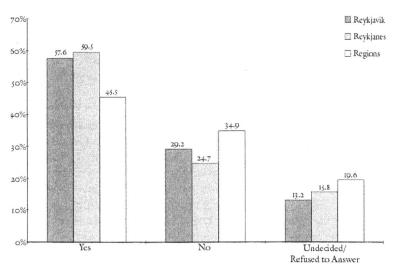

Chart 5. Do you think Iceland should start discussions with the EU concerning membership? Attitude divided by regions. May 2001. PricewaterhouseCoopers.

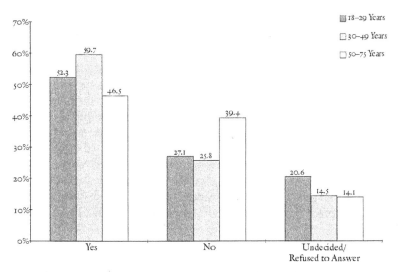

Chart 6. Attitude divided by age. May 2001. PricewaterhouseCoopers.

starting discussion with the EU, men also tend to oppose discussion in greater numbers. On the other hand, half as many women are unde-cided or refuse to answer the question. The majority of both men and women want to start discussion with the EU (see Chart 7). The survey also demonstrates that just over a quarter of women oppose discussion while one-third of men oppose it.

Chart 8 indicates that people with high and middle income are more likely to support discussion with the EU concerning membership than those with low income. More than two-thirds of the population with high income support discussion with the EU, while only 37 percent of those with low income support discussion. Around 36 percent of those with low income oppose discussion, while only 23 percent of those with high income do so. Moreover, there is a striking difference concerning income in the category "do not know" and "refuse to answer." More than quarter of those with low income fall into that category, while only around 10 percent of those with middle or high income are undecided or refuse to answer.

Further proof of the pro-European attitude of around half of the electorate is their response to the question as to whether they agree or disagree with Iceland's taking the euro as a national currency. Chart 9 demonstrates that 40 percent of Icelanders want to adopt the single cur-rency, and over 14 percent are neutral. Thirty-five percent do not want to take on the euro, and almost 10 percent refuse to answer. It is interesting how many support taking the euro as a national currency since there has not been any serious debate on its costs and benefits.

Furthermore, not a single politician has proposed adopting the euro. There is, however, a growing concern within the business community about the Icelandic crown and increased discussion on whether Iceland should take on the euro as a currency. The chairman of the Confedera-tion of Employers, including vessel and fish-factory owners, stated in its annual conference in 2001 that adopting the euro should not be ruled out.[21] Also the Federation of Icelandic Industry, which has advocated EU membership for a number of years, wants to adopt the euro. Its chairman has called on the government to make a detailed study of the pros and cons.[22] It has to be kept in mind, however, that the euro will

---

[21] Speech by Finnur Geirsson, chairman of the Confederation of Icelandic Employers, at its annual conference 15 May 2001. Available at <www.sa.is/frettir>.
[22] See "Erlend lán eða áhættufé" (July 2001) at the Federation of Icelandic Industry home page: <www.si.is>.

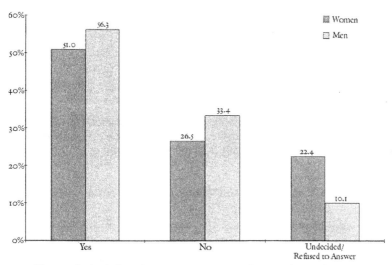

Chart 7. Attitude based on sex. May 2001. PricewaterhouseCoopers.

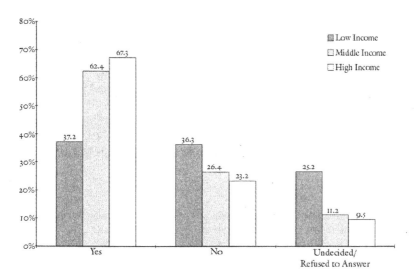

Chart 8. Attitude divided by income. May 2001. Pricewaterhouse-Coopers.

SCANDINAVIAN STUDIES

not be adopted without membership in the EU. The discussion within the business community about adopting the euro is therefore of a purely hypothetical nature.

During the last couple of months, the exchange rate of the Icelandic crown has been unfavorable to those who borrow money in a foreign currency and import raw material and goods as it has fallen by nearly 20 percent in just one year.[23] Also, the interest rates are much higher in Iceland than in other European counties.[24] If this trend continues, it is more likely that the business community will press the government to adopt the euro as a national currency and join the EU.

WHY IS THE ELECTORATE RELATIVELY PRO-EUROPEAN?

Three factors help to explain the relatively pro-European attitude of around half of the electorate in Iceland, and they also provide an explanation for the gap between the electorate and the political elite concerning EU membership. First, 87 percent of Icelanders are employed in economic sectors other than fisheries and agriculture (Statistics Iceland. Vinnumarkaður 2000). Their attitude toward EU application reflects this fact. Second, a considerable number of Icelanders seem to be more concerned with their economic prosperity than the political discourse of the political elite. Third, a part of the electorate fears that Iceland will become isolated by not taking an active part in European integration.

Icelanders generally do not link themselves closely with farming and fishing interests. Only 8.2 percent of Icelanders are employed in fishing and fish processing, and only 4.4 percent are employed in agriculture (see Chart 10).[25] This is a dramatic shift from 1970 when almost 28 percent of Icelanders were employed by the fishing, fish processing, and agricultural sectors and from 1940 when over half of Icelanders were employed by these sectors.

---

[23] The Icelandic crown fell by 19.66 percent in a twelve month period from 1 July 2000 to 1 July 2001. Information from The Icelandic Central Bank.

[24] For example, three months LIBOR interest rates in Icelandic crowns is 12.27% but in euros 4.48%.

[25] 3.9 percent of Icelanders are employed in the fishing and 4.3 percent are employed in fish processing, all together 8.2 percent (Statistics Iceland: Vinnumarkaður 2000. <www.hagstofa.is>).

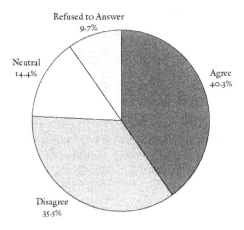

Chart 9. Do you agree or disagree to Iceland taking the euro as a national currency? May 2001. PricewaterhouseCoopers.

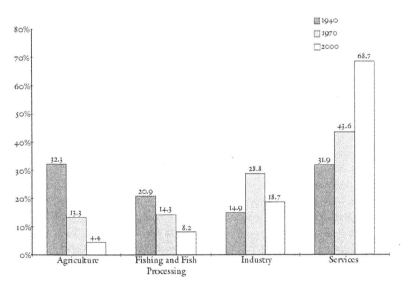

Chart 10. Employed persons by economic activity percent. Source: Statistics Iceland and National Economic Institute.

Occupation partly explains voters' attitudes to EU application. Opposition to membership is strongest in the primary industries. A survey conducted in 1999 indicates that 69 percent of farmers are against application and that only 12 percent support it; the rest are undecided. Opponents of EU application narrowly outnumber supporters among fishermen, the only occupation sharing the view of the farmers. Furthermore, fishermen are in greater number undecided than other employees. On the other hand, non-manual workers tend to support EU application in greater number than manual workers.[26] Nearly 44 percent of non-manual workers support application, while only 24 percent of them oppose it. Nearly 35 percent of manual workers support application, and around 28 percent of them oppose it. The rest are undecided, manual workers in greater numbers than non-manual workers.[27]

Second, Icelanders who support discussion with the EU are more concerned with economic prosperity than the political discourse concerning independence and sovereignty. The fact that four out of ten Icelanders state that they want to abandon the Icelandic crown and adopt the single currency points toward this fact. It is, thus, no wonder that more than half of voters want to adopt the euro or are neutral to the idea at times when the Icelandic crown has fallen so dramatically. In such a situation, it should not come as a surprise that voters were concerned about their budget and future income and that they questioned the viability of the crown and the ability of the government and the central bank of Iceland to manage it. Economic benefits seem to be their highest priority.

Voters with middle and high income are much more likely to support discussion with the EU than voters with little income, as shown earlier. Also, members of the younger generations are to a much greater extent in favor of full participation in European integration than the older generation, age fifty and above. The political discourse of the political elite concerning independence and sovereignty seems not to be as widely accepted by the younger generation as the older. However, it must be kept in mind that a considerable number of voters accept the nationalistic political discourse as the protest against the EEA-agreement proved. A survey conducted in June 1994 indicates that 25 percent of all opponents of application were opposed because the EU is a colossus or that Iceland is small and 23 percent mention the importance of

---

[26] Excluding farmers and fishermen.
[27] From an Icelandic Election Study (1999) courtesy of Ólafur Th. Harðarson.

independence or self-reliance. On the other hand, 19 percent of the respondents stated that they want to apply for EU membership because of economic improvement and 7 percent because of increased freedom/openness (Social Science Research Institute, U Iceland 1994. Cited in Kristinsson 1996:158).

The third reason behind voters' willingness to apply for membership in the EU seems to be their fear of isolation. The 1994 survey indicates that as 37 percent of respondents who favor EU membership do so because they fear that Iceland is becoming isolated. The government is aware of this concern of the electorate. The main reason behind its decision to join Schengen was the fear that Icelanders would no longer be allowed to travel without passport to the other Nordic states. One of the fundamental features of Nordic cooperation, the region to which 90 percent of Icelanders feel closest (Harðarson 1995:310), would have been put in jeopardy. If Icelanders were hindered in traveling without a passport, it could clearly been interpreted as a sign of Iceland being an increasingly isolated state.

Finally, the findings that around one-third of the population wanted to apply for EU membership in 1998 and 1999 and more than half wanted to start discussions with the EU concerning membership in 2001 do not necessarily mean that all of those favorably disposed would vote for membership in a referendum. The outcome of the negotiations would be decisive, particularly in terms of how the Icelandic fishing industry was to be treated in an association agreement. This support of membership is also not based on a great deal of information since debate concerning membership so far has been limited. Moreover, in 1991 when the Progressive Party hinted that the Social Democratic Party and the Independence Party "could not be trusted to keep Iceland out of the EC," very negative discussion took place concerning membership, and surveys indicated that support for application fell dramatically (Kristinsson 1996:155–7). It is clear that around half of the electorate wants to explore the possibility of membership, but whether it would be transferred into an affirmative vote in a national referendum remains to be seen.

PRESSURE FOR A POLICY CHANGE TOWARD EUROPE

There seem to be three main reasons for increased discussion of EU membership in Iceland. First, the stronghold of the primary industries on the Progressive Party is diminishing and the Alliance has more limited connections to the primary industries than other parties. The leadership of the Progressive Party—traditionally a farmers' party—is increasingly aware of the fact that half of the party's electorate now comes from Reykjavík and its surroundings. The party has to keep these voters onboard and, if the party is to increase its share of the votes, it has to appeal to the growing population in urban areas. The newly-decided changes to the electoral system motivate the party to appeal to voters in the urban areas. The Alliance, like the Social Democratic Party, has looser ties to the primary industries than other parties. None of its MPS has direct connections with agrarian interests, and though some of them have connections to fisheries interests, they are more indirect and cover a broader scope of all the fisheries sectors compared to those of the Independence Party and the Progressive Party. They tend to have direct connection with vessel owners and fish processing companies (Vignisson 2001:23). In the last general election, moreover, the Alliance gained over 71 percent of its votes in the urban areas—Reykjavík and its surroundings (Statistics Iceland, Election Statistics).[28]

Secondly, Ásgrímsson and the leadership of the Alliance have questioned the ability of Iceland to defend its interests within the decision-making structure of the EEA. Moreover, they increasingly question whether the EEA-agreement satisfies Icelandic economic interests. These factors became evident in Iceland's attempt to reject proposals by the European Commission concerning a ban on bone and meat meal in animal feed including fishmeal and fish oil as a response to the BSE crisis in Europe at the end of 2000.[29] The institutional structure of the EEA-agreement was not of much use to the Icelandic government in its attempt to get EU members to reject the proposals. The case shows how difficult it is to influence decision making of the EU without being a full member.[30] Furthermore, a new report by the Ministry for Foreign Affairs on the effect of the EU enlargement on the EEA-agreement states that though the enlargement will not entail any practical problems for Iceland, the enlargement will make the functioning of the agreement

---

[28] Available at <www.hagstofa.is>.

[29] If accepted, the proposals would have been a devastating blow for the Icelandic fish industry as 7 to 10 percent of Iceland's export value has been fish meal and fish oil during the past five years. Fish meal and fish oil rank third in marine export, only salted fish and frozen fish rank higher (see Statistics Iceland. External Trade. <www.hagstofa.is>).

[30] Preliminary findings from crisis management research by Baldur Thorhallsson and Elva Ellertsdóttir.

more difficult and the EFTA countries will have to make more efforts to safeguard their interests (Ministry for Foreign Affairs 5/15 2001:13). Moreover, the unsatisfactory influence of the EFTA/EEA states on decision making in the EEA has led to a call for "technical changes" to the EEA-agreement in an internal report from the EFTA headquarters and by high-ranking civil servants of the EFTA/EEA states. These changes should coincide with the changes that have been made to the decision-making structure of the EU.[31] Ásgrímsson has also stated that one of the issues that can be discussed in relation to the development of the EEA is the possibility of adopting the euro.[32]

Third, interest groups in Iceland such as the Confederation of Icelandic Employers and the Icelandic Federation of Labor are becoming more critical of the EEA-agreement. They increasingly worry that the EEA does not guarantee their interests as the EU changes and the potential influence of Iceland diminishes. Thus, interesting policy changes have been undertaken concerning the question of EU membership. They now demand that the issue of EU membership be placed on the political agenda where Icelandic negotiation objectives for a possible membership application can be defined.[33] This moves them closer to the position of the Federation of Icelandic Industries and the Chamber of Commerce, which have advocated EU membership for a decade.[34] The Icelandic Federation of Labor has also demanded a referendum on membership application. It states that Iceland has to increase its influence within the EEA either by strengthening the EEA-agreement or by joining the EU. However, the Icelandic Federation of Labor argues that the possibility of strengthening the EEA-agreement is a far-fetched political utopia ("Ísland í Dag: Greining og leiðsögn" November 2000). Furthermore,

---

[31] See "Samið við ESB um uppfærslu EES-samningsins." 27 June 2001: <www.mbl.is>.

[32] Taken from a newspaper interview with H. Ásgrímsson entitled: "Sláandi hversu mikið hefur farið úr landi." 27 June 2001: See *Fréttablaðið*: <www.visir.is>. However, Ásgrímsson argues that there is a limited possibility to take the euro as a currency without membership in the EU. But he states that if Britain, Sweden, and Denmark adopt the euro, it would have great influence on the debate in Iceland. It would provoke many questions about the possibilities of keeping the crown considerably stronger in the future.

[33] The Confederation of Icelandic Employers' policy change took place in May 2001 and the Icelandic Federation of Labor altered its policy toward the EU in November 2000.

[34] The Federation of Icelandic Industries has enthusiastically campaigned for membership, while the Chamber of Commerce has kept a lower profile particularly in the last few years. This has happened as the fisheries sector has gained a greater number of seats on the board of the Chamber of Commerce (see Vignisson 2001:34), and the Independence Party has taken a firm position against membership.

the EEA-agreement has led to important changes within the national administration. Membership in the EEA has strengthened the position of officials and limited the traditionally strong position of ministers because the institutional structure of the EEA only involves ministers in decision making to a limited degree. Competent officials are needed to press Icelandic interests in Brussels forward and in implementing EEA rules. As a consequence, the recruitment of officials is becoming more professionally oriented, and a number of specialists in European affairs have been employed. "This increases the potential for the development of a more autonomous civil service that serves the citizens rather than the whims of their political masters" (S. Kristjánsson and R. Kristjánsson 2000:123). For instance, the Ministry for Foreign Affairs has published detailed reports on the position of Iceland in Europe in the last year. The reports have increased and influenced the EU debate.

CONCLUSION

This paper has argued that the heavy reliance of Iceland on its fish resources and the importance of agrarian and fisheries lobby partly explain the distinctive strategy of the Icelandic political elite toward European integration. Icelandic governments have responded to European integration by an *ad hoc* response. The strategy has been to secure Iceland's immediate interests, particularly those of fishing by limited involvement in the European project. The priority has been to secure markets for Icelandic fish and protect the domestic market from agricultural imports; domestic control over the primary industries is the main goal. This coincides with Ingebritsen's argument that the divergent approach of the Nordic states toward European integration can be explained by their different economic sectors because economic interest groups representing leading sectors influence the responses of Nordic governments to European integration (Ingebritsen 1998:155, 162). However, particular domestic characteristics, which add to the strength of the primary industries, have to be taken into account such as the electoral system and special characteristics of the national administration. Also, the lack of corporatism in Iceland compared to the other Scandinavian states contributes to the important role of the primary sectors and helps the government in sidelining other economic sectors, which are adopting a more pro-European policy (Thorhallsson 2001).

The paper indicates, moreover, that the political discourse in Iceland concerning independence and sovereignty is a key variable in explaining the elites' approach to the European project. Neumann states "one should think of national identity as an independent variable" (2001:92) in explaining the Norwegian nation's response to Europe. The paper also indicates that a part of the skepticism of the political elite is related to the geographical position of Iceland and the defense treaty with the US, which have neutralized the question of Iceland's security in the debate on EU membership and supports Ingebritsen's arguments that three of the Nordic states—Iceland, Denmark, and Norway—align themselves with British intergovernmentalism as a vision of European unity. They prefer power to be located at the state level and security decisions to be made with the US (Ingebritsen 1998:118–21).

Iceland is moving from an economy based on the primary sectors. The fact that over 87 percent of Icelanders are employed in other economic sectors helps to explanation the pro-European attitude of the public. Supporters of EU application outnumber opponents in all occupations except farmers and fishermen. Also, the ties of the urban population to the regions seem to be diminishing. The pro-European electorate seems to be more concerned with their economic prosperity than the political discourse of the political elite. Furthermore, they fear isolation from Europe by not being fully integrated in the European project.

There are factions within all parties, except for the Left Green Movement, which support EU membership or want to examine the possibility of membership. Support for membership is most noticeable within the Alliance, and supporters can be found among its MPs, prominent leaders outside parliament, and general party members. Some industrial and business leaders within the Independence Party want to examine the possibility of membership along with some younger party members. One of the party's twenty-six MPs, who is the executive director of the Chamber of Commerce, advocates membership and some others are seen as potential supporters. The leader of the Progressive Party is clearly the driving force behind the policy turn of the party, but the three choices concerning European integration outlined in the party's report, show how the party is split on the issue of membership. The commitment of the leader of the Progressive Party to examine the party policy toward Europe critically has in fact surprized many, as it has not only created division within the party but also within the government. The parties are afraid of an internal split. This explains the cautious internal debate within the three largest parties and the Liberal Party. The Independence Party, for instance, is not prepared to take the chance of splitting the right wing of the political spectrum on such a sensitive issue as long as its leaders see no immediate pressure to join the EU.

It remains to be seen whether the primary industries in Iceland can continue to influence the attitude of the political elite toward the question of membership. But their influence seems to be diminishing. The Alliance and the Progressive Party are moving toward a more pro-European policy as they loosen their ties to the agrarian and fishing interests.

The Independence Party is now the key player. It is doubtful that the other parties will press for EU membership in a government without its support or a more neutral position. The Independence Party has moved from a "wait and see" approach to firm opposition to membership. A policy change under the leadership of David Oddsson is unlikely. As long as the EEA-agreement satisfies the primary economic sectors and Iceland is not hit by an economic recession or continuing fall of the crown, the party is bound to stick to its position under the present leadership occupied with the political discourse of independence and sovereignty.

WORKS CITED

Archer, C., and I. Sogner. *Norway, European Integration and Atlantic Security.* London: SAGE Publications, 1998.

"Ályktanir Búnaðarþings." *Freyr* 97.3: 2001.

Ásgrímsson, H. "Europeisk Sikkerhet og Islands Sikkerhetspolitikk." *Norsk Militært Tidsskrift* 12 (1996).

"Erlend lán eða áhættufé." Federation of Icelandic Industry Home page. July 2001. <http://www.si.is>.

European Commission. "The European Union 'A View From the Top': Top Decision Makers and the European Union." *Eurobarometer* Web site. 1996. <europa.eu.int/comm/public_opinion/archives/top/top_en.htm>.

Evrópunefnd Framsóknarmanna. "Nefndarálit." Jan. 2001. <www.maddaman.is/efni/evr.pdf>.

Geirsson, Finnur. Speech. Annual Conference of the Confederation of Icelandic Employers. 15 May 2001. <www.sa.is/frettir>.

Hálfdánarson, G. "Hver á sér fegra föðurland. Staða náttúrunnar í íslenskri þjóðarvitund." *Skírnir* 173 (1999): 304–36.

___. "Iceland and Europe." *European Peripheries in Interaction: The Nordic Countries and th Iberian Peninsula.* Eds. L. Beltrán, J. Maestro, and L. Salo-Lee. Spain: U Alcalá, 2002.

Harðarson, Ólafur Th. "Icelandic Security and Foreign Policy: The Public Attitude." *Cooperation & Conflict* 20 (1995).

___. "Icelandic Election Study" (1999). U Iceland. Unpublished paper.

Hjartarson, S.H. "ESB og forræðið yfir fiskimiðunum." *Fiskifréttir* 6 Oct. 2000. <www.liu.is>.

Ingebritsen, C. *The Nordic States and European Unity.* Ithaca: Cornell UP, 1998.

Ingimundarson V. *Í eldlínu kalda stríðsins.* Reykjavík: Vaka Helgafell, 1996.

"Ísland í Dag: Greining og leiðsögn." *Stefnumörkun 39. þings ASÍ í Alþjóðamálum.* November 2000.

Katzenstein, P. "The Smaller European States: Germany and Europe." *Tamed Power: Germany in Europe.* Ed. P. Katzenstein. Ithaca: Cornell UP, 1997.

Kristinsson, G.H. "Valdakerfið fram til viðreisnar 1900-1959." *Íslensk Þjóðfélagsþróun 1880–1990.* Eds.G. Hálfdánarson and S. Kristjánsson. Reykjavík: Félagsvísindastofnun og Sagnfræðistofnun, 1993.

___. "Iceland and the European Union: Non-decision on Membership." *The European Union and the Nordic Countries.* Ed. L. Miles. London: Routhledge, 1996.

___. Jónsson H., and H. Th. Sveinsdóttir. *Atvinnustefna á Íslandi 1951–1991.* Reykjavík: Félagsvísindastofun Háskóla Íslands, 1992.

Kristjánsson, S. *Corporatism in Iceland.* Reykjavík: Félagsvísindadeild, 1979.

___., and R. Kristjánsson. "Delegation and Accountability in an Ambiguous System: Iceland and the European Economic Area (EEA)." *The Journal of Legislative Studies* 6.1 (2000).

Liberal Party. Home page. <www.xf.is/evropumal.htm>.

The Ministry for Foreign Affairs. *Stækkun Evrópusambandsins: Áhrif á stöðu Íslands innan ees.* Reykjavík: Ministry for Foreign Affairs, 2001.

Neumann, I.B. "The Nordic States and European Unity." *Cooperation & Conflict* 36.1 (2001): 87–94.

PricewaterhouseCoopers. "News release: Iceland, the EU, and the Euro." 25 May 2001. PricewaterhouseCoopers, Iceland. Unpublished Survey.

"Samið við ESB um uppfærslu EES-samningsins." 27 June 2001. <www.mbl.is>.

"Sláandi hversu mikið hefur farið úr landi." Interview with H. Ásgrímsson. 27 June 2001. *Fréttablaðið*. <www.visir.is>.

Statistics Iceland. Vinnumarkaður 2000. <www.hagstofa.is>.

Svåsand, L., and U. Lindström. "Scandinavian Political Parties and the European Union." *Political Parties and the European Union*. Ed. J. Gaffney. London: Routledge, 1996.

"Telur samningsmarkmiða raunhof." *Morgunblaðið*. 24 June 2001.

Thorhallsson, B. "The Distinctive Domestic Characteristics of Iceland and the Rejection of Membership of the European Union." *Journal of Political Integration* 23.3 (2001): 257–80.

Verslunarrað Íslands. "Alþjóðavoðing Atvinnulifsins Skýrsla til viðskiptaþings 1999." Reykjavík: Verslunarrað Íslands, 1999.

___. "Atvinnulif Fram tiðarinnar Ísland meðal tiu bestu Skýrsla til viðskipta þings 2000." Reykjavík: Verslunarrað Íslands, 2000.

Vignisson, H.T. "The Influence of Economic Sectors on the Policy-Making of Governments in Iceland." *Concerning European Integration*. Study sponsored by the Icelandic Students' Innovative Fund. Supervised by Baldur Thorhallsson. Unpublished report, 2001.

The Battle Over Denmark
Denmark and the European Union

Lykke Friis
Danish Institute of International Affairs

"Something Rotten in the State of Denmark?"

IN 1998, Denmark and the EU celebrated their silver wedding. Unlike most couples, which, unless they decide to split, manage to smooth out the wrinkles after several decades of wedlock, Denmark's EU-marriage remains a rocky one. Indeed, for the last decade, Denmark has behaved like an EU-member that is often toying with the idea of heading to the divorce lawyer. This image was accentuated when the Danish electorate voted no in two important EU-referenda. In 1992, voters rejected the Maastricht Treaty and in 2000 said no to Denmark's participation in the single currency, the euro.

This rocky marriage is anything but a new phenomenon. As a matter fact, one can easily make the case that Denmark's EU-membership in 1973 was a marriage of convenience. At least it is striking how the Danish EU debate was dominated for several decades by twinges of bad conscience very similar to the ones experienced by a bride who ends up marrying the affluent graduate student instead of her true (but rather impecunious) love from her hometown. In Denmark's case, the affluent groom was the European Union, which offered the prosperous economic future that Denmark's true love, the remaining Nordic countries, was not able to provide.

The core argument of this article is that Denmark's "matrimonial" difficulties must be seen mainly as the result of a constant battle over identity. As far back as 1972, Danish governments have struggled to find a positive fit between what is perceived as Danish identity and the

The author wishes to thank Christine Ingebritsen and Rachel Lutz for usual comments and criticism.

European Union. Although there are special features in the Danish case, such as the tradition to have national referenda on all key EU-decisions,[1] this identity battle is not unique for Denmark but is rather a phenomenon which characterizes all Nordic countries. With the possible exception of Finland, whose relationship with the EU has been dominated by the all-important security argument, all Nordic countries are struggling to find a credible fit between their national identity and the EU. Indeed, as Ole Wæver has provocatively pointed out, this fit is especially difficult to find in the Nordic countries particularly because Nordic identity is partly "about being *better* than Europe" (Wæver 1992: 77; emphasis in the original). Hence, Denmark and the other Nordic countries could lose some of the advantages of their "Nordic Model" by co-operating closely with the rest of Europe.

The above argument of this article is laid out in four sections. We start by looking specifically at Denmark's road to the European Union and the journey afterwards. After this flashback, section two brings the analysis up-to-date by analyzing the latest EU-referendum in Denmark. A central argument here is that this referendum was very much decided by the no-side's ability to construct a far more credible fit between Danish identity and the EU than the so-called yes-side.[2] In section three, we look at Denmark's position after the latest "no:" is Danish EU-policy about to change or rather will it be business as usual? The final section takes a more comparative approach and ties the analysis together by asking the following question: What role does Nordic co-operation play in terms of improving the fit between EU integration and national identity?

THE DANISH PATH TO THE EU

A Nordic Sprinter—A European Latecomer

Compared to the rest of the Nordic region, Denmark was quick to find its way to what was then the European Community (EC). Yet

---

[1] According to the Danish constitution (art. 20), EU-treaties shall be put to a national referendum—unless the treaty has the backing of a 5/6 majority in the *Folketing*. Some scholars, however, have argued that the tradition to hold referenda has developed into a political norm, disconnected from the actual legal content of the constitution as such.
[2] In principle, it is a generalization to use the expressions yes and no side. Over time, substantial variations have emerged within both camps. In this broad and general article, however, we will still stick to the concepts.

considering that the integration process had started in 1951, Denmark, which entered the EC in 1973, was in reality a European latecomer. For the first few decades, Denmark, together with its core trading partners, namely the UK and the other Nordic countries, preferred to stay outside the European integration process. The very fact that Denmark was a latecomer is a core reason why the overall EU issue quickly turned into a battle over identity.

In 1973, most of the political arguments for membership, which had played an important role elsewhere such as in the Benelux countries, were either outdated or used as crucial yes-arguments for other institutions. A telling example of this is the "peace and stability argument" (or, phrased less politically correct, the argument about containing Germany). In 1973, peace and stability seen from Copenhagen appeared either as a goal fulfilled or as a task that another organization that Denmark had joined, NATO, was in charge of. As a result, the yes-side's arguments for EC-membership were highly focused on the economic benefits—"We must join in order to protect our bacon exports to the EU."

The problem with this economic approach was that it failed to link EC-membership to Danish identity. This was in clear contrast to the no-side, which linked its argumentation to "Danishness" and even to continuation of the Danish State. Not only would Denmark be transformed into a municipality in Europe as the EC gradually developed into a federation or even a state, but it would also be tied down in a Union, in which Danish values (such as its welfare system and participatory democracy) could not be accommodated. Indeed, the no-side's rhetoric was thick with references to the capitalistic common market and its non-democratic character, all features that were looked upon as the opposite of what Denmark stood for. Moreover, the no-side portrayed the yes-politicians as an elite out of touch with the general public. Instead of joining this very "un-Danish" and "un-Nordic Club," Denmark should rather join forces with its soul mates, Sweden, Norway, Finland, and Iceland.

All the yes-side could do to counter this rhetoric was to emphasize the promise of economic gains and point out that the EC—since it was simply a normal, intergovernmental organization just like the free trade organization, EFTA, which Denmark had joined in the early '60s—was not a threat to Danish identity. In practice, this led to a situation in which the government downplayed all supranational and political features of the EC. For the voter, the many statements that the EC was "just" an intergovernmental organization, which in any case could be kept at bay by using the national veto, must have left the impression that the EC was indeed a threat to Danish identity. If not, why was it so important for yes-politicians to underline that they could keep Brussels at bay? At least it is safe to argue that, from the beginning, any new integration steps promised to cause problems for the various Danish governments since they ran counter to the promises issued in the initial campaign.

During the first years of Danish EC-membership, the various promises were not severely tested. Partly due to the oil crisis, the integration process stuttered through most of the 1970s. When the integration process picked up speed again during the 1980s, the new dynamism was centered around an economic project (The Single Market), which, according to the Danish Government, could be portrayed as a confirmation of its yes-campaign in the early 1970s—"You see, the EC *is* only about economics." All political features of the so-called Single European Act were downplayed to such a degree that the Danish prime minister, on the day before election night, promised the voters that the Single European Act had buried all ambitions to create a political union. Or, to quote the prime minister directly, "The Union was stone dead" (Friis 255) Largely because the EC was portrayed as only about economics—and hence no real threat to Danish identity—was the government able to secure a yes in the national referendum.[3]

From Maastricht to Edinburgh

The Maastricht Treaty in 1992 was a much stiffer test for the Danish yes-side. A treaty that contained a common currency, a common foreign and security policy, union citizenship, etc., could hardly be portrayed as solely an economic enterprise. Hence, the yes-side was pushed to develop a new strategy. A core feature here was the tendency to abandon the de-politicized strategy. Essentially, the yes-side acknowledged that there were no clear dividing lines between politics and economics. In particular, the Social Democratic Party took the view that the EU should also be seen as an instrument replacing the Darwinism of the market with common EU rules, for instance on the environment. Inspired by the fall of the Berlin Wall, leading Social Democrats also played

---

[3] As a curiosity, the Danish Parliament actually rejected the Single European Act. This caused the prime minister to call a political referendum in order to overrule the majority in parliament. The no to the Single European Act by the parliament was largely seen as domestic politics—i.e. political positioning in the run up to national elections.

the security card. According to the spokesperson of the party, there were three arguments for a yes to the Maastricht Treaty—Germany, Germany, and Germany. Although these arguments seemed to ease the traditional confrontation between "us in Denmark" and "them in Brussels," no yes-politician went so far as to argue that the EC was an extension of Denmark or an instrument which would allow Denmark to protect its model.

As highlighted by the "no" to the Maastricht Treaty in the referendum in June 1992, the shift toward a more political yes did not go down well with the public. A large part of the 1992 campaign centered on old referenda promises. The no-parties were thus eager to point out that the yes-side had tricked the public into voting yes in 1972 and 1986 by downplaying the political implications. This strategy of the no-side pushed the yes-side into a strategy of denial. Referenda promises had not been broken since the EC (even with Maastricht) was not on the road to statehood. Indeed, the EC was still largely an intergovernmental co-operation with sovereign states as members.

Although the referendum in 1993 approved the Edinburgh Agreement (the Maastricht Treaty with Danish reservations on union citizenship, a common currency, defense policy, and supranational co-operation on justice and home affairs), the situation was anything but stable. To a large extent, the yes-side had moved away from its purely economic, utilitarian way of reasoning but had not been able to convince the public that European integration was not a threat to Danish national identity. To put it mildly, the decision to hold another referendum in 1993 after the no in 1992 had also caused considerable bad blood.

A More Danish EC

In view of this unstable situation, the Danish yes-side embarked on a new two-fold strategy in the run to the next EC referendum on the Amsterdam Treaty in May 1998. The new strategy was combined with a third, more traditional, feature.

The first part of the strategy was directly linked to Sweden's and Finland's membership in the Union in 1995. Since the EC was now endowed with three Scandinavian members, it appeared far more realistic to embark upon a pro-active line of action—trying to transform the EC into a more Nordic enterprise. To be sure, it was also more difficult for the Danish no-side to maintain the argument that EC-membership was undermining the Nordic alternative for co-operation.

More specifically, this first part of the strategy was aimed at bridging the classical dichotomy in the Danish EU-debate—between "us" in Scandinavia and "them" in the EU. In close co-ordination with Sweden and Finland, Denmark pushed several "Nordic" issues onto the agenda for the Amsterdam conference (unemployment, consumer policy, environment, and social policy). As a result, the Danish government was, for the first time, able to construe the EU as an extension of and not as a threat to Danish values. What the Amsterdam Treaty aimed at doing was spreading these values to the whole of Europe. Or, to quote the slogan of the Danish Social Democratic Party, "The Danish Road is now also the road of the EU;" the EU is "becoming more Nordic and more Danish."

The second part of the strategy was, once again, a novelty, namely to stress the EU's important role in maintaining peace and stability in central and eastern Europe. The integration project was no longer just about economics and cool cash, but a project guided by strong ideals—doing unto central Europe what the EU had done for itself. In reality, this was the first time Danish politicians presented voters with a vision of why EU integration was important.[4]

This new twofold strategy was combined with a true classic in Danish governments' attempts to deal with EU-skepticism. In the run up to and during the Amsterdam referendum, the government was busy in pointing out powerful roadblocks, which would ensure that Denmark would not be tied down by more integration. The first roadblock was the four reservations obtained in the Edinburgh Agreement. Already before the Amsterdam Intergovernmental Conference (IGC), the prime minister promised that the four reservations would "stand before, during, and after the IGC" (DUPI 200:261). Hence, they were not in any way up for discussion.

As far as the reservations were even discussed, the government concentrated on emphasizing that the euro, European defense, and co-operation within justice and home affairs were still theoretical projects, which had just been placed on the drawing board. In any case, non-acceptance of the euro would, according to the Danish prime minister, only lead to marginally higher interest rates in Denmark than in the euro-zone (*Weekendavisen* 28 May 1998).

---

[4] The fact that the Amsterdam Treaty did not really fulfill its task of gearing the EU's institutions toward enlargement was heavily downplayed by the yes-side. Not surprisingly, the no-side did its best to draw attention to this fact.

The second roadblock was the overall development in the EU as such. The core yes-parties spent considerable time arguing that the EU-integration train was running out of steam. Indeed, in the final days before the referendum, Prime Minister Poul Nyrup Rasmussen issued a kind of guarantee that Amsterdam was the last IGC of its kind (*Weekendavisen* 28 May 1998).[5]

TO EURO OR NOT TO EURO?

If one looks at the Amsterdam referendum result (see Table 1), it is easy to make the case that the new strategy paid off. After all, the yes-side managed to win the referendum with a (for Danish circumstances) safe margin. In practice, it is however just as valid to argue that the victory of 1998 bore the seed for the defeat in the euro-referendum in 2000. Many of the promises issued during the 1998 campaign came back as boomerangs just as in 1992 when voters remembered promises that the "Union was stone dead." This fact shows how Denmark's relationship with the EU is affected not just by the battle over national identity, but also by a referendum factor. In Denmark, unlike in most other EU member states, including Sweden and Finland, the protagonists in the national identity battle are regularly endowed with a perfect arena for their quarrels—an arena, which makes the infighting even fiercer and triggers a self-perpetuating process. Just as in elections, EU referenda tend to become black-and-white. And just as in national elections, a number of election promises are issued that come back to haunt the politicians in the next election. Perhaps due to the complexity of EU-affairs, this tendency is even more pronounced when EU-issues are on the agenda in a referendum.

In principle, this referendum factor can also be explained as follows: it is obviously far easier for a government to pursue a pro-European policy (like Finland, for instance) if all important EU-decisions are not supposed to be ratified by the citizens. If Denmark had not developed

---

[5] The "guarantee" was issued despite the fact that the Amsterdam Treaty clearly did not prepare the EU's institutions for enlargement, leaving it to another IGC to finish this job. To be fair, Poul Nyrup Rasmussen was, however, not alone but was strongly supported by the new leader of the Liberal party, Anders Fogh Rasmussen. Moreover, both politicians opened for "future technical adjustments" to the EU's institutions in connection with enlargement.

the referendum tradition, Denmark would probably today have been a member without reservations. In order to shed more light on this referendum factor (and also to show how the battle over national identity continued), we will now turn to the euro-referendum in more detail.

	1972	1986	1992	1993	1998	2000
Yes	63.3%	56.2%	49.3%	56.7%	55.1%	46.8%
No	36.7%	43.8%	50.7%	43.3%	44.9%	53.2%
Turn out	90.1%	75.4%	83.1%	86.5%	74.8%	87.6%

Table 1: Denmark's six EU-referenda. Source: L. Friis.

Old and New Promises

The Amsterdam referendum was barely over before the Danish prime minister changed his tune on the euro. In October 1998, the prime minister stated that there would be a referendum on the euro, although it was uncertain when. In March 2000, Prime Minister Rasmussen set September 28 as the date.

This rather sudden turnaround immediately triggered a fierce debate on broken campaign promises. Why was it suddenly so vital for Denmark to join the euro— the "most important foreign policy decision since the Second World War" (Danish Parliament 25 May 2000)—when the same prime minister, in May 1998, had argued that the euro would only affect Denmark marginally? And what had happened to the prime minister's campaign promises, which had barely been able to gather dust?

The prime minister maintained that things had changed since May. The euro was now about to be launched, and speculation against the Danish krone in August 1998 had proven that non-membership carried a stiff price. Unlike weaker countries within the euro-zone, Denmark was subject to speculation from the "wild birds of the financial markets" (*Berlingske Tidende* 1998). Considering the tradition of election promises that were not kept in their entirety ("the Union is stone dead"), this explanation was apparently not able to convince the majority of the voters. At least it is striking how the overall question of why Denmark should vote on the euro never left the agenda all the way up to September 28. In contrast, it breathed new life into the overall question of the credibility of the yes-side.

The credibility issue only gained in prominence when attention turned to the prime minister's so-called "divorce promise." At a seminar in February 2000, the prime minister made the case that the euro-decision was not necessarily final. If Denmark were to regret its decision at a later stage, it could reintroduce the krone. The fierce discussion as to whether this was a credible promise culminated in May 2000, when the president of the Commission, Romano Prodi, during a visit to Denmark questioned the divorce clause. Besides feeding into the credibility discussion, the immediate debate on divorce can hardly have reassured voters in doubt. Why was it so important for the prime minister to stress that divorce was an option? Didn't this imply that the project in itself was insecure and possibly a threat to Denmark?

A similar discussion took place in the final days of the campaign. Here, the prime minister, after heavy pressure from the no-side, guaranteed that the Danish pension system would be maintained more or less indefinitely. Almost in parallel, the Danish foreign minister issued a veto-guarantee: Denmark would veto any proposals in the ongoing IGC that would negatively affect the Danish pension and social system. Although the purpose of both initiatives was to calm the voters, it actually seemed to have the opposite effect. Why would ministers promise to veto proposals if they did not themselves look upon them as a threat to the Danish model?

Most likely, the various promises (old and new) contributed to the "no" on September 28. The fact that most promises centered on economics points to another explanation, namely the fact that the government reverted to a very economic approach of discussing EU-affairs. It, therefore, became difficult for the yes-side to present a stable fit between Danish identity and the euro—or at least a fit which could compete with that offered by the no-side.

Who's More Danish?

Unlike in the Amsterdam campaign, the government decided very early on to run a campaign that mainly stressed the economic benefits. This became clear in the first debate in parliament in April 2000 when the prime minister launched four arguments for a yes: (1) securing economic progress, (2) an "insurance" against currency speculation, (3) job safety, and (4) Danish dignity—"Denmark cannot be on the sideline" (*Folketinget* 11 Apr. 2000). Although political arguments were not absent (see argument 4), they trailed far behind the economic arguments. Apparently, the government was convinced that such a pragmatic, utilitarian approach would pay off. After all, weren't the Danes skeptical of more political integration?

Reasons for voting no:
    37% No to more union
    23% Wish to defend Danish identity, such as the krone
    23% Mistrust of the EU as such
    17% Other

Reasons for voting yes:
    50% To protect Danish influence
    23% Deepen political integration
    11% Economic advantages
    16% Other

Figure 1: "The Danish No—Politics Beats Economics." Source: *Politiken* 15 Oct. 2000.

The opinion polls conducted after the euro-referendum suggest this economic strategy misfired. For both yes- and no-voters, economics only played a marginal role. As a matter of fact, only every ninth yes-sayer ticked the yes-box on the ballot paper due to economic advantages (see Figure 1). Even more damaging was the fact that the economic strategy, as hinted above, failed to present a credible fit between the euro and Danish identity. Obviously, the yes-side tried to make the claim that rhe EMU was the best way to insure the Danish model and economic success. After having portrayed Denmark as a "pioneering country" for years, this message was, however, difficult to put across.[6] As a matter of fact, by having labeled Denmark as "the best welfare state in the world," the government was put on the defensive. If the Danish model was so superior, surely then Denmark could only be pulled down by the rest of Europe in an economic and monetary union? The credibility of this danger was increased by the fact that most Danes, apparently as a reflex, accepted the assertion that the Danish pension scheme (*folkepension*) was better than those in, for instance, Germany, Sweden, and France, hence confirming Ole Wæver's quip cited at the beginning of this article that Nordic identity is "about being *better* than Europe."

---

[6] The pioneer argument dominated the prime minister's address to the nation on 1 January 2000—just on the brink of the referendum campaign ("It is our duty to take care of the welfare society, which everyone is looking upon as the best in the world").

Conversely, the no-side had no similar problems. On the contrary, they presented a no as the best way to protect Danish identity. If voters rejected the euro, everything would be business as usual and the Danish success model would continue. If they voted yes, Denmark would more or less disappear from the map as an independent state, as a national currency is part and parcel of national statehood.

How successful this argument was can be seen not only from the opinion poll but also from the actual debate on the euro. Throughout the entire campaign, the no-side was never pushed to present an alternative vision for Denmark beyond the euro. The alternative was simply that the status quo was also promoted by many Danish symbols — from the Queen (whose image adorns the obverse of many Danish coins) to the flag—whereas the yes-side could only refer to a lowering of interest rates. Especially the right-wing Danish People's Party's attempts to invoke the symbols of Danishness frustrated the prime minister. After the party had launched its campaign slogan, "For Krone and Country," he made the following appeal in Parliament:

> We are all Danish, and we are Danish all day long, and no one is more Danish than others here in Denmark.... So I hope we will not hit each other over the head with statements that persons who take a particular point of view are indeed almost traitors, and that they are definitely not Danish.... (*Folketinget* 11 Apr. 2000)

Although the yes-side's inability to link the euro to Danish identity is a crucial factor that explains the no, it should be mentioned that the government was also dogged by simple bad luck. Just after the government had decided to launch a public debate on the euro, the sanctions against Austria's new right-wing coalition government were agreed upon. Although the sanctions were not formally an EU decision, it seemed to provide Danish no-sayers with the final proof that the EU was developing into a strong political body, which even interfered in national elections.

The next misfortune was the biannual report of the Danish Economic Council. As early as the spring of 2000, this report, in strong language, torpedoed the yes-side's core argument that euro-membership was important for the Danish economy. According to the independent economists, the economic effects of joining were "small and uncertain" (*Det økonomiske Sekretariat* 2000). Perhaps not surprisingly, the report became the new focal point of the debate.

Finally, the continuing fall of the euro also undermined the yes-side's strategy. Most important here was that it triggered the image of the

Titanic, which the no-side used again and again. Why should Denmark join a sinking ship? Wasn't Denmark much safer staying on shore? The argument that the krone, pegged to the euro, would not be affected by an eventual collapse, could not compete with the image of a sinking ship.

The bad luck coupled with the overall campaign led to a situation in which the no-vote hardly came as a surprise. Unlike June 1992, when the no shocked the Danish government and the entire EU, the surprise in 2000 was not that the voters rejected the motion, but rather the clarity with which this was done.

BUSINESS AS USUAL? —AFTER THE NO

In the immediate aftermath of the referendum, the Danish government took the view that the voters had not turned their backs on Europe; the vote on 28 September was only about the euro. Although this attempt to encapsulate the rejection of the euro was quite understandable, it was not fully carried out in practice. Despite the fact that the vote had only been on the euro, the government came to the conclusion that none of the other reservations could now be put to a referendum for some time. After having lost the referendum on the euro, it was simply looked upon as suicidal to ask the voters to consider any of the other reservations.

As a result, the no to the euro will have broader consequences for Denmark, in that the country is *not* on its way back to full-fledged membership. Instead of putting the reservation concerning defense policy to a national vote (as was generally expected before 28 September), the issue of another referendum has been taken off the agenda.

The fact that Denmark still retained certain reservations could easily be seen as a business-as-usual argument. Before September 2000, Denmark had four reservations; after September 2000 the number was exactly the same. The argument here, though, is different: the four reservations had been seen ever since 1992 by Denmark's EU-partners as a provisional arrangement or as breathing space which Denmark needed after the 1992-referendum before catching up with the other member states. As a result, Denmark was generally looked upon as a full-fledged member in waiting. Hence, Denmark's views on, for instance, the defense questions remained of interest to the other member states. After the no, the situation was different: Denmark had indicated to the other member states that the reservations were here to stay. Very likely, this will make the other member states less attentive when a Danish representative is given the floor on a policy issue about which Denmark has a reservation.

Secondly, it must be stressed that the EU post-2001 is very different from the EU of 1993. In 1993, when the Danish reservations were accepted, the three important areas (euro, justice and home affairs, and defense) were still dormant. After 2000, they stand out as important aspects of European integration or as features that define the EU. Hence, non-membership in these particular areas will probably also have broader consequences for a country's influence and agenda-setting capacity.

As a matter of fact, the Danish position after the no is unique. Although the EU is generally developing into a more flexible union (with enhanced co-operation and various special protocols), no other country has three reservations. Denmark is the only country that cannot participate in the defense initiatives and the only country which cannot accept supranational legislation on justice and home affairs. Finally, whereas Denmark has said no to EMU, Sweden and the UK are still seen as members waiting in the wings.[7]

This unique position of Denmark does, however, not necessarily imply that Denmark will change its EU-policy. On the one hand, it will be difficult to pursue a far more pro-EU policy considering the present climate of opinion. On the other hand, the Danish government will still push for its traditional policy concerns: enlargement, employment, greater involvement of the national parliaments in the EU, etc. When Denmark takes over the EU presidency in the second half of 2002, one can therefore already be sure that it will put enlargement at the top of its agenda. Indeed, what could be more appealing for a Danish prime minister than being able to give the "From Copenhagen to Copenhagen Address"? "The membership perspective for central and eastern Europe was extended here in Copenhagen in 1993, and now, here in the same city, we are able to sign the first accession treaties."

That everything has remained more or less business as usual in terms of policy, if not in terms of influence, can be seen from the results of the Nice intergovernmental conference, which was concluded in December 2000. After the no, Denmark pursued almost the same policy as before. The only explicit change was Denmark's view on enhanced co-operation.

---

[7] Since union citizenship is very undeveloped, the reservation on this matter does not really play a role in practice.

As pointed out by the Danish foreign minister, it was hardly tenable for Denmark to use flexibility itself and deny other member states any kind of flexibility.

In practice, Denmark was, however, not really tested in Nice. In the most important areas, such as the size of the Commission or qualified majority voting on social affairs, Denmark was anything but isolated. Indeed, the hard work was often left for others to carry out. Since these efforts meant that the new treaty did not contain any transfer of sovereignty, Denmark ratified the Treaty of Nice in parliament on 1 June 2001. Ironically, Denmark, which is usually pictured as the most euro-skeptical country, was the first to ratify the treaty, while Ireland— generally viewed as an EU-enthusiast—rejected it in a referendum in June 2001.

Even though it is difficult to see major changes in the actual policy of Denmark in the immediate future, such is not the case with regard to the Danish EU-debate in general. After the massive defeat, all yes-parties have stated that one should dare to embark upon a more politically oriented debate on European integration instead of leaving this flank open to the no-side. Skeptics point to similar statements by yes-politicians after the Danish no in 1992. The point is, however, that new developments within the EU leave the government with no real choice. After all, in 2004 the IGC is scheduled to discuss issues such as a European constitution and catalogue of competencies, which can hardly be portrayed as economic initiatives. Secondly, and more positively seen from a Danish perspective, the EU is finally moving into a stage of the enlargement process, where accession is indeed around the corner. Since enlargement, unlike general opinion in most other member states, is popular in Denmark, it provides the government with some powerful political arguments.

As a matter of fact, one can argue that Denmark is facing an all or nothing referendum where membership as such is at stake. Two possible scenarios can already be seen on the horizon. In scenario one, the new IGC produces a completely new EU-treaty (or constitutional treaty), that replaces the existing ones. If Denmark rejects the new treaty, it would therefore be left without any legal connection to the EU and would be forced to negotiate a new kind of agreement. Scenario two is less radical. Here the IGC does not produce a completely new treaty, but only a treaty, which amends the existing ones. Formally, the Danish referendum would therefore only center upon a single issue. Should Denmark remain at the present level of integration (the Treaty of Nice), or should it implement the new treaty? In practice, Denmark would once again be facing an all or nothing referendum. The basic reason is that another Danish no would in practice require Denmark to find new EU-reservations in order to be able to ratify the new treaty.[8]

Since the new IGC will most likely only deal with constitutional issues, such as the charter of fundamental rights or a catalogue of competencies, it is difficult to see what areas would qualify as potential new reservations. Hence, in the event that Denmark votes no, it would once again face a situation where it would have to negotiate a new, separate agreement with the EU — possibly similar to Norway's. Indeed, the Norwegian way or full membership could very well be the crucial question in the coming years for Denmark. Although it is far too early to predict the answer to this question, a possible indicator is the fact that actual support for EU-membership is generally rather high (see Table 2): 65 percent are of the opinion that Denmark has gained from membership.

Luxembourg	79%
Ireland	75%
Netherlands	71%
Spain	63%
Belgium	62%
Portugal	61%
Greece	61%
Italy	59%
Denmark	51%
Germany	48%
France	48%
Finland	39%
Austria	38%
Sweden	34%
UK	28%

Table 2: Support for European Union Membership.
Source: *Eurobarometer* 54:34–50.

---

[8] On paper, a re-negotiation of the entire treaty is also a possibility. This was, however, not possible in 1992. Neither were the other member states willing to re-open the treaty when Ireland rejected the Treaty of Nice in June 2001.

CONCLUSION—A MORE NORDIC EU?

The core argument of this article is that Denmark is not really an anomaly in Scandinavia. On the contrary, Denmark's relationship to the European Union is dominated by a feature, which also plays a major role in all the other Nordic countries (with the possible exception of Finland)—namely the difficulties of finding a credible fit between national identity and the EU project. Since the Nordic countries have traditionally been characterized by a strong belief in their exceptionalism (the Nordic model), the road to Europe has often been bumpy. However, judging from the European debate as such, all member states are presently struggling to make the EU compatible with national identity. The Irish no in the referendum to the Treaty of Nice is only one example; German concerns for the common currency another. Or to quote a leading British EU-expert:

> Governance is becoming increasingly a multi-level, intricately institutionalized activity, while representation, loyalty and identity remain stubbornly rooted in the traditional institutions of the nation state. Much of the substance of European state sovereignty has now fallen away; the symbols, the sense of national solidarity, the focus for political representation and accountability, nevertheless remain." (Wallace 1999:521)

Where Denmark differs from the other Nordic countries and most of the member states is in its tradition of putting important EU decisions to referenda. Unlike in Germany, for instance, the referendum practice provides an effective channel for euro-skepticism or just an excellent opportunity to give the government a black eye. As we have shown, the black-and-white referenda lead to a self-perpetuating process where election promises in one referendum are transformed into a boomerang in the following.

The conclusion that the Nordic countries, despite some variation, are not really that different seems to be confirmed by the recent development within Nordic co-operation. Despite the Danish euro referendum, which could have enticed the more pro-EU Finland to give up on Nordic co-operation within the EU, we have witnessed the opposite. In spring 2001, Sweden's Prime Minister, Göran Persson, for the first time acknowledged that "the Nordic countries have lost a lot by not co-ordinating sufficiently in the EU" (*Norden i veckan måndag* 2001). Since Denmark and Finland have generally been more positive about Nordic co-operation within the EU than Sweden, a new door seems to have been opened since no major forces in the Nordic countries any longer look upon Nordic co-operation as a real alternative to the EU. The essence of the game now is how Nordic co-operation can be used as a platform within the European integration process. Although not all Nordic countries are members of the EU, they are all affected by EU directives.

It is still unclear what produced the change of heart in Sweden. A likely explanation is the forthcoming enlargement of the EU. Accession of up to thirteen new members will undoubtedly produce a very different Union, which in itself could provide the Nordic countries with the all-important incentive for closer co-operation. A likely scenario here is that the EU (at least on some issues) would move to group negotiations, where countries would speak with one voice—simply in order to ensure that negotiations among twenty-eight member states will not go on indefinitely. Although this may sound far fetched, the Franco-German axis and the Benelux countries already today speak with one voice on certain matters. Austria, the Czech Republic, Hungary, Poland, Slovakia, and Slovenia have also made preparations to move in a similar direction (Ferrero 2001).

If this scenario turns into reality, the three Nordic countries would risk loosing a substantial part of their influence if they insist on putting forward exactly identical policy statements—on, for instance, the environment—but only in three Nordic languages. At least, one could hardly blame the EU-partners for taking off their earphones after the first Nordic presentation. To be sure, increased Nordic co-ordination would not amount to a Nordic bloc but would only lead to formal co-operation on those issues upon which the countries would argue along similar lines anyway, such as transparency, environment, enlargement, and employment.

Another possible explanation for the Swedish turnaround is the realization that Nordic co-operation within the EU could provide the Nordic countries with help in the identity battle. Since the Nordic countries are very proud of their model, what could be sweeter than exporting this it to the rest of Europe? Or, to paraphrase the slogan of the Danish Social Democratic Party in the run up to the Amsterdam referendum: Why not try to make the EU more Nordic—a continuation of the Nordic region—rather than a threat to the region and its identity? At least it should be very clear that the region's future relationship with the EU will very much depend on finding a better fit between Nordic identity and the EU as such.

WORKS CITED

Berlingske Tidende. "Nyrup: Danskerne skal stemme om ØMU'en." 24 Oct. 1998.
Det økonomiske Råds Sekretariat. *Dansk Økonomi.* Spring 2000. Chapter 2.
Danish Parliament. Closing Speech. 25 May 2000. <www.nyrup.dk/taler>.
DUPI. *Udviklingen i EU siden 1992 på de områder, der er omfattet af de danske forbehold.* Danish Institute of Internaional Affairs, 2000.
Eurobarometer 54 (Autumn 2000): 34–50.
Ferrero-Waldner, Benita. "Austria and Its Neighbors—The Concept of Partnership." 6 June 2001. <www.bmaa.gv.at>.
Folketinget. F51, Speech 4. 11 Apr. 2000. <www.folketinget.dk>.
Friis, L. (1999). "EU and Legitimacy—The Challenge of Compability." *Co-operation & Conflict* 34.3: 243–71.
Norden i veckan. "Ökad nordisk samordning i EU." 28 May 2001. <www.norden.org>.
Politiken. "Mange i tvivl om euroen." 15 Oct. 2000.
———. "Vilstrup: Et nej til mere union." 15 Oct. 2000.
Wallace, W. (1999). "The Sharing of Sovereignty: The European Paradox." *Political Studies* 47: 503–21.
Wæver, O. (1992). "Nordic Nostalgia: Northern Europe after the Cold War." *International Affairs* 68.1: 77–102.
Weekendavisen. "Nyrup: Ikke flere traktater." 28 May 1998.

Integration by Different Means
Finland and Sweden in the EU

Ann-Cathrine Jungar
Uppsala University

THE EXPECTATIONS WERE MIXED when Sweden and Finland joined the EU in 1995. On one hand, it was expected that the two small Nordic states would bring policies that are connected with the so-called "Nordic model"[1] onto the European agenda and thereby supplement the market-making community with a stronger social and democratic dimension. On the other hand, some predicted that the Nordic states would become minimalist members of the EU since they were supposed to be reluctant about the further transfer of sovereignty to the EU, i.e. negative to deeper European integration (Gstöhl 1996; Mouritzen 1997; Miles 2000).

The initial expectation that Sweden and Finland would act quite similarly in the EU has not been entirely fulfilled. Sweden is said to be a reluctant European, whereas the perception of Finland is that of a successful adapter to the EU and consequently as more influential. Various metaphors have been used to illustrate this perceived difference: Finland has been depicted as a "model pupil" that has socialized the norms and rules of the EU and is more prone to compromise—even core interests—whereas Sweden is described as a hesitant but simultaneously "preachy" member that wants to export the Swedish way of doing things to the EU (von Sydow 1999; Novack 2000).[2]

Research has been financed by The Bank of Sweden Tercentenary Foundation.
[1] The characteristics of the Nordic model are described on pages 404–8.
[2] See also Raunio and Wiberg (2000:10) where Charlemagne, a columnist for *The Economist,* is quoted: "Since joining the EU in 1995, and despite coming from its most distant edge [the Finns] have displayed an almost uncanny mastery of its workings. Many point to them as the very model of how a 'small country' (vast in land mass, but with only 5.2 million people) should operate within the EU's insitutions: not preachy like the Swedes, not difficult like the Danes, not over-ambitious like the Austrians, merely modest and purposeful, matching a sense of principle with a sense of proportion."

However, of what this difference actually consists is seldom spelled out. The aim of this article is to provide a picture of Sweden and Finland in the EU—both in terms of similarities *and* differences. The paper begins with a presentation of the widespread EU skepticism in the two countries. Naturally, this constitutes a heavy constraint on the behavior of political leadership, which has had to prove the legitimacy of the EU for the voters. Nevertheless, the Finnish and Swedish politicians have reacted somewhat differently to their predominantly negative domestic opinions. This does not apply primarily to the substantive policies the two countries have pursued so far in the EU: the two states have indeed brought up issues that are particular Scandinavian concerns on the European agenda, i.e. transparency, environment, gender equality, etc. Sweden has been particularly keen on introducing and developing EU policies that can be characterized as belonging to the core competence of the state, e.g. employment and social welfare, and consequently cannot from this point of view be characterized as a reluctant European.

Rather, Finland and Sweden have diverged with regard to the means by which these policies should be realized in Europe, i.e. the mix of intergovernmental and supranational elements. Moreover, they emphasize somewhat differently the future priorities for the EU. The Finnish government, on the one hand, has been more keen on protecting what is already in place by empowering the EU with efficient means for the successful implementation of policies, for instance the increased use of majority voting and a strong Commission that can supervise compliance, etc. The Swedish government, on the other hand, has manifested greater preparedness to extend the competencies of the EU. However, this cannot come about by transferring formal decision-making power to the EU. Consequently, Sweden is more concerned about harmonizing policies by the means of intergovernmental negotiations and is therefore negative to the transfer of formal decision making competence to the EU, whereas Finland has to a greater degree supported supranational solutions. One indicator of this difference is that Sweden does not take part in the EMU although fulfilling the required criteria, whereas Finland does. As a matter of fact, those who characterize Sweden as a reluctant and Finland as an active member of the EU tend—often tacitly—to equate pro-integration with pro-EU. Given this underlying assumption, Sweden can indeed be described as a more-reluctant European than Finland, but if one departs from the issues that the Swedish government would like the EU to handle, such a statement is not justified.

The disposition of this article is the following. Firstly, the public opinion on the EU membership is presented. Secondly, the policies Finland and Sweden have pursued in the EU are discussed in general terms. Finally, the third and main part focuses on the major difference between Finland and Sweden, i.e. the proportion of intergovernmental as opposed to supranational elements in the EU, a difference clearly manifested in the intensifying debate on the future of the EU.

PUBLIC OPINION AND THE EU: THE REFERENDUM AND THE FIRST FIVE YEARS

The behavior of national governments in the EU is enhanced or constrained by domestic public opinion. Since the EU is not a democracy with a government that can be held accountable, the democratic control and legitimization of EU policies takes place within the member states. That is, the national governments negotiating in the EU act with the knowledge that the parliament and ultimately the voters can hold the government accountable for actions taken in the EU.[3] It is therefore quite reasonable to assume that public opinion—on specific issues as well as with regard to further integration—should matter for how governments actually behave in the EU. The purpose here is to describe the perceptions and attitudes of the Swedish and Finnish citizens toward the EU at the time of the referendum as well as during the first years of membership.

THE REFERENDA ON MEMBERSHIP

National referenda on membership in the EU were carried out in Finland, Sweden, and Norway in the autumn of 1994. The parliaments, which possessed the decisive powers, had promised to follow the results even though the referenda were not decisive.[4] Fifty-seven percent of the

---

[3] EU Advisory Committees were set up in the Finnish and Swedish parliaments. Since norm-giving power in a number of policy areas has been transferred from the national parliaments to the EU institutions, these bodies are meant to give the parliamentarians an opportunity to follow and control the decision-making process in the EU.

[4] The Finnish and Swedish parliaments approved of the EU membership agreement in November and December 1994. However, even though the Finnish parliamentarians had promised to respect the result of the referendum, forty-five parliamentarians voted against membership in the EU, whereas 152 voted in favor. The parliamentary procedure preceding the vote in Finland was characterized by obstruction from the EU opposition.

Finnish citizens and 53 percent of the Swedish citizens voted in favor for membership in the EU, whereas the Norwegians for the second time decided to remain outside.[5] The sequence of the referenda correlated to proportion of public opinion in favor of the EU, thus Norway, as the most "insecure card," was the last in the row (Jahn and Storsved 1995:239–40).[6] In a number of opinion polls during the early 1990s, this pattern was evident: the Finns were, in general, more pro-EU, whereas the Swedes and the Norwegians tended to be more skeptical (Paloheimo 1995:114–5).[7]

The typical yes-voter was a well-educated male living in an urban environment, whereas women and those with less education, or rural backgrounds correlated with a negative vote to the EU in the two countries (Ringdahl and Valen 1998:178–80; Paloheimo 1995). Hence, the *identikits* of the supporters and opponents to EU membership were quite similar in both countries.

The main arguments of both supporters and opponents of EU membership concerned different aspects of democracy and economy, i.e. neither side succeeded in monopolizing any one of these two arguments. However, different aspects of democracy and economy were utilized by the supporters and the opponents, respectively (Oskarsson 1996:219–24). The supporters, on the one hand, conceived of the EU as a means of improving decision-making capability by increasing the democratic control of issues that transcended national borders and that, therefore, could no longer be efficiently handled at the national level. Hence, democracy was equated with decision-making efficiency rather than with procedure.[8] The opponents, on the other hand, were more concerned about democracy at the national level, i.e. that norm-giving power that rightly resided with the national political institutions was being transferred to supranational bodies that are not democratic. The pro-EU economic arguments consisted in the perception that trade and

---

[5] A consultative referendum was also carried out in the Åland Islands, which is an autonomous part of Finland.

[6] Austria voted on June 12; Finland, October 16; Sweden, November 16; and Norway, Novermber 28.

[7] For instance 51 percent of the Finns, 37 percent of the Swedes, and 30 percent of the Norwegians supported membership in 1992 according to the *Eurobarometer*.

[8] Kerstin Jakobsson (1997) has illustrated how the political leadership in Sweden gave a new and different meaning to democracy during the EU referendum; in the debates democracy was viewed as parallel with decision-making capability and efficiency and focused on specific issues rather than procedures.

exports would improve and that membership would guarantee access to more markets, whereas the opponents feared that economic growth would deteriorate and unemployment increase others. No other group of arguments dominated like these two though others relating to the maintenance of peace and military security were mentioned by many EU supporters in both Finland and Sweden.

One noteworthy difference is that the Finnish EU supporters mentioned culture or belonging to western Europe as a reason for membership in the EU—an argument that was only of marginal importance among the Swedish supporters. For some of the Finns, membership in the EU was conceived of both as a manifestation of identity and a recognition of Finland as belonging to the west. Throughout its existence Finland has had a dual nature as a bridge between east and west, and the emphasis on the two has varied over time and been constrained by external circumstances (Heininen 1999:23–4). Even though Finland since independence has been characterized by traditional liberal and democratic institutions and western cultural heritage, there was an urge to choose more authentic identity and be recognized, especially after decades of being perceived as the model of Finlandization or Soviet subordination.

THE EU SKEPTICS

The Swedish and Finnish citizens are, together with the Danish and British citizens, the most EU-skeptical members of the Union: the legitimacy of the EU is low when measured with the images that the citizens hold of the EU and the perceived benefits that have accrued as a result of their membership. As a matter of fact, a majority in favor of membership in the EU has never been registered in the opinion polls after the referenda in Finland and Sweden.

The legitimacy of the EU is often measured as the citizens' support of their own country's membership in the EU. Roughly half the population support their country's membership: 48 percent of the citizens in the fifteen member states supported EU membership in 2001 (*Eurobarometer* 55).[9] Finland as well as Sweden are situated below the European average:

---

[9] The question reads as follows: Generally speaking, do you think (our country's) membership in the European Union is a good thing, a bad thing, or neither good nor bad? (The alternative don't know was also available).

36 percent of Finns and 33 percent of Swedes considered membership a good thing, whereas membership was perceived as a bad experience by 23 percent of the Finns and 37 percent of the Swedes. The two Nordic member states are more similar with respect to their number of EU supporters, whereas the number of those who have a critical view of the EU is higher in Sweden than in Finland, i.e. that EU criticism is more widespread in Sweden. The countries also differ in regard to the number of those who perceive that the EU has been "neither good nor bad": 27 percent of Swedes and 35 percent of Finns consider that the EU has been neither a positive nor a negative experience. That is, the citizens in the two member states differ somewhat with respect to their attitudes toward the EU after five years of membership. The largest difference is that EU criticism is more widespread in Sweden than in Finland, whereas the gap between the number of EU supporters is somewhat smaller—the EU support is 6 percent higher in Finland than in Sweden.

An important difference is that the relationship between the three above-mentioned categories of EU support and opposition has been more stable in Finland than in Sweden (Holmberg 1996). The EU supporters have outweighed the EU critics in number in Finland throughout the period of EU membership. Support for the EU dropped immediately after the referendum but increased again in 1998, though it has never surpassed 50 percent. The number of those who conceive of the EU in negative terms has been quite constant in Finland over time as well as those who say that the EU has been "neither good nor bad." The picture in Sweden, however, is completely different since the number of supporters and opponents has varied over time. Until 1998, EU critics outstripped supporters, whereas the opposite was the case between 1998 and 2001 when the trend of decreasing support was reversed and the number of EU supporters was once again higher than that of EU opponents. Between 1996 and 1997, the EU critics outweighed the supporters by almost 15 percent. A temporary change came about in 1998: the number of EU critics has decreased steadily, whereas the support has been quite stable.

A difference also prevails with regard to how the Finnish and Swedish citizens evaluate the benefits their countries have experienced from membership in the EU: in 2001, 38 percent of the citizens in Finland considered that Finland had benefited, whereas according to 44 per-

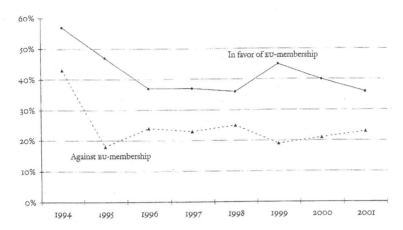

Table 1. The proportion of citizens in favor or against membership in the EU in Finland 1994-2001. Source: *Eurobarometer* (43, 45, 47, 49, 52, 53, 55), except for 1995, which is the result in the national referenda.

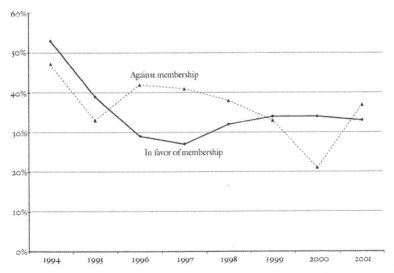

Table 2. The proportion of citizens in favor or against membership in the EU in Sweden 1994–2001. Source: *Eurobarometer* (43, 45, 47, 49, 52, 53, 55), except for 1995, which is the result in the national referenda.

cent Finland had not (*Eurobarometer* 55).[10] The Finnish citizens are quite close to the EU average since 45 percent EU citizens perceive that their respective member states have benefited from membership. The gap between those who perceive that Finland had benefited or not decreased compared to previous measurements. During the first years as members, far more Finns considered that Finland had not benefited rather than benefited, but over the years the proportion of those who believe that EU membership is beneficial has increased. The Swedes are far more negative with regard to Sweden's having benefited from EU membership: 27 percent of the Swedish citizens perceived that Sweden had benefited from being part of the EU after five years as members. On only one previous occasion has the number of those who conceive of the EU as having positive effects for Sweden been higher, 29 percent in 1999: an overwhelming majority of the Swedes believe that Sweden would be as well—or even better?—off by not being a member of the EU. The proportion of Swedish citizens who consider that Sweden has not benefited has varied between 53 and 60 percent during the five membership years.

To sum up, the popular legitimacy of the EU is low both in Finland and Sweden when compared to the EU average. However, the Swedish citizens are even more critical of membership in the EU than the Finns. In addition, the Swedes feel that they have benefited less from EU membership than their eastern neighbor. In the following parts of the article, we will indirectly address the question if—and in that case how—the EU criticism has affected the behavior of the political leadership in Finland and Sweden.

THE NORDIC MODEL FOR EXPORT

It was widely expected that Finland and Sweden as newcomers in the European Union in 1995 would put issues connected with the Nordic model on the European agenda. As a matter of fact, the two Nordic member states have introduced new and developed old policies in the EU, as well as contributed to the ongoing discussions on how to improve

---

[10] The question in the *Eurobarometer* is the following: Taking everything into consideration, would you say that (our country) has on balance benefited or not from being a member of the European Union?

and develop the institutional framework of the EU. The Nordic model is indeed a debatable collection of ideas, but is usually used as both a distinct set of political values and a distinct way of carrying out politics (Petersson 1994, chapter 2).

Firstly, both inside as well as outside, the Nordic model is primarily associated with a well-developed welfare state with the aim to guarantee the individual security at different stages of life. The Nordic model is characterized by universality and a striving toward equality (Esping-Andersen 1990).[11] A noteworthy characteristic of the Scandinavian welfare model has thus been to counteract large differences in society by attempting to give individuals with various backgrounds and experiences the same opportunity—not only economically—but also educationally, culturally, etc. (Hatland, Kuhnle and Romrren 1994; Kuhnle 1983; Heckscher 1984).[12] Until quite recently, the EU was predominantly a market making community[13] since it was mainly occupied with the removal of barriers to trade (Scharpf 1999:45-6), i.e. the policies connected with the core characteristics of the Nordic model have not been issues at the EU level. However, they have gained increased importance partly as a consequence of the fulfilment of the EMU.[14] For instance, in the Treaty of Amsterdam, policy areas thought to bring the EU "closer to the citizens" were strengthened: labor market and in particular employment, social policy, gender equality, environ-

[11] Esping-Andersen contrasts the Scandinavian welfare model with the conservative and liberal welfare models. In the conservative welfare regime the family is the basic unit, while the individual is in the center in the Scandinavian model, and in addition welfare rests in the former to a large degree on institutions in the civil society, such as the church. The liberal welfare regime is characterized by being minimal, the aim is only to support the most needy.

[12] The above model is to be understood as a stylized starting point for the current project, and not as an unexceptionable characterization of the Nordic systems of government.

[13] Scharpf states that market making is predominantly reflected in negative integration, i.e. the removal of barriers to trade, but also in positive integration of the harmonization of product standards at the EU level. However, market correcting measures are also part of positive integration since minimin rules are set up to regulate working conditions or pollution control.

[14] The Social Protocol, decided in Maastricht, has been considered as an important take-off for activist social policy at the EU level. In many issues related to working conditions, gender equality and so on, majority voting was allowed and the Commission has made use of the Protocol in order to push through initiatives. See Pierson, who illustrates the limited explanatory capacity of intergovernmental theories to explain integration by a focus on the case of EU social policy (54).

ment protection, consumer protection, and so forth.[15] With the new Nordic member states, progress could be made in these policy areas where sufficient majorities previously had been difficult to find.[16] The establishment of common rules and practices in these areas where the domestic standards are higher is for the Nordic countries primarily a means whereby vital national interests can be protected and harmful social and economic dumping can be avoided.

Secondly, the Nordic model is associated with a particular form of decision-making: popular participation in the decision-making process through various institutional solutions has been sought, and the aim has often been to reach a high degree of political consensus and wide political agreement (Esaiasson and Heidar 2000).[17] A very concrete expression of the institutionalized openness is the principle of public access to official documents. The Nordic model has been a deliberative form of democracy where efforts have been made to give the citizens knowledge and tools to take part in the public discussion (Allardt 1981). Finland and Sweden have been united in their aspiration to increase the openness of the EU institutions (Novack 1999) both as a means of decreasing parts of the democratic deficit of the EU, but also in order to defend the maintenance of these principles, which are crucial parts of the Nordic democratic identity at the national level. However, regarding the issue of democratizing the EU and making it directly accountable to a European electorate, there has so far been no broad support. On the contrary, the nation-state is considered and defended as the focal point of democratic institutions by the Scandinavian governments.

Thirdly, whereas Norway and Denmark have been and still are members of NATO, Sweden and Finland have maintained a foreign political policy of neutrality. They have aspired—under somewhat different conditions—to act as bridge builders and mediators between

[15] As a matter of fact, of the two newcomers Sweden has been more concerned to develop an employment dimension in the EU (now synthesisized in the Luxembourg process); during the Swedish presidency in the first half of 2001, employment was one of the prioritized policy areas (see page one of *Program för Sveriges ordförandeskap i EUs ministerråde 2000-07-07*).

[16] The environmental and gender equality lobbies have been particularly disappointed since the two new member states have not been prepared to increase the power of the supranational EU bodies in these policy spheres, but have rather preferred intergovernmental and consequently less powerful instruments.

[17] The existence of a common Nordic political model is questioned. According to the authors in the volume there are no distinct characteristics that differentiate the Nordic political systems as a group from the other west European states.

east and west as well as south and north during the bipolar world order. Hence, neutrality has been defined and rendered credible by international activism and has simultaneously been an efficient means for guaranteeing security. With the evolution of a new international order in the 1990s the feasibility of the neutral status of Finland and Sweden was repeatedly cast in doubt. Whereas Finland to a larger extent has acknowledged that the present EU cooperation in foreign and security policies in practice is not consistent with a neutral status, Sweden has until very recently clung firmly to its dogma of neutrality. The process of foreign political redefinition is somewhat less troublesome in Finland (Forsberg 2000:267)[18] than in Sweden (Strömvik 1999:252–3).[19] Now a process of change seems to be on its way in Sweden: in the proposal for a new Social Democratic Party program the term neutrality is no longer mentioned[20] and a more intense parliamentary debate has been initiated. Nevertheless, the two states have actively contributed to the establishment of a new foreign and security political dimension to the EU: Finland and Sweden jointly proposed setting up an EU crisis prevention capacity and have been keen supporters of providing the means for an EU crisis management capacity, i.e. humanitarian and peace-keeping operations. Hence, the two previous neutral states actively take part in the development of common European security politics but are still not prepared to take part in any collective military defense, i.e. military cooperation that prescribes reciprocal obligations, be it in NATO or in an EU military force. If that were the case, it would mean a final break with the neutral past. One of the prioritized issues during the Finnish presidency in 1999 was the development of a "Northern Dimension" to the EU agenda. The "Northern Dimension" encompasses economic and infrastructural cooperation in the broad Baltic Sea territory as a means of enhancing stability in the area, as well as counteracting the Mediterranean groups in the EU (see Antola 1999). One of the most important achievements of the Swedish presidency was the coordination of the

---

[18] In Finland the concept of neutrality was replaced with "military nonalignment and independent defense" at the time of the membership in the EU and toward the closing of the millennium the military defense was no longer presented as independent, but only credible.

[19] In Sweden the neutrality doctrine was downplayed with the membership in the EU, but officially the political leadership has nevertheless clung to the doctrine of nonalignment in peace, but modified as the maintenance of a neutral status during war in the *neighboring areas* of Sweden.

[20] See also Swedish Social Democratic Party Home page < www.sap.se/ >.

EU's common foreign policies, and the importance of Sweden's histori-cal experience as an international mediator cannot be overlooked.

To summarize, Finland and Sweden have embraced the EU as a means whereby political issues, which no longer can be solved at the national level, can be more efficiently dealt with. The goals and the policy interests they pursue are not diverging to any greater extent, but they differ on the methods. More precisely, Sweden has to a higher degree prioritized the protection of formal decision making power as a means of defending national interests, whereas Finland has traded some sovereignty in the conviction that such a strategy will bring about greater influence and sensitivity to Finnish interests in the Union. Even though it was expected that the new member states would become minimalist members of the EU, they have chosen somewhat different strategies. This is illustrated in the following part of the article.

INTERGOVERNMENTALISM AND SUPRANATIONALISM

The EU is not a full-fledged federation, nor is it a pure intergovernmental organization. On the one hand, the EU cannot be characterized as a federation since the competencies between the various levels, i.e. the EU and the member states, are not well defined. The EU is an organization that, so far, has been in constant movement toward an unknown future destination. Moreover, the EU is not in itself a democratic political system since the main decision-making bodies in the EU are not at all or only indirectly responsible to the citizens. Hence, the voters can hold their respective governments accountable for their behavior in the Council, and they can decide who of their fellow citizens is to represent them in the European parliament. There is as of yet no full parliamentarism in the EU even though the European Parliament has increased its control over the Commission: the EP can make the Commission resign by a vote of non-confidence, and the commissioners have to gain the approval of the EP in order to take office. Moreover, the decision-making influence of the European Parliament varies considerably in various policy areas. On the other hand, the EU is not an intergovernmental body since the organization carries distinct supranational traits. More precisely, individual member states do not possess a veto in a large number of policy areas where the ultimate decision-making power is with the EU, i.e. individual member states have to comply with the decisions taken in the Council even though they might have opposed them. The reason for this is that decisions are taken by qualified majorities in certain policy areas, above all in the first pillar. The discussions on the democratic deficit of the EU relate overwhelmingly to this particular institutional design and these specific decision rules. Other aspects of the EU's democratic deficit are the dominance of experts in the decision making, the lack of a common European political community, and the lack of a European identity (Laffan, O'Donnell, and Smith 2000:202–4; Eriksen and Fossum 2000).

Hence, the EU is not a federation but represents a delicate balance of intergovernmental and supranational elements. There has always been tension between those who are prepared to move the EU in a more supranational direction and those who want to maintain the EU as a predominantly intergovernmental organization. In the three-pillar structure of EU, these elements are differently distributed: the supranational elements are strongest in the first pillar and have gradually been strengthened in the third pillar with the increased use of majority voting, while intergovernmental elements dominate in the second pillar. Since the purpose of this article is to analyze whether the political leadership wants to move the EU in a more supranational or intergovernmental direction in the future, we need to operationalize these concepts.

Supranationalism is here understood as a set of decision making rules, i.e. the status of supranational institutions in the decision-making process with regard to initiation, decision-making, and (control of the) implementation.[21] Firstly, supranationality requires that the decisions are binding for the member states, not optional, as would be the case in an intergovernmental organization. In addition, the monitoring and sanctioning of obstruction is primarily with the supranational institutions in a supranational organization, whereas the member states exclusively control this part of the decision-making process in an intergovernmental model. In a purely intergovernmental model, the compliance is voluntary (see Streeck on neo-voluntarism). Secondly, the use of majority voting is a distinct character of supranationalism; that is, individual member states face the risk of being voted down even though they oppose the decisions. In the intergovernmental

---

[21] See Jon Hovi for a more detailed characterization of supranationalism. According to Förland and Claes, particular attention should be paid to the following two elements: (1) the organization has to be able to make decisions that are binding for the national administrations; (2) the decisions can be made against the will of individual members, i.e. majority voting is used (1991:127–8).

model, unanimity is the rule. Thirdly, the existence of independent supranational institutions is a vital element in a supranational model. The supranational institutions possess autonomous power *vis-à-vis* the initiation, the decision-making, or the monitoring. For instance, the Commission has the sole right for initiatives in the first pillar, the European Parliament is a co-decision maker in a number of areas, and the European Court of Justice is the supreme interpreter of the Treaties. In an intergovernmental body, the common institutions have the character of administrative agencies supporting the member states or discussion forums possessing no formal power in the decision-making process.

The Future of the EU

The upcoming enlargement of the EU has been a catalyst for a number of discussions of the future EU—how should the EU develop in the shorter as well as in the longer run. Joschka Fischer was the first in a series of prominent European political leaders, who have given voice to their future visions of the EU during the six months preceding the Nice IGC that should pave the way for EU enlargement. Fischer's proposal was that the EU should develop into a full-fledged democratic federation (Fischer).[22] Firstly, the competencies between the EU, on one hand, and the member states, on the other, should be regulated in a European constitution. Secondly, the prevailing asymmetry between the execution of power and accountability—i.e. power is exercised at the EU level, whereas the national governments are held responsible—should be nullified by making the EU a democracy: a European parliament consisting of two chambers—the first with directly elected members and the second with elected representatives from the member states—should hold an EU government accountable. Naturally, none of the other prominent European political leaders agreed with the federalist vision, but he initiated a political debate on the future of EU.[23]

Obviously, the two Nordic social democratic prime ministers, Paavo Lipponen and Göran Persson from Finland and Sweden, have taken the occasion—or have been pressed?—to formulate their visions of both the present day and future EU as well. Their primary point of departure for

[22] For academic responses on the Fischer speech see Joerges, Mény, and Weiler (2000).
[23] This debate has also had repercussions inside the Union, see the White paper on European governance from the Commission.

the discussion is how to make the EU a more legitimate project. Since the Finnish and Swedish voters are the most EU-skeptic Europeans, this challenge of particular concern for the political leadership in the respective countries. In the debate the need for institutional reform has been connected to the future enlargement of the EU: a common argument is that institutional reforms are necessary in order to guarantee efficiency in the decision-making when the number of member states increases. As warm supporters of enlargement, the two Nordic party leaders connected the discussion of EU institutional reforms to the widening of the Union.[24] It is claimed that the use of majority voting should increase in order to avoid deadlock and that the position of the Commission as an initiator and a guardian of the Treaties must be protected (European University Institute 2000). This is the main argument of the Finnish prime minister, Paavo Lipponen, and a parliamentary majority at home backs him up. A second line of reasoning is that there is a trade-off between widening and deepening the EU: when new member states join the EU, it cannot become as encompassing. The Swedish prime minister, Göran Persson, does not see that enlargement necessitates institutional reforms that strengthen the supranational characteristics of the EU as a means to increase efficiency, neither does he believe that the widening of the EU is a restriction with regard to the number of policy areas with which EU can deal. Rather, the EU should engage in issues that concern the citizens more closely and since these issues in fact belong to the core competence of the nation-state, new policy making methods are required. Hence, the two social democratic party leaders and prime ministers sketch somewhat different future scenarios for the EU. The remainder of the article is therefore dedicated to a description of the future visions of Göran Persson and Paavo Lipponen, as well as an account of the broader parliamentary debate in these issues carried out in the parliaments of the two countries.

THE SEARCH FOR LEGITIMACY

The political leadership in Finland and Sweden agree that increased legitimacy is needed in the EU. How then can the legitimacy of the Union be strengthened? How does the political leadership that is constrained

---

[24] However, whereas the Swedes (together with the Danes) are the strongest supporters of enlargement, 61 percent of the Swedish citizens are in favor for enlargement, the Finns are more relutant: 48 percent support enlargement (*Eurobarometer* 53).

by domestic EU-negative opinions, but simultaneously recognizes the need for joint actions, formulate their visions for a more legitimate Union? How can the "joint decision trap" be resolved: more cooperation is needed, but the preparedness among the citizens to give up sovereignty is weaker (Scharpf 1996:361–73). Even though the prime ministers from Finland and Sweden consider that the EU is suffering from the same illness, they propose somewhat different therapies. Let us start with the description of the symptoms of the disease. The illness from which the present EU is suffering is the lack of popular support and participation in the EU, the complexity of the EU institutions, and the lack of capability to deal with pressing political problems. The Finnish prime minister, Paavo Lipponen, states that

> the European Union has two fundamental problems: first, alienation from the people which is due to lack of democratic legitimacy, lack of transparency and too much bureaucracy; and second, an incapability to adapt to a changing world. (Lipponen 2000)

The Swedish prime minister points to the same features but adds that if the EU project is not reformed it will contribute to a mistrust in politics and democracy at the national levels as well: the legitimacy of the EU is intimately related to the trust in politics in general. If precautions are not taken to make the EU a legitimate project among the citizens, a somewhat different "spill over" consisting of mistrust in politics will materialize at the member-state level. Hence, if matters deteriorate the EU will no longer "rescue the nation-states," but contribute to their deterioration.

> The real danger threatening the EU does not proceed from enlargement and the concomitant risk of impoverishing effective cooperation. The threat to the EU project, which is basically about strengthening the national democracies which make up the Union, is an altogether different one. There has been a steady decline in public confidence and credibility in our elected representatives. Active involvement in party political activities is diminishing. These developments are taking place at national and international levels. This is a truth we must face squarely in any discussion about the future European Union. We must have the courage to probe the weaknesses in our national democracies—just as we are doing with our European institutions. We must address the work of reform from the standpoint of people's everyday problems, and of the need for greater transparency and public participation. (Persson 2000B)

INPUT- AND OUTPUT-ORIENTED LEGITIMIZATION

Hence, according to the Nordic political leadership, the EU lacks what Fritz Scharpf has termed both "input-oriented legitimacy" and "output-oriented legitimacy" (1999:6–13). Input-oriented legitimization can be paraphrased as "government by the people," whereas output-oriented legitimization is "government for the people." In the first case, the decisions taken are legitimate because they reflect the will of the people. The realization of the will of the people requires some kind of democratic institutions in order to aggregate and allocate preferences. In the present EU, the democratic legitimization is indirect, i.e. through the national parliaments. Scharpf does not see any prospects for an increased input legitimization in the EU, that is increased direct public participation and influence due to the lack of European political community with a sense of collective identity (Scharpf 1999:10).[25] The Nordic prime ministers stress the weak popular participation in the EU decision making. The questions are if and how the Nordic politicians would decrease the lack of input-oriented legitimization and thus reduce the democratic deficit? By a stronger involvement at the national level, i.e. by the national parliaments and/or by strengthening direct popular participation and democracy at the European level?

Output-oriented legitimization prevails if the political choices promote the common welfare of the "constituency in question" and requires a capacity to solve problems that need collective solutions. In that case, Scharpf argues, a thick identity is not required but only "a range of *common interests* that is sufficiently broad and stable to justify institutional arrangements for collective action" (1999:11, emphasis in original).[26] What can be done to increase the output oriented legitimacy? Should the legitimacy of the EU increase if other policy issues are dealt with at the European level? Or should the Union in the present form be rendered more efficient, and are clearer divisions of competence between the Union and the member states required?

---

[25] "Original European legitimization might eventually evolve as processes of European-wide political communication and opinion formation [and] would be facilitated by European political parties, European associations, and European media."

[26] Output-oriented legitimacy is interest based rather than identity based. However, the proponents of deliberative forms of democracy would not agree with that a thick identity is a prerequisite for democracy in the EU (see Eriksen and Fossum 2000).

The two types of legitimization do not preclude one another, and they can here provide a background for the discussions that have taken place in Finland and Sweden. Göran Persson, on the one hand, stresses the need of the EU to deal with issues that are closer to the citizens. However, some of the (mainly anti-EU) political parties in the Swedish parliament do not see why policy areas such as employment, culture, and education have to considered at the EU level (EU Advisory Committee 2000/01:10). Since these new areas belong to core responsibilities of the nation-state, new decision-making methods are required. Hence, Göran Persson advocates that a new *co-operative method* should be increasingly utilized in the EU decision making, whereby issues that are central to the national governments can be coordinated and dealt with jointly, but the ultimate decision-making powers still reside at the national level. Hence, the Swedish prime minister advocates an intergovernmental method for the "new" policy areas, but also proposes a strengthening of intergovernmentalism in other areas as well. Paavo Lipponen, on the other hand, defends the traditional *community method* where the Commission is a central institution as an initiator and a guardian of the implementation of EU policies. Therefore the position of the Commission, which has been weakened in the late 1990s, needs to be restored. The Finnish parliament supports the prime minister's defense of the community method but does not agree in his more federalist visions or the proposal that the EU has to become a federation where the Commission is accountable to the European Parliament, whose position needs to strengthened by an increased use of co-decision making (Suomen Eduskunta, verbal PTK 148/2000 vp, 29 Nov. 2000). However, they agree with the prime minister that the debate on the future of Europe has to be carried out in a broader European context and not only restricted to the national parliaments. Hence, Lipponen is more concerned about defending and ameliorating what already is in place and considers the new co-decision making method as an interesting instrument worth testing. However, in comparison with his Swedish colleague, he is much more critical to intergovernmental solutions.

INTEGRATION BY COORDINATION

An indicative illustration that Finland and Sweden do not diverge with regard to the goals they seek but rather the means is seen in how Göran

Persson motivated the Swedish veto of common decisions on taxes by qualified majorities in the EU. During the EU Advisory Committee meeting when the parliament had the last chance to comment upon the Swedish positions to be taken in the IGC the prime minister stated:

> I believe that everyone, or almost everyone, present here wants a har-monization of these taxes [carbon dioxide]. Those of us who oppose the use of majority decisions in the decision-making on taxation are not opponents to tax harmonization. We oppose the principle of abandon-ing the current decision-making procedure of unanimity and replacing it with a majority decision. Hence, it is the principle we are opposing and not the harmonization of environmental taxes. That [harmonize taxes] we can do, in unanimity. (EU Advisory Committee 2000/01:10)

Hence, for Persson the issue is the protection of sovereignty or formal decision-making power. Various kinds of criticisms arose in the Com-mittee as a result from this statement. The political parties on the right did not fully agree with the need to harmonize taxes. The Left Party (*Vänsterpartiet*), which is the strongest critic of the EU, does not see that the Swedish government, despite numerous statements, strengthens the intergovernmental character since Sweden has supported the use of majority voting in a number of other issues. The Green Party (*Miljöpar-tiet*), the second largest anti-EU party, contrary to the parliamentary majority supported the use of majority voting regarding environmental pollution. In order to increase efficiency in this area, national sovereignty could be compromised. Persson recognizes, thus, the increased need of joint action in a number of policy areas, which belong to the core tasks of the national parliaments, but does not want to give up formal decision making power. According to the prime minister, the successful Nordic economic cooperation is an example to follow.[27]

THE NEW AND OPEN METHOD OF COOPERATION

The Nordic cooperation has been based on shared values and goals and contrary to the EU did not deprive the national governments of ulti-mate decision-making power. Since the EU, according to the Swedish prime minister, must develop a capability to deal with other issues than market making by means of negative integration, new decision-making

---

[27] See Peterson (1994:210–22) for a brief overview of the Nordic cooperation.

methods are required. The community method has been instrumental with regard to the making of the Common Market, but when it comes to issues closer to the citizens such as welfare and labor market policies, this method is flawed.[28]

> Issues at the center of attention are how to realize the goal of full employment throughout Europe, how to manage increasingly globalized capital, how to struggle against environmental degradation, xenophobia, international crime, and trafficking in human beings is to be pursued, and how the challenge of an increasingly aging population is to be met without lowering our ambitions for security and welfare. A larger Union with ambitions in new areas calls for the further development of our working methods. (Persson 2000B; 2000A)

On the one hand, a number of policy issues need joint action in order to be dealt with efficiently. Hence, the "running to the bottom" like social and economic dumping must be counteracted by joint action. On the other hand, many of the measures that need to be taken belong to the core tasks of the national parliaments. The method by which this dilemma between problem solving capability and the protection of ultimate norm-giving power can be resolved is the "new and open method of co-ordination." It is characterized,

> by common objectives but with national decision-making authority maintained. Initiatives are drawn up jointly by the Member States and the Commission. Comparative methods are incorporated into the system. The initiatives are compiled and become political objectives that complement then Union's supranational legislation. The aim of this form of cooperation is to get the Member States to move in the same direction in the long term—even in areas where Member States cannot accept that the national right of decision is transferred to a formal European decision-making level. (Persson 2000B; 2000A)

The aim is to achieve harmonization, but without letting national decision-making authority go. The goals are set up, but the individual member states can decide on the means. Hence, the cooperation is based on soft law, i.e. non-binding rules and regulations, which were earlier the case in social policy making in the Union, and "neo-voluntarism" (Jakobsson

---

[28] This has been characterized by Scharpf (1998) as a "threshold of perception." The citizens can accept supranational solutions in decision making in macroeconomic policies in which they do not take much interest. But supranational decision making is not accepted in issues related to welfare, civil rights, etc.—in which citizens take a direct interest.

and Johansson 2001). The right of initiative belongs jointly to the Commission and the member states. The main weakness in this method is that since the rules are not binding, the Commission does not supervise compliance. If there are no material punishments for the member states that do not fulfil their obligations or take measures to reach the objectives, there is an obvious risk of failure.[29] Hence, co-ordination will not materialize. However, soft control mechanisms such as benchmarking and peer review are to be used. The control consists in that the member states compile reports and statistics, which are compared among them. Group pressure and good examples are conceived as bringing about compliance (Hjelm-Wallén 2000). The reason why the Swedish prime minister believes that this model can be quite successful is that there is a strong "measure of unity and interdependence" among the EU countries. Hence, the prerequisites guaranteeing successful Nordic cooperation prevail in the EU of today. This is perhaps true in the present EU where a majority of the member states are governed by social democratic governments, but the question is if the method would be as successful in a more pluralist political landscape?

As a matter of fact, this method is already practised in the EU. A revised model was launched at the Lisbon meeting in March 2000 when it also was named the "new and open method of co-ordination," but it has been used in policy making in employment for several years. The novelty in Lisbon was the use of the model in other policy areas as well, for instance, research, education, social exclusion, and information technology.[30] Prime Minister Persson was very satisfied when he reported the latest news from Lisbon to the Swedish Parliament:

> The process is political, not juridical. If an individual state fails it does not have to face the European Court of Justice. The direction that has been taken in Lisbon means more cooperation, but does not result in more supranationality. (Swedish Parliament, Snabbprotokoll 1999/2000:92)

Hence, the output legitimacy of the Union could be ameliorated without abandoning national sovereignty. There is no mention whatsoever

---

[29] For instance, the Swedish commissioner (for environment) Margot Wallström criticized Persson severely and claimed that Persson's proposal poses a threat to European integration.

[30] The first benchmarking report—on information technology—was presented at the European Council in Biarrirz, 13–14 Oct. 2000. Naturally, Sweden was the best in class....

of increasing the input legitimacy at the EU level; for instance, he welcomes the participation of the European parliament in the discussion, but is not prepared to increase its power. Theoretically, one might be opposed and say that it is quite obvious that party leaders are more prone to defend intergovernmentalism in these particular policy areas, and therefore Göran Persson has no more of an intergovernmental bias than Lipponen. However, Persson advocates a rebalancing of the member states and the EU institutions in other spheres as well.

A FUTURE REBALANCE?

In spite of the fact that Göran Persson recognizes that the mix of supranational and intergovernmental elements has been quite successful, he sketches a rebalance in the long run—"the model is not static" (2000A). The intergovernmental character of the EU needs to be strengthened. The power of the Council needs to be increased, whereas that of the Commission is to be weakened, although the prime minister gives credit to the Commission as a body that has protected the interests of the smaller states:[31]

> The Commission suffers from a democratic deficit. It is neither a government nor an intergovernmental secretariat. The construction is and has been valuable, but in the long term a more mature model that relates to the national democratic systems will materialize. (Persson 2000A)

Therefore Göran Persson proposes that the Commission should be subordinated to the Council in the future: the Commission should grow together with the Council secretariat and develop into an intergovernmental body. The main problem Persson sees with the Commission is that it is not democratic, and by subordinating that body to the Council, accountability can be achieved. This is a clear example that input legitimization should not be realized at the EU level but rather through increasing participation in the member states. The intergovernmental conviction is reflected in that EU should not develop into a democracy, but that democratic accountability should take place at the national level. The Council should therefore be the

---

[31] See Thorhallsson (2000:154–5) and Geurts (1998:58–9) for academic accounts of the relationship between small states and the Commission.

main political body of the EU, and input or democratic legitimization should take place at the national levels.[32]

> When we seek to increase public participation in the decision-making process, we must proceed on the assumption that the identities of each and every one of us are, first and foremost, rooted in our experience as citizens in the nation-states. At present, the body with the clearest links to the citizens of the Union is the Council, with ministers from all member countries. If voters consider that their representatives are not advancing their interests, it is to their governments and national assemblies they turn. (Persson 2000B; 2000A)

Hence, the so-called democratic deficit is to be reduced at the member state levels, i.e. in the national parliament and through national opinion mobilization. There is a determination not to entangle the Swedish and European levels of governance from an institutional, but also an informal point of view. The proposals to institutionalize the cooperation between national and European parliamentarians — for instance to give the MEPs the right to take part in the parliamentary sessions — have been rejected (Riksdagskommittén IV, Promemorior från Referensgruppens arbete med fråga om riksdagens hantering av EU-frågorna 2000). Moreover, the Swedish prime minister recognizes the value of the European Parliament as a discussion partner but has not announced any preparedness to increase its formal power. To summarize, the Swedish political leadership is a stern advocate of intergovernmental solutions, i.e. of protecting the unanimity voting, thereby reducing the influence of the Commission and the Court of Justice. A European Union that also solves problems that are closer to the citizens, i.e. output legitimacy, should reduce the legitimacy deficit. As a consequence, the Swedish prime minister has not been enthusiastic about regulating the competencies between the EU and the member states respectively. According to the prime minister, input or democratic legitimization is to be channelled through the national parliamentary institutions.

STRONG INSTITUTIONS GUARANTEE INFLUENCE

According to the Finnish government, the increased use of majority voting was the most important prerequisite for a successful enlarge-

---

[32] It is indicative that when Persson states that a public debate on the EU is needed he is talking about a "national debate" (see EU Advisory Committee 2000/01:10).

ment of the EU (Finnish parliament, PTK 148/2000vp, 29 Nov. 2000). This standpoint is consistent with the Finnish interest in ameliorating the efficiency of the EU institutions. That is, an efficient Union is said to be in the interest of a small state. The Finnish political leadership to a much greater extent than their Swedish colleagues gives voice to a small state identity in how they conceive of the Union (Tiilikainen 1998: 172–3). This position is represented in how they combine institutional guarantees for representation in supranational bodies together with a concern for gaining credibility (and indirectly, influence) among the member states and EU institutions as constructive supporters of the integration project and the existing institutional structure. Hence, the historical legacy of trading sovereignty for the protection of the state interest(s) while simultaneously requiring constitutional guarantees is reflected in the Finnish behavior, whereas it has been claimed that the Swedish form of democracy (pragmatism, corporatism, interest representation, etc.) is a crucial parameter for Swedish behavior.[33] However, Finland and Sweden are quite similar in this respect, and, as a matter of fact, the corporate decision-making procedures have been strengthened in Finland during the membership in the EU. What is evident is that the Swedish democratic conviction is, as was illustrated above, firmly rooted in the nation-state.

THE COMMUNITY METHOD

The Finnish prime minister, Paavo Lipponen, is very concerned about the present intergovernmental trend in the EU. The existing institutional framework of the EU—or more precisely a strong and independent Commission, the European Parliament as a co-decision maker, and an active Council—finds a stern defender in Paavo Lipponen. According to Lipponen the recent development has witnessed "a strengthening of the European Parliament, a weakening of the Commission, and a tendency toward intergovernmentalism" (Lipponen 2000). He welcomes the increased and even strengthened position of the European parliament as a co-decision maker but deplores the other two developments. The *community method*, which reflects this particular institutional balance,

---

[33] An editorial in *Hufvudstadsbladet* 27 November 2000 (Peterson 2000:25) points to lack of constitutional awareness in the Swedish democratic system, i.e. "everything can be negotiated."

should, according to the Finnish prime minister, constitute the present as well as the future basis for the EU. According to Lipponen, it has worked well in the past as it has brought enormous benefits to the EU, for instance the single market and the EMU. A backlash or a return to an intergovernmental method may jeopardize the integration project and is a bad alternative since it is "often inefficient, lacks transparency and leads to the domination of some over others. It is also a potentially destabilizing factor because strong institutions are less prone to pressure from political changes and crises in the member states" (Lipponen 2000). The arguments against the intergovernmental method is that transparency is weakened and decision making efficiency is threatened because of the question of "who is going to guarantee that rules are being adhered to and commitments made together are being met by all member states?" (Lipponen 2000; see also Finnish parliament PTK, 148/2000 vp 28 Nov. 2000). Above all, the "equality" of the member states is disturbed. The Commission is perceived to be an ally of the smaller member states due to its independent status. According to Lipponen, the Commission "protects small states since it takes care that the preparation is objective and that the basic treaties are equally respected. If that were not be the case, we would have to use the law of the jungle" (Lipponen 2000; see also Finnish parliament PTK, 148/2000 vp 28 Nov. 2000).

Lipponen succeeds even in convincing the sternest anti-EU party, the Center, of the advantage of an independent Commission to a small member state. He advises the parliamentarians to ask the Benelux countries why such an institution as the Commission was created in the first place and naturally provides them with the means to counteract the influence and aspirations of the larger member states. Hence, the Finnish political leadership embraces the idea that this particular institutional balance provides a better guarantee for small state influence than intergovernmental solutions where the larger member states decide which tune to play. The Finnish acceptance of and sympathy for this supranational institution is related to both output and a "particular" input legitimacy. First, the Commission guarantees efficiency in terms of control of compliance. Second, even though the Commission is not democratically accountable, it enhances through its various committee systems many interests that are taken into consideration during various phases of the decision making process. In fact, the latter aspect is in the Finnish debate also a strategic argument since it is linked to the protection of the national interest.

The difference between the Swedish and Finnish prime ministers with regard to the status of the Commission is remarkable. In addition, the Finnish prime minister is not as enthusiastic about the new open method of cooperation as his Swedish colleague since this form of cooperation suffers from the weaknesses that accompany the intergovernmental method. Even though the need for cooperation and even harmonization could be required in certain policies, the Finnish parliamentarians are more concerned about a clearer division of competencies between the EU and member states (Finnish parliament PTK, 148/2000 vp 29 Nov. 2000). The Swedish idea of more integration, or rather harmonization in term of policies but by other means, is not discussed at any length among the Finnish parliamentarians. Hence, one could argue that subsidiarity is somewhat differently interpreted: subsidiarity in Finland is equated with a clear division of competencies where pluralism is acknowledged at the member state level, whereas subsidiarity in Sweden means formal decision-making power is guaranteed even though policies are harmonized throughout the Union.

THE LONG TERM STRATEGY—FEDERALIZATION?

What about input legitimization, then? The Finnish parliament agreed with the short-term program for EU that the prime minister presented. However, the parliamentarians are lukewarm about his long term reforms consisting of increased popular participation and EU democracy, particularly as articulated in his speeches given abroad. They agree in that an EU constitution is needed in order to regulate competencies, but the political majority cannot accept an EU constitution in which

> the parliament would represent democratic legitimacy from an equally fundamental point of view as a directly elected body with considerable powers. The Commission should enjoy the confidence of the Parliament, with a President with powers to appoint members of the Commission. And in this institutional set-up, just like in national decision-making, all aspects of civil society should be involved. (Lipponen 2000)

Input legitimization should not take place exclusively within the borders of the member states, according to Lipponen, but to a greater extent at the EU level as well. Democracy should not just be reflected within the borders of the nation-state. The domestic criticism toward Lipponen's federalist project was stark in his own party as well as among the parliamentarians of the opposition. The best way to reduce the democratic deficit is to strengthen the national parliaments in the decision making since

> the legitimacy of the Union is and will also in the future be channelled through the Member States and the national parliaments. Hence, in order to reduce the democratic deficit the participation of the national parliaments in the decision-making must be developed. It was a mistake to make the elections to the European parliament direct when there was no popular demand for such a change. (Tuomioja 2000)

Even though the Finnish system for making the parliamentarians participate in the preparation of EU affairs has been considered among the best functioning, the parliamentarians (as can be expected) demanded improvements. In sum, the Finnish parliament cannot accept the proposal to make the Commission responsible for a European parliament (Finnish parliament PTK, 148/2000 vp 29 Nov. 2000).

Paavo Lipponen recognizes that there is no popular support for such a change for the time being but advocates that small steps can be taken to involve the population in the decision making. For instance, the public could play a greater role in the future revision of the Treaties.

> A good starting point for shifting toward a bottom-up approach would be to change the way we revise the treaties. In the past fifteen years we have prepared, negotiated, or ratified a treaty. The problem is that many of the IGCs are detached from the public sphere and proceed on the basis of the lowest common denominator. Last minute deals are struck so that everyone can bring something home. (Lipponen 2000)

The new charter on human rights was prepared in a convention in which representatives from the EU institutions, the member state parliaments, and the civil society took part. The process was open and invited, therefore, deliberation. The question is what status these conventions in fact will have when the decisions are made, since they are not entrusted with any formal decision-making power. The Finnish parliament is positive about these types of deliberative multilevel practices, i.e. input legitimization by deliberation, but is not prepared to establish an independent democratic structure where formal decision-making power is transferred to a supranational parliament. Hence, even though the Finnish parliamentarians are positive about a federal constitution in which competencies are divided between the EU and the member states—they take no interest in democratizing it.

To summarize, Finland has a more positive view of the supranational elements in the EU: they guarantee efficiency and protect the interest of small member states. Hence, the support for supranational features in the EU is linked to output legitimization. In addition, the Finnish political leadership takes an interest in the creation of a European public room but does not support the proposal of the prime minister to make the EU a democratic political system.

CONCLUSION

This paper has illustrated that the two new member states have embraced different positions with regard to the mix of intergovernmental and supranational elements in the EU even though they are quite similar with respect to the policy interests and the domestic popular support for the EU. The Nordic countries recognize that a variety of decision-making methods need to be used in the EU, but they propose a somewhat different balance between intergovernmental and supranational features. That is, Sweden has taken a stronger intergovernmental position, whereas Finland is more positive to the supranational elements in the EU. The Swedish intergovernmental inclination by the political leadership is related to the protection of sovereignty, whereas the Finnish support of supranationalism is related to efficiency and the protection of small-state interests.

WORKS CITED

Antola, Esko. 1999B. "From the European Rim to the Core: The European Policy of Finland in the 1990's." *Northern Dimensions Yearbook 1999*. Helsinki: Finnish Institute of International Affairs.

Allardt, Erik, *et al*, eds. 1981. *Nordic Democracy: Ideas, Issues, and Institutions in Politics, Economy, Education, Social and Cultural Affairs of Denmark, Finland, Iceland, Norway, and Sweden*. Copenhagen: Det Danske Selskab.

Eriksen, Erik Oddvar, and John Erik Fossum, eds. 2000. *Democracy in the European Union*. London: Routledge.

Esaiasson, Peter, and Knut Heidar, eds. 2000. *Beyond Westminster and Congress: The Nordic Experience*. Columbus: Ohio State UP.

Esping-Andersen, Gøsta. 1990. *The Three Worlds of Welfare Capitalism*. Princeton: Princeton UP.

EU Advisory Commitee. Minutes. 2000/01:10 (1 Dec. 2000).

Eurobarometer. 43 (Spring 1995).
___. 45 (Spring 1996).
___. 47 (Spring 1997).
___. 49 (Spring 1998).
___. 51 (Spring 1999).
___. 53 (Spring 2000).
___. 55 (Spring 2001).
European Council. 2000. "Europa." Nicefördraget, bilaga IV. Home page. 9 Sept. 2002. <europa.eu.int>. PDF available at <europa.eu.int/futurum/documents/offtext/declaration_sv.pdf>.
European University Institute. 2000. *Reforming the Treaties Amendment Procedures.* Second Report on the Reorganization of the European Union Treaties. Submitted to the European Commission on 31 July 2000.
Finnish parliament, verbal. PTK 148/2000 vp, 28–29 Nov. 2000.
Fischer, Joschka. 2000. "From Confederacy to Federation—Thoughts of the Finality of European Integration." 12 May 2000: Speech at the Humboldt University in Berlin.
Forsberg, Tuomas. 2000. "Ulkopolitiikka: Puolueettomasta pohjoismaasta tavalliseksi eurooppalaiseksi." *EU ja Suomi.* Eds. Raunio and Wiberg. Helsinki: Edita.
Førland, Tor Egil, and Dag Harald Claes. 1999. *Europeisk integration.* Lund: Studentlitteratur.
Geurts. 1998. "The European Commission: A Natural Ally of Small States in the EU Institutional Framework." *Small States inside and outside the European Union: Interests and Policies.* Ed. Laurent Goetschel. Boston: Kluwer Academic Publishers.
Gstöhl, Sieglinde. 1996. "The Nordic Countries and the European Economic Area." *The European Union and the Nordic Countries.* Ed. Lee Miles. London: Routledge.
Heininen, Lassi. 1999. "Den nordliga dimensionen i finländsk utrikespolitik." *Perspektiv på den nordliga dimensionen.* Eds. Esko Antola, et al. Helsinki: Edita.
Hjelm-Wallén, Lena. 2000. Tal av vice statsminister Lena Hjelm-Wallén vid Svenska Paneuropeföreningens seminarium den 4 oktober 2000.
Holmberg, Sören. 1996. "Den rörliga EU-opinionen." *Ett knappt ja till EU. Väljarna och folkomröstningen 1994.* Eds. Mikael Gilljam and Sören Holmberg. Stockholm: Norstedts. 112–24.
Hovi, Jon. 1991. "Overnasjonalitet." *Internasjonal Politikk* 49: 5–17.
Jahn, Detlef, and Ann-Sofie Storsved. 1995. "Domino-strategin i praktiken: EU-folkomröstningarna i Österrike, Finland, Sverige och Norge." *Politiikka* 37.4: 238–251.
Jakobsson, Kerstin. 1997. *Så gott som demokrati.* Umeå: Boréa.
Jakobsson, Kerstin, and Karl-Magnus Johansson, eds. 2001. *Från social dimension till välfärdspolitik: Ny politik och nya samarbetsformer i EU.* Stockholm: SNS Förlag.
Joerges, Christian, Yves Mény, and J.H.H. Weiler, eds. 2000. *What kind of Constitution for What Kind of Polity? Responses to Joschka Fischer.* Cambridge: Harvard Law School.
Laffan, Bridgid, Rory O'Donnell, and Michael Smith. 2000. *Europe's Experimental Union: Rethinking Integration.* London: Routledge.
Lipponen, Paavo. 2000. Speech given at the College of Europe. Bruges, Belgium: 10 Nov. 2000.
Miles, Lee. 1996. *The European Union and the Nordic Countries.* London: Routledge.
Mouritzen, Hans, Ole Waever, et al. 1996. *European Integration and National Adaptations: A Theoretical Inquiry.* Commack, NY: Nova Science Publishers.

Novack, Jennifer. 2000. "Finland as the Model Pupil and Sweden as the Reluctant European? Insights from Their Attempts to increase Public Access to Documents in the EU." Unpublished paper.

Oskarsson, Maria. 1996. "Skeptiska kvinnor—Entusiastiska Män." *Ett knappt ja till EU. Väljarna och folkomröstningen 1994*. Eds. Mikael Gilljam and Sören Holmberg. Stockholm: Norstedts. 112–24.

Paloheimo, Heikki. 1995. "Pohjoismaiden kansanäänestykset: puolueiden peruslinjat ja kansalaisten mielipiteet Suomessa, Ruotsissa ja Norjassa." *Politiikka* 37.2: 113–27.

Persson, Göran. 2000A. Statsminister Göras Perssons tal inför Klubb Norden den 5 oktober 2000. 26 Jan. 2001. <www.statsradsberedningen.regeringen.se/persson/>.

___. 2000B. "EUS framtid—ett Europea i förändring." *Tiden* 6. 26 Jan. 2001. <www.sta tsradsberedningen.regeringen.se/persson/>.

Pierson, Paul. 1998. "The Path to European Integration: A Historical-Institutionalist Analysis." *European Integration and Supranational Governance*. Eds. Wayne Sandholtz and Alec Stone Sweet. Oxford: Oxford UP.

Peterson, Olof. 1994. *Swedish Government and Politics*. Stockholm: Fritzes.

___. 2000. *Svensk Europadebatt*. Groupement d'ètudes et de recherches. 25 Jan. 2001. <www.sns.se>.

Raunio, Tapio, and Matti Wiberg, eds. 2000. *EU ja Suomi*. Helsinki: Edita.

Riksdagskommittén. Promemorior från Referensgruppens arbete med fråga om riksdagens hantering av EU-frågorna. Sverige, 2000.

Scharpf, Fritz. 1996. "Can there be a Stable Federal Balance in Europe." *Federalizing Europe? The Costs, Benefits and Preconditions of Federal Political Systems*. Eds. J.J. Hesse and V. Wright. New York: Oxford UP.

___. 1999. *Governing in Europe: Effective and Democratic?* Oxford: Oxford UP.

Streeck, Wolfgang. 1996. "Neo-Vountarism: A New European Social Policy Regime?" *Governance in the European Union*. Eds. Marks and Scharpf. London: Sage.

Strömvik, Maria. 1999. "Sverige och EUS utrikes—och säkerhetspolitik: ett intensivt men hemligt förhållande?" *Sverige i EU*. Ed. Karl-Magnus Johansson. Stockholm: SNS.

Swedish Parliament, verbal. 1999/2000:118.

Swedish Parliament, verbal snabbprotokoll. 1999/2000:92.

Swedish Social Democratic Party. Home page. 20 Jan. 2001. <www.sap.se>.

Sydow, Emily von. 1999. *När Luther kom till Bryssel: Sveriges första år i EU*. Stockholm: Bokförlaget Arena.

Tiilikainen, Teija. 1998. *Europe and Finland : Defining the Political Identity of Finland in Western Europe*. Aldershot: Ashgate.

Thorhallsson, Baldur. 2000. *The Role of Small States in the European Union*. Aldershot: Ashgate.

Tuomioja, Eero. Ulkoministeri Erkki Tuomiojan puhe Ranskan ulkopoliittisessa instituutiossa. 15 Nov. 2000.

Wallström, Margot. 2000. "Perssons idé hotar EUS framtid." *Dagens Nyheter*. 22 Oct. 2000.

Finland's European Vocation

Robert Rinehart
Foreign Service Institute

IN 1843, ZACHARIUS TOPELIUS, then a twenty-five year old student of natural philosophy, gave a public lecture entitled "Do the Finnish People Possess a History?" at the Imperial Alexander University, which in time became the University of Helsinki. He answered in the negative. Because Finland had no political existence, he argued, it was not a legitimate topic of historical investigation. The Finns had not been sovereign agents. They had never acted politically on their own behalf but always as part of another political entity.

Topelius was the youngest of a small group of writers and intellectuals who set about to create a Finnish national identity where none had existed before. In many countries, that would have been an organic development or the task of kings, soldiers, and statesmen, but, in Finland, it was a conscious act and the work of a philosopher (and economist), Johan Vilhelm Snellman, a linguist (and physician) Elias Lönnrot, a poet (and teacher) Johan Ludvig Runeberg, and Topelius, a playwright and popular historian, who taught young Finns what it meant to be Finnish. Runeberg gave Finland a modern heroic historical poem, "Tales of Enisgn Stål." Lönnrot complied a folk epic, *Kalevala*, from an oral tradition of considerable antiquity. Writing in Swedish for the most part, they gave Finland a past and a myth distinct from that of other countries.

And Snellman provided a Hegelian ideological framework for nation building. In his essay "On the Theory of the State" (1861), he invoked Adolf Ivar Arwidsson's familiar syllogism: "Swedes we are no more, Russians we can never be, so let us be Finns." But the synthesis was ambiguous. It could be taken as a moral imperative: "we *must* be Finns" or as a logical inference: since we are not Swedes or Russians, we have to be Finns. Or, as Arwidsson and Snellman most likely intended, it can be read as indicating an on-going process of becoming Finnish that can be helped along by practical actions.

The Grand Duchy of Finland was a state, created in 1809 when the Diet swore fealty to the czar-grand duke at Porvoo. Of that, Snelllman and the others were certain. But Finland and the Finns were not yet a nation. That required cultural consciousness and a distinct identity. Swedes in Finland, like Snellman, who were the politically effective portion of the population, identified themselves as Finnish, but their culture like their mother tongue was Swedish. The Finnish heroes of Topelius's stories were, in fact, super-Swedes. Snellman argued that there was a fundamental link between culture, language, and the national identity, without which the nation-state could not exist, and, to fix the link, he proposed to "educate the nation and nationalize the educated." To achieve that end, he advocated accepting Finnish as the national language for use in administration and as a medium for cultural expression. When, however, in 1863, Finnish was officially recognized as having equal status with Swedish, most of Snellman's contemporaries in the Swedish-speaking elite opposed the move on the grounds that adopting Finnish, an obscure "Asiatic" language, at the expense of Swedish would isolate Finland, alienate it from the other Nordic countries, and cut it off from access to the European mainstream.

In the 1890s, the Finns—Finnish- and Swedish-speaking together—successfully blocked the Russification of their country. Reforms in 1906 introduced a deliberative national legislature, universal suffrage, and the first fully democratic electorate in Europe. At the end of 1917, Finland declared itself an independent country and, after a cruel civil war, adopted a liberal, democratic, republican constitution, consistent with the Wilsonian ideal. Despite deep political cleavages among its people left in the aftermath of the civil war, Finland was both a nation and a state.

How Finland Survived

In succeeding decades, Finland took risks to defend its sovereignty and territorial integrity and, arguably, its existence as a nation-state. Against impossible odds, the Finns resisted invasion alone in 1939–40 rather than

concede to Soviet territorial demands. Territory was lost, but defeated
Finland escaped the occupation that befell its Baltic neighbors. Democratic Finland became a cobelligerent with Nazi Germany against the
Soviet Union during the Continuation War to recover territory seized
during the earlier Winter War. When it became clear that it would share
in Germany's unconditional defeat, endure a Soviet occupation, and,
perhaps, lose its independence, Finland negotiated an armistice with
the Soviets and switched sides in the war.

Following the war, Finland concluded treaties with the Soviet Union
that confirmed territorial losses, imposed reparations, limited the size
of the Finnish armed forces, and left open the possibility of Soviet
intervention, if requested, in the event of threat of aggression from
the West. The Treaty of Friendship and Mutual Cooperation (1948)
also set in place a Finnish-Soviet trade regime that eventually worked
to Finland's advantage. The Finnish media practiced self-censorship
as an accommodation to Soviet sensitivities. Finland adopted a foreign policy based on neutrality and non-alignment (although Finnish
neutrality was not formally admitted until 1986 by the Soviet Union,
which contended unofficially that Finland's treaty obligations to it were
a type of alignment). Finland's votes in the United Nations during the
Cold War sometimes reflected an understanding of Soviet positions
that suggested to American observers that Finland was not always an
independent operator in its foreign policy. The term "Finlandization"
was coined to describe the process by which a country accommodating the Soviet Union became subservient to it. The Finns rejected the
inference that Finland was in any way a satellite country or included in
the Soviet sphere of influence. Whatever Finland did, they responded,
was done by choice and because it was the wisest policy for a small
country living next to a super-power to pursue and not as the result of
coercion. Ten years after the collapse of the Soviet Union, most Finns
still agree that the policy was necessary and appropriate, but some are
ready to concede that the price paid was greater than needed in order
to be credible.

The idea of nationhood had not come as early or as naturally to
Finland as it had to the other Nordic countries, and, given the reality
of geography, it had remained precarious even after independence. The
task of Finnish political skill, diplomatic ingenuity, military readiness,
and popular will was to assure that, to repeat Max Jakobson's words,
"Finland survived" at whatever cost, compromise, or concession was

necessary, short of sacrificing sovereignty and essential institutions, democracy, social welfare, and a free economy.

FINLAND AND EUROPE

This is a simplistic rendition of modern Finnish history, which may seem extraneous to a discussion of Finland's participation in the European Union (EU) at the beginning of the twenty-first century. It is intended, however, to demonstrate a rationale for Finland's EU membership and for the role it plays today as the one fully integrated Nordic member state. (In fact, the Finns do not see themselves as "playing a role." Pragmatic to the core, there is nothing theatrical in their approach to the European integration process.) The historical record might suggest that Finland's quick transition from a non-aligned Nordic neutral to an "Ultra-European" core member state is another example of its ability to recognize the realities of a situation and accommodate to them. In order for Finland to "survive," the Finns embraced a new modality, in this case the EU, merging their national identity with that of a broader European identity. In this way, they are assured political security and a piece of the economic action, and they preserve their Finnishness, albeit in a European context. This studied pursuit of a "European vocation" could be a clear and logical explanation of the course Finland has taken toward core participation and one certainly based on historical precedents. But historical precedents can be read in different ways, and political decisions often produce their own logic. Finnish national identity is not an issue, and the argument for "cultural survival" through a merger of identities is not satisfying.

But have the Finns also assumed a "European identity" to complement their Finnish identity? Certainly, it would be hard to find willingness among the Finns to be "better Europeans" than anyone else. They are not in competition with the Italians or Luxembourgers. Finns will readily admit to suffering form an inferiority complex in relation to people on the "Continent." They are also sensitive that they are not taken seriously enough, especially by the larger countries in the EU, and dismayed that the rest of Europe seems to know so little about them. What Finns say they expect from Europe is recognition on their own terms, on the basis of what they are, not what other

Europeans expect them to become.[1] Indeed, they are not inclined to change and generally believe they have more to contribute to the rest of Europe than to learn from it.

How do the Finns expect to attract that recognition and to extend that influence? Finland's real "European vocation" is to be an actor in the EU as a core country that has a seat at every table, involved in every decision whether monetary policy, voting procedures, trade policy, or crisis management. Finland moved straight to the core of the EU once it had acceded to membership because, as Finns argue, it was the only course that made sense for a small country always wary of being marginalized. It was an entirely pragmatic course to take. Idealism and enthusiasms were not necessarily involved. Being a conspicuous member of the "inner circle" greatly expands the options available to a small country. "They (the Europeans)," it is pointed out, "can't ignore us now."

Finland's application for EU membership was a completely political decision. That economics was an important consideration, especially given Sweden's earlier application, goes without saying. That having been said, however, the overriding consideration for Finland was one of security. As Max Jakobson succinctly described his country's security deficit in comparison with the physical assets of the other Nordic countries, "Norway has NATO and Sweden has Finland, but Finland faces a land border of 800 miles with Russia" (6). When Finland joined the EU that border became Europe's border.

FINLAND AND EUROPEAN SECURITY

The extent of Finland's core participation in the common European Security and Defense Policy (ESDP) and cooperation with the North Atlantic Treaty Organization (NATO) are developing issues in a political environment that has seldom in the past countenanced debate on national security.[2] Two reasons for this departure are: (1) national

---

[1] A case in point was a remark by Belgian Prime Minister Guy Verhofstadt made during his country's EU presidency that he regarded Finland as the number-one supporter of European federalism, so much so that he believed the Finns would actually put their "culture in EU hands" (US Press release 25–27 Aug. 2001). Finns were puzzled what he meant by that.

[2] The Finnish debate of "post-neutrality" security policy is described in an (1 Oct. 2001) unpublished paper, "Paradoxes of Post-Neutrality: Finnish and Swedish Views of NATO and ESDP," prepared at the Finnish Foreign Policy Research Institute (UPI-FIIA), Helsinki.

security and foreign policy issues, until recently the prerogatives of the president of the republic, are increasingly areas of concern for the prime minister and the government and have, hence, been drawn into the political arena, and (2) security related questions are no longer national but are European. Additionally, European security questions no longer come under the rubric of "foreign" policy. Important changes in Finland's defense orientation are underway, and the pace of those changes has been rapid. The 1997 reorganization of the Finnish Defense Forces (FDF) has, in some respects, already been rendered obsolete. Questions that arose subsequently about how to develop the capabilities required by responsibilities imposed by the ESDP were addressed in the 2001 White Paper on security and defense policy.[3]

From 1994 to 2000, defense and foreign policies were directed by then president, Matti Ahtisaari, and Prime Minister Paavo Lipponen, both moderate Social Democrats. Both also viewed the world through similar prisms — pragmatic realists, strongly Atlanticist, committed to European integration, skeptical of Russia, and supportive of a strong defense posture. Their basic position was that an American presence is a stabilizing factor vital for European security and that NATO is the basic guarantee of that presence. Under current circumstances, Finland did not need to join NATO, although neutrality and non-alignment were abandoned in 1995 in favor of an "all-options-are-open" policy. Instead, Ahtisaari and Lipponen moved Finland as close as was feasible to NATO militarily through Partnership for Peace (PfP) and politically through EU channels. It was a process intended to close the gap between membership and non-membership that both its critics and supporters recognized as "sliding" into NATO.

Meanwhile, EU membership had provided major new security benefits for Finland. In effect, bilateral relations with Russia could be reduced, if not altogether eliminated, superceded by an EU-Russia relationship. It was to Finland's advantage as a core member of the EU that the club's foreign policy/security pillar should be as strong as possible. Hence, Finland supported the ESDP — provided it did not compromise the link to NATO (i.e. the United States).

Two positions emerged in discussions regarding the ESDP. One favored a strong common foreign and security policy specifically in the event of tensions involving Russia that might unhinge the EU

---

[3] See Finland, *The European Security Development and Finnish Defense,* and Finland, *The Finnish Security and Defense Policy 2001.*

unless foreign policy and security mechanisms were in place to confront them. The second cautioned restraint out of concern that the common policy could draw Finland into confrontations it might otherwise have avoided.

Similarly, two further contrasting positions were evident regarding the consequences of an enhanced relationship with NATO. One regarded the common policy as a positive development only if it moved deliberately toward convergence with NATO, thereby permitting Finland to "slide" closer to the Atlantic Alliance through the EU apparatus. The other school of thought, however, expressed misgivings that the French approach (subsequently embodied in the French presidency report: "It remains essential to the credibility and effectiveness of the European Security and Defense Policy that the Union's military capabilities for crisis management be reinforced so that the Union is in a position to intervene with or without recourse to NATO assets" [Riggle par. 30]) would dominate the ESDP and weaken the essential American linkage to Europe through NATO.

Once Britain and France had jump-started the stalled common security policy with the St. Malo Agreement in 1998, Finland stepped on board to support a common policy shaped along the lines proposed by Ahtisaari and Lipponen. The Finnish presidency report following the Helsinki Inter-Governmental Conference (IGC) in December 1999 reflected their position insisting on strengthening the ESDP as part of a convergence with NATO. It was a particularly constructive contribution of the Finnish presidency (July-December 1999) to the common policy in avoid alienating quarrels among members over irrelevant issues.

Finnish security doctrine is illustrated by three concentric circles, each representing areas of defense and foreign policy responsibility (see *Finnish Security*). They are: (1) The traditional defense of Finnish national territory by a large reserve force; (2) Regional (European) security involving participation by specially designated standing units in crisis management situations under an EU command proposed as part of the ESDP; and (3) Global peacemaking under the authority of the United Nations (UN) commands.

Consensus exists in Finland about the value of maintaining a defense force capable of accomplishing all three missions. The decision has been made to raise a three-brigade NATO-compatible force that could be deployed both for crisis management tasks abroad under the ESDP and also for territorial defense. The change will require a larger number of professional personnel equipped with high-tech assets not currently found in Finland's arsenal, both expensive. The officially stated policy is to retain the cost-effective old system of territorial defense while developing the expensive new rapid reaction force, but, in the light of continued budget restraints, it is deemed likely by analysts that the traditional territorial defense system will be abandoned by steps. The argument for territorial defense has always been that it gave Finland a claim to having a credible independent defense ability against an aggressor. However, it is a force that cannot be made NATO-compatible nor contribute to the ESDP. Nor is Russia, the only conceivable enemy against which it was arrayed, any more considered to be a potential military threat. Giving up the territorial defense system in order to afford participation in the ESDP means practically that Finland becomes explicitly dependent on NATO for its defense. Hence the logic of Finland's concern about decoupling the Atlantic link.

Tarja Halonen, an unconventional foreign minister in the Lipponen government, who succeeded Ahtisaari as president in February 2000, initially brought views radically different from those of the prime minister with her to the office. Coming out of the Social Democratic left wing and, by reputation, a pacifist, she was adamantly anti-NATO and antagonistic toward the military establishment. She was pro-EU but criticized what she called the "militarization of the EU" as a result of its collaboration with NATO in the ESDP. For the first time since World War II, an apparent rift in the country's leadership on security policy that also had serious implications for Finland's EU missions opened up. As a result of amendments made to the Finnish constitution, the president now shares responsibility for foreign policy and defense with the head of government, a relationship in principle still to be ironed out in practice, particularly regarding Finland's relations within the EU.[4] The government has responsibility for EU affairs, which now involves the common foreign and security policy, while the president remains commander of the FDF.

Since taking office, the views that President Halonen expressed as foreign minister on European security have evolved to a softer position regarding its relationship to NATO. In March 2000, addressing the

---

[4] Prime Minister Lipponen explained that Finland's foreign policy is conducted by the president of the republic in collaboration with the council of state (government) headed by the prime minister. He rejected the idea that the president, prime minister, and foreign minister formed a policymaking triangle (see US Press release 13–15 Oct. 2001).

opening session of the Eduskunta, she stated that consideration of NATO membership for Finland was irrelevant and would not be entertained during her presidency. In May, she delivered a speech in Stockholm on the topic of "military non-alignment in the heart of Europe." In the August 2000 foreign policy review, she was silent on the question, but, later that same month in an address before the Paasikivi Society in Helsinki, Halonen conceded that long-term American involvement through NATO was vital for European security.

Just prior to the Nice IGC, the Finnish press commented editorially on the contradictory views on foreign policy and European security presented by Lipponen and Foreign Minister Erkki Tuomioja. On the same day that Lipponen reiterated his vision of Finland working at the EU's core on all points involving integration, Tuomioja elegantly formulated a dissenting opinion: "Others should not count on Finland and the Finns always being ready to accept all pursuits of enhancing integration or participating in all arrangements" (*Helsingin Sanomat* 19 Dec. 2000).[5]

Finland, together with Sweden, sponsored expanding the scope of the Common Foreign and Security Policy (CFSP) as provided in the Amsterdam Treaty by adding crisis management, humanitarian and rescue tasks, and peacekeeping measures, the so-called Petersberg Tasks, to the EU's competence. Finland is now too securely fixed at the core of the EU's crisis management efforts for another government to pull out of it. The current government supports continuing development of the ESDP concept while ensuring that it leads to EU-NATO convergence. The Nice IGC removed "interim" status from the EU military command structure giving the go ahead for the creation of a "permanent" staff on which Finland is represented. Finnish personnel participate in Headline Task Force Plus, a staff of NATO and EU experts responsible for compiling the Headline Goal Catalogue that lists assets available for operations under ESDP.[6] At the EU Capabilities Commitment Conference in November 2000, Finland pledged two mechanized battalions, headquarters staff from all three services, and a naval command vessel,

---

[5] Tuomioja is Lipponen's rival from the left within the Social Democratic party, and their disagreements extend to domestic issues as well. It should be noted that Finland does not have a tradition of collective ministerial responsibility.

[6] The EU's Military Committee is chaired by General Gustave Hägglund, former chief-of-staff of the FDF, who has emphasized that his mission depends on close cooperation with NATO.

with a total complement of 1500 personnel to be included in the catalogue. For the first time, Finland, together with the three additional non-NATO EU members, was invited to attend the annual NATO planning conference convened at Oberammergau in January 2001. Finnish personnel will join those from the other Nordic countries—three NATO members and Sweden—on a permanent basis at NATO headquarters in Brussels to coordinate planning for EU-led operations. This participation gives the Finns access to NATO planning outside of Article 5 contingencies. Application for NATO membership, however, is unlikely during Halonen's presidency. Finland will continue to cooperate closely with NATO, however, through the ESDP.[7]

FROM HELSINKI TO NICE

The priorities of Finland's EU presidency reflected President Ahtisaari's hopes for the future of European integration and for the part Finland would play in it. Among them was building structures for the common foreign and security policy. Heading the list, however, was the Northern Dimension Program that aimed at focusing the EU's attention on the particular concerns of northern European member countries and reminding Brussels that there was indeed a Europe beyond the Mediterranean. Primary in the program were measures intended to improve the EU's ties to Russia through a series of joint projects. Much of the most important work of that presidency was interrupted when its resources were diverted to cope with the crisis in Kosovo.

---

[7] Subsequent to the preparation of this article in January 2001, President Halonen has spoken often on the question of Finland's relationship with NATO further clarifying without noticeably modifying her position on the questions. In a television interview, for example, she dismissed claims that Finnish foreign policy had become more favorable to NATO membership (reported in *Helsingin Sanomat* 7 Sept. 2001). Prime Minister Lipponen stated, however, that the NATO relationship was a subject fit to be addressed in the 2004 security and defense policy report and suggested that it should be openly discussed. His remarks were interpreted as his "not rejecting" the idea of NATO membership (Lipponen). A week later, Foreign Minister Tuomioja addressing the Paasikivi Society opined that Finland could join NATO only with approval by a referendum (*Helsingin Sanomat* 24 Oct. 2001). The Edukunta debated on security policy on 5–6 September for more than fourteen hours, an unprecedented event. In the wake of the events of September 11, public support for Finnish NATO membership dropped from 21 percent on 1 September to only 17 percent by the end of the month. Support for membership peaked at 30 percent in 1998 and declined sharply following the Kosovo campaign.

The Finnish agenda also concentrated on improving the efficiency of EU institutions as a prelude to enlargement. That meant dealing with leftovers from the Austrian presidency that included such important items as majority voting, the size and composition of the Commission, and the CFSP, all of which needed to be resolved before the proposed first round of enlargement in 2002. The Helsinki IGC succeeded at least in determining that enlargement would take place on schedule, although most of the items remaining from the previous presidency including agreement on majority voting and the Commission were still unresolved.

Finland's mission at the Nice IGC was to impress on the conference the importance of improving the efficiency of EU operations prior to enlargement. Finland proposed requiring a double majority for voting in an expanded Council, one vote for each country plus the support of countries accounting for half the population of the EU. (Had someone in the Ministry for Foreign Affairs been reading the *Federalist Papers*?) Finland approved extending majority voting to twenty areas, including matters touching service-sector trade, but it opposed its extension to fiscal policy (i.e. taxation), environmental concerns, and third pillar matters affected "consular affairs" (i.e. immigration, refugees, and asylum). These are areas where the Finns have concluded that national administration is more efficient, more appropriate to Finnish conditions, or, as in the case of environmental issues, more stringent than policies likely to come from Brussels.

Finland regarded the results of the Nice IGC as only generally favorable. Enlargement can go forward with the reforms proposed, but, according to the Finns, the enlarged EU will not be as efficient as it could have been, and an opportunity has been lost to increase institutional flexibility. In contrast to the simple voting system recommended by the Finns, Nice approved a three-tiered qualified voting majority that continues to allow three large countries or two large countries and one small to block passage of measures, even as the EU enlarges. This complex voting system is far from the Finnish-backed idea of a double majority.

FINNISH PUBLIC OPINION AND EUROPE

It is a paradox that the way for Finland, a small country of the periphery, to maintain its identity has been to give up some sovereignty within the EU and to keep a seat at the table where decisions are made for the

EU. And that is Finland's real "European vocation," to be a core actor in the EU.

How well is this understood by the Finnish public opinion? Fifty-eight percent of the Finnish electorate approved Finland's application for EU admission, a higher percentage than in Sweden or, earlier, in Denmark. But neither the electorate nor the government that brought Finland into the EU could have foreseen the pace of European integration. Polls indicate that a majority of public opinion continues to support EU membership. It is not a large majority, but it is a clear one. In the past five years, there have been no dramatic changes affecting public support for membership. Keijo Korhonen, an outspoken critic of the EU, received only 4 percent of the vote in the first round of the 2000 presidential election. (His slogan: "We can make it on our own into eternity.") The same majority does not exist, however, when pollsters ask Finns if they lay claim to a European identity. It has been suggested that, if Finns understood what "Europe" means or may come to mean as a consequence of deeper EU integration, the majority favoring the membership would evaporate.[8]

Finnish public opinion is led by elite opinion. There is a tradition that wisdom comes from above—from Swedish kings, Russian czars, and from "people who know about these things." Juho Paasikivi, Finland's deeply revered president (1946–56), once remarked that the "Finns are blockheads" who look for guidance. Runeberg's character Sven Dufa is the archetype of the brave and simple Finnish peasant, who does what he is told and does it well without always knowing why he is doing it. But even elite opinion, which is overwhelmingly positive regarding the EU, almost uniformly rejects the idea of creating independent European structures "in the French sense," as Finns invariably describe them, or of

---

[8] This paragraph was written in January 2001. In July, one poll showed that 49 percent of the Finns, less than an absolute majority for the first time since accession to the EU, considered that membership was having a positive impact in Finland, a drop of 13 percent from July 2000. The *Eurobarometer* 55, published on 17 Oct. 2001 by the European Commission, indicated that the 23 percent of Finns interviewed found nothing positive in EU membership. According to the poll, conducted in April-May, 36 percent gave unqualified support to EU membership. Half of those polled lacked trust in the EU. As indicated above, the level of support for the EU at the beginning of 2001 had been stable since Finland's accession. Commentators explain that recent polls show Finns are, in fact, becoming more accustomed to EU institutions and systems and increasingly recognize European issues as domestic issues and are, therefore, more open to criticism.

federal constitutional structures for Europe as proposed by the German chancellor and foreign minister. If Finnish elite opinion has produced few Euro-skeptics, neither has is provided many Euro-enthusiasts.

WORKS CITED

Eurobarometer 55 (Autumn 2001).

Finland. *The European Security Development and Finnish Defence.* Helsinki: Council of State to Parliament. 1997.

___. *The Finnish Security and Defence Policy 2001.* Helsinki: Council of State to Parliament. 2001.

Helsingin Sanomat. 19 Dec. 2000. Op-Ed.

___. 7 Sept. 2001.

___. 24 Oct. 2001.

Jakobson, Max. *Finland in the New Europe.* Washington DC: Center for Strategic and International Studies/Praeger, 1998.

Paradoxes of Post-Neutrality: Finnish and Swedish Views of NATO *and* ESDP. Unpublished paper. Helsinki: Finnish Foreign Policy Research Institute (UPI-FIIA).

Riggle, Sharon. EU *Officially Adopts Military Tasks: A Summary of the Nice Conclusions.* Briefing paper. Centre for European Security and Disarmament, 18 Dec. 2000. <www.cesd.org/eu/nicebrief.htm>.

United States. Press release. US Embassy, Helsinki. 13–15 Oct. 2001, quoting Paavo Lipponen.

___. Press release. US Embassy, Helsinki. 25–27 Aug. 2001, quoting Guy Verhofstadt.

Contributors

Eric Einhorn is professor of political science, University of Massachusetts, Amherst. He has written extensively on the Scandinavian welfare state and foreign policy making.

Lyyke Friis is senior research fellow and project director for European Studies at the Danish Institute of International Affairs (DUPI). She is the author of numerous books and articles on European integration and Denmark's relationship to the EU.

Christine Ingebritsen is chair of the European Studies Program, and associate professor in the Department of Scandinavian Studies, University of Washington. Her work examines Scandinavia's role in international politics, and she is the author of *The Nordic States and European Unity* (Ithaca: Cornell UP, 1998).

Anne-Cathrine Jungar is a research scholar, Department of Government, Uppsala University and lecturer at the University College, Stockholm, Sweden. She is currently heading a project on the EU and Nordic democracy.

Annica Kronsell is assistant professor, Department of Political Science, Lund University, Sweden. She has published in the field of EU environmental politics, the Europeanization of Swedish environmental policy making, as well as gender and international relations.

Paulette Kurzer is associate professor of political science at the University of Arizona. She is the author of *Markets and Moral Regulation: Cultural Change in Europe* (Cambridge: Cambridge UP, 1991).

Robert Rinehart is chairman of Northern European Area Studies Programs at the Foreign Service Institute. He is also on the faculty of The

Graduate School of Political Management at The George Washington University and teaches at Växjö University in Sweden.

Lars Svåsand is professor of political science at the Institute of Comparative Politics, University of Bergen, Norway. He has written numerous books and articles on Norwegian political parties and Europeanization.

Baldur Thorhallsson is associate professor of politics and head of the Department of Politics at the University of Iceland. His research focus is "Small States and European Integration," and he has published numerous articles on Iceland and the EU. The title of his recent book is *The Role of Small States in the European Union* (Aldershot: Ashgate, 2000).